Scientology: A to Xenu

An Insider's Guide to What Scientology is Really All About

Chris Shelton

Published by
GraphicsWerks
Denver, CO
www.graphicswerks.com

DEDICATION

This book is dedicated to the survivors of Scientology. May every one of your voices be heard and your stories told.

Table of Contents

Forward by Jon Atack   i

Preface   v

Introduction: How to Read This Book   viii

1. Why Should Anyone Listen to Me?   1

2. Bitter, Defrocked Apostates (or Why Customer   41
    Reviews Matter)

3. How Scientology Presents Itself to the World   49

4. Scientology: Bona Fide Religion or Destructive   59
    Cult?

5. Why Scientology is Imploding   75

6. Who was L. Ron Hubbard?   93

7. An Important Aspect of the Brainwashing   125

8. Is There Anything Good in Scientology?   131

9. The KSW Mind Trap   135

10. Pseudoscience and the Purification Rundown   151

11. Why Scientologists Believe They are Saving the   161
    World (or Here's the Part about Xenu)

12. Scientology's PR Problem (Let's talk about OSA)   193

13. The Insanity that is Scientology's Organizational   207
    Structure

14. Scientology's Most Powerful Lie   227

15. Converting the Converted   263

16. N is for Narcissism   265

17. Recovering from Scientology   275

    References and Notes   283

    Appendix 1: A Scientology Glossary   293

    Appendix 2: The Affirmations of L. Ron Hubbard   310

    Appendix 3: The Scientology Organizational   339
    Hierarchy

    Bibliography   341

Foreword by Jon Atack

My own experience of Scientology was mild compared to Chris'. Although I reached the lofty heights of Level V of the Operating Thetan Course, and took a bunch of training courses over my nine years of believing, I was never a live-in member. I went home to my own bed at night, always ate properly and spent most of my time in the real world, speaking English rather than Scientologese. On the two occasions Scientology staffers yelled at me, I yelled right back. I had not realised I was not supposed to.

Chris, on the other hand, survived the rigors of the Sea Organization, where rice and bean diets were imposed for weeks on end; there were screamed 'severe reality adjustments,' and the threat of Scientology's internal prison hung over his head every single day. Chris was even physically assaulted while on the 'Road to Freedom,' as Hubbard styled his bizarre system of psychological thralldom.

I left over thirty years ago, and spent a dozen years exposing the truth about the Scientology cult. Inevitably, I was harassed on a daily basis and ultimately steamrollered into withdrawal. Tony Ortega's *The Unbreakable Miss Lovely* gives a dramatic and accurate picture of the harassment meted out to critics; twelve years was quite enough for me.

By the time I withdrew, I'd published the first comprehensive history of Scientology and helped with the first truthful biography of its leader – *Bare-Face Messiah* by Russell Miller. I'd written tens of articles and papers and helped with hundreds of media pieces and as many court cases. I'd also spoken to hundreds of former members, many of whom expressed gratitude for my part in liberating them from the

i

Scientology trap. That gratitude was all that kept me going. They were hard years, because there were only a handful of us protesting.

In 2013, after a 17-year hiatus, I reluctantly rejoined the fray, hoping to help survivors overcome some of the worst after-effects of Scientology's remarkably intrusive thought reform program. In their study of over a thousand former cult members, academics Conway and Siegelman reckoned Scientology the most "debilitating" of the destructive cults. Where victims of the Moonies or the Krishnas return to normality within a few months, Conway and Siegelman determined that, unaided, Scientologists take over 12 years to recover. Recently, they have agreed with me this estimate is conservative: many who have been exposed to Scientology never fully regain their critical faculties and continue to live in the half-world of Suppressives, missed withholds and body thetans. Scientology is a self-perpetuating psychological trap.

The problem is compounded by the phobia of psychology and psychotherapy induced by the cult, and by the failure of most therapists to understand the mechanics of such indoctrination. There are very, very few people out here who know how to help, and many who busily undo our efforts because they are still under Hubbard's enchantment.

I first heard about Chris Shelton in 2013 when I began blogging at the Underground Bunker. I was pleasantly surprised to find someone who had survived such a profound involvement and managed to dig himself out. Believe me, it is highly unusual: more usually, former members spend years embroiled in the halfway-house of the self-styled Independent movement, until some external event triggers reflection.

Of course, recovery from prolonged trauma does not happen overnight, and Chris has the humility to admit he has further to travel – as do we all – but that very humility marks him out from most former members, who retain the phoney élite status implanted by the cult into its devotees.

Unlike 99% of former Scientologists, Chris was prepared to consider other explanations and to leave the cage of phobias induced by Scientology. I remember my own trepidation when I first read about the brain, a few months after leaving the cult. It seemed like heresy to question Hubbard's dictum that the brain is simply a switching mechanism between the spirit and the body and of no consequence whatsoever.

All forms of psychology were also taboo, but Chris has managed to plunge headlong into the relevant material. I had the privilege of working with him at the Getting Clear seminar in Toronto, and his good humour and his intelligence impressed me. He is a natural educator, because he makes no claim to superiority, despite his quick wit and ready articulation.

My friend Christian Szurko, who is surely as expert about cults as anyone else alive, has pointed out former Scientologists tend to be even more arrogant than escapees from other groups. Chris is a notable exception. He has no pretensions to guru hood nor any need to form his own cult of personality. He has done remarkable work thus far, and I have no doubt that he will make many more contributions beyond this exceptional book.

Chris is driven by the compassionate urge to help those who have been harmed by Scientology. He has understood the fundamental principles of manipulation and managed to articulate them without jargon. His journey and the insights it has provoked will help many others to understand not only the tricks and traps of Scientology, but the dark nature of undue influence wherever it exists.

This book deserves a wide readership. It is a blow for freedom against the oppression of totalitarian practices.

Jon Atack, Nottingham, November 2015

Preface

I was a Scientologist for 27 years.

For a quarter of a century I worked as a staff member for the Church, starting at its lowest levels in a local church organization in Santa Barbara. After eight years there, I moved up to the Sea Organization (aka the "SO"). The Sea Org has been called the "clergy" of Scientology, and in reality is a paramilitary group of only the most dedicated Scientologists who promise to do whatever the current leader of Scientology says to do, regardless of whether those actions would be considered moral or even legal. I spent seventeen years in the SO doing what amounted to slave labor under the guise of the "greatest good for the greatest number".

As I write this, I've been out of the Sea Org for almost three years and out of Scientology entirely for two. These have been the best two years of my life, recovering my sanity, enhancing my emotional stability and creating a new life outside of the destructive cult mind control I was so heavily steeped in.

I've been told I have recovered very quickly from the mind control, but this isn't really true. Cult indoctrination is no joke and it takes a very long time for former members of any destructive cult to recognize all the various things which were done to us, all the mental and emotional land mines laid in place by the cult leader or leaders. I have been very proactive in my recovery by taking a lot of time to educate myself about how destructive cults work and I think that is one thing which helped me enormously.

What I did do differently from most other ex-cult members is I started speaking out almost immediately after I was "expelled" from that group. Most people apparently don't do that. They retreat and disappear for a long while, either to try to make sense of what the hell happened to them or to just try to forget about the whole thing. If there is anything which makes me different from most other people I've met, it's that I like to talk. A lot. I've always been that way from when I was very young. I was pretty upset about what happened to me but I was also very interested in why it happened and what I could do to help other people who were in my same situation.

At first I did so through blog articles and then, when I realized that wasn't reaching as many people as I wanted, I started making videos on a YouTube channel I set up for just that purpose.

This book is a culmination of the work I've done over the past two years in my recovery process. I say "recovery process" because I came to realize not only were my articles and videos a way for me to help and warn others about the dangers of Scientology, but they were also providing me catharsis. It was a way for me to unload a lot of the emotional pain and duress Scientology put me through.

This book and everything in it has been a labor of love and healing. I have a ton of people to thank, most especially my family for being there for me in every way whenever I needed them (which was a lot). I lost a lot of people when I decided to speak out against Scientology – friends and relationships I had for decades and even lost my fiancé, a woman I loved more than life itself; but the new ones I've made since have more than made up for those losses because now I have real friends and closer family ties than ever before and I'm sure someday I will find someone to love again too.

In the world of Scientology, a friend is defined simply as a "fellow cult member" and if you aren't that, you aren't anything to a Scientologist. They will abandon you utterly, "disconnect" you from every part of their life, if one of Scientology's "Ethics Officers" tells them to. That is not a friend by any real definition of the word, but this is what destructive cults do to people, as I will describe in great detail in this book. The good news is I've rediscovered what real friendship, real care and compassion actually mean since I've left Scientology behind me. It is for this reason, more than any other, I have no regrets about the sacrifices I had to make in leaving and am so very thankful I did manage to come to my senses and get out of Scientology.

I hope you find this book interesting and engaging, and I hope it helps you too.

Introduction: How to Read This Book

I have tried to write this book as both something to be read like any regular book, from beginning to end, but can also be used as a sort of reference work with chapters which stand alone.

I start by talking about myself and my own story, an effort to "establish my credentials" so to speak and make it clear why I am an expert when it comes to Scientology. I can't say I'm an expert on very many things, but on this subject I most definitely have more than my fair share of knowledge and experience.

I then go into Scientology broadly, what it is and why it is a destructive cult and what L. Ron Hubbard was trying to do in establishing it in the first place.

I then cover specific aspects of it, such as the pseudoscience of the Purification Rundown and the confidential upper-level services as well as its asinine management hierarchy and fraudulent tax-exempt status.

Finally, I go into the recovery process and what it has taken me to flush Scientology out of my system and move on with my life.

Some of this material is not brand new but is based on articles and videos I've made in the past about different topics or subjects within the world of Scientology. However, that doesn't mean there is nothing new here. On the contrary, everything has been revised and updated and even someone who has seen everything I've created up to now will find a lot of brand new material here.

By necessity and because each chapter is its own unit, there are places where it might seem like I'm repeating myself. That is merely because I'm making some of the same points in different ways about Scientology's nature and activities.

Where key Scientology-specific terms are used, I've done my best to define them in the text itself but I may not have done this over and over again in each chapter because after a while that just becomes redundant and ridiculous. There is an extensive glossary at the end which can be used to define any specific Scientology terms used here.

1. Why Should Anyone Listen to Me?

My Life Into and Out of Scientology

Who am I and what makes me such an expert on Scientology?

Well, I have the unique but unenviable distinction of having been involved in a destructive cult for most of my life and escaping on my own bat. Life in a cult like Scientology is not an easy experience, especially when you get involved in the Sea Organization, and escaping from it can be pretty rough.

Having done so, I like to think I have some knowledge and experience worth sharing. How did I get involved in this in the first place, and how did it take over my entire life? Let's start at the beginning.

Growing Up in Scientology

My parents got involved in Scientology when I was four years old. I was California-born and -raised and we were living up in Oxnard or thereabouts at the time. The thing is, my parents divorced when I was only two years old. As best as I can remember, life was alright for me, shuttling back and forth between them. Somehow my dad's brother got involved in Scientology out in Las Vegas and he told my dad about it. Mom and Dad were still connected by me and whatever other ties they shared and my Dad ended up getting my Mom and his best friend into it. Mom was not having a great time being a single mother in 1974. I don't have all the rest of the details, but I've gleaned that much.

They started doing courses and counselling, which in Scientology is called auditing, and I think they got some marriage counselling as well. Now the amazing thing is my parents got back together and they remarried in 1976. I always credited Scientology with that, and it was only the first of many differences Scientology made in my life. We had moved to Pasadena, California at that point and my parents started working for the Pasadena mission. Missions are a sort of lower-level franchise operation which are privately owned and licensed to deliver basic Scientology services. Missions are supposed to be the front line of Scientology, getting people in and eventually sending them up to the higher level churches where the real money is made. However, back in the 1970s, the privately owned missions were actually doing much better than the official Scientology churches and Pasadena was one such operation. But I digress.

I grew up around Scientology but I was never a part of it because I didn't understand it and was having a hard enough time just growing up and trying to be normal. I was kind of a nerdy intellectual type and was the sort of annoying kid who teachers seemed to like but other kids didn't so much. I had a few friends (also nerds) but I was never ever let into the cool kid circles. More honestly, my annoying ways and intellectually superior attitude kept me out of those circles and I never could seem to learn how to fit in. I developed an attitude it was better to be noticed and annoying than to be ignored. This was not exactly the path to popularity and so school dances, dates with girls and social success were completely foreign activities.

By the time high school rolled around in the mid-80s, my parents were no longer on staff but were still ardent Scientologists and were spending their money and time doing Scientology's advanced spiritual levels, called OT levels. First these were done in Los Angeles and then my Dad got up to OT VI and VII and was travelling to a place called the Flag Service Org in Clearwater, Florida for those. They'd invested a lot of time and money in it but I hadn't really been paying a lot of attention. I heard some things from other kids about how kooky Scientology was but I knew they didn't know what they were talking about, and I didn't know what I was talking about in defending it, so I just ignored it for the most part. It was never really an issue.

Getting Suckered In

At the tail end of completing middle school, we moved up to Santa Maria, California for a number of reasons; the primary one being Los Angeles was a really sucky place. My dad was going into business with some other Scientologists up there, the cost of living was less and we would have a much nicer home. I think the idea was everything would be better there. Truthfully, it was.

Santa Maria is not a big town. It's kind of a farming-type community trying to grow into something more when we got there. It's inland, about halfway between Santa Barbara and San Luis Obispo. Little did I know we had moved to within an hour's drive of where L. Ron Hubbard was living out his last years in seclusion at his Creston ranch, a bit north of San Luis Obispo. I was just a short drive away from the man who would end up influencing my life more than any other person. This was not something I would be aware of until decades later.

High school was, well, high school. I was shy and awkward, not athletic and not someone who any girls ever wanted to have anything to do with. My dorky wardrobe and amazingly inept social graces had a lot to do with that, I'm sure.

So when I was 15 years old, during the summer between my sophomore and junior years, my Dad suggested out of the blue that I go down to the closest Church of Scientology, which was about an hour's drive away in Santa Barbara. A young co-worker at my Dad's company, the son of my Dad's business partner, in fact, was going down on Monday and Tuesday nights and all day Sunday taking classes and he could drive me down with him. So it was I ended up in front of Lynn, a gorgeous blond who worked the front desk at the Santa Barbara church, who reeled me in like a fish.

The personality test, or more officially the "Oxford Capacity Analysis," is one of the primary means Scientology uses to sucker people in to take services. It consists of 200 pretty odd questions which they use to graph your personality and tell you about yourself. There are questions such as "Do you sleep well?" or "Do you spend much time on needless worries" or "Do you browse railway timetables, dictionaries and such just for pleasure?" It's basically one step up from a total cold reading (the kind psychics do) in that you have given them some information about yourself and then they go over the results with you and get you to tell them even more about yourself. The whole point is for you to open up and tell them what it is about yourself you want to change or improve. This is called your "ruin". They then use this information to sell you any beginning Scientology which you think will help you with that problem. Once you have your foot in the door, it's then a matter of keeping you in with service after service, all costing progressively more money the further along you go.

Me being who and what I was – a shy, introverted 15 year old who could barely look at people when I was talking to them, especially if they were pretty – I was putty in Lynn's hands. She told me what I already knew about myself but couldn't believe she somehow magically found out. When she said I had a problem with girls, but they had a way of solving that problem for me, it was like the Second Coming of Christ. The clouds parted, the angels sang and I swore I could see an angelic halo around her face. I just about fell out of my chair, because it was inconceivable to me I would ever be able to overcome my awkwardness or figure out how to ever get a date.

Lynn assured me all that and much more was possible if I did their communications course. I couldn't sign up fast enough.

Was I a stupid person? No, I wasn't. I was quite smart actually and got good grades and even at 15 years old, I knew a lot of things. I wasn't stupid but I was naïve and reckless. I didn't know con men really existed, people can lie without knowing they are lying and just because someone says they are your friend, doesn't make it so. If I have any "weakness" in my life, it's my trust and optimism. Even after everything I've been through, I still believe people are basically good and are worthy of my trust before they prove me wrong. Of course, that is now tempered by all my experience so I'm no fool anymore but back then, yeah. I was a fool. I was also desperate to be thought well of and I would do anything, repeat anything, to be popular.

The communications course did help me overcome my shyness and I was able to start talking to girls. What I said to them was not any better, though, and this class did not really help me to become more popular or get any more dates than I had before. What it did do is help me become a little bit more self aware though. I stopped dressing like a total nerd and I walked with my head a little higher and I felt a bit more confident. My friends noticed this and remarked on it and that was all the proof I needed Scientology indeed could work miracles.

Scientology as a Career

Two years later, with not only the communications course under my belt but a slew of other courses including their Study Technology, a course on their system of Ethics and even basic training on the E-meter, I graduated high school and was just starting college.

I was always creative, developed some writing skills and wanted very much to be a novelist in the tradition of Stephen King. This was so much the case, I determined my career trajectory would be to get an English degree and teach in school while I wrote whatever Great American Novel I had in me. Alas, this was not to be.

It was September of 1987 and I was doing Scientology's detox program, what they call the Purification Rundown, even though I'd never taken any street drugs or been exposed to real toxins in my entire life. The extent of my "drug history" was anesthesia from having my tonsils removed when I was 5 years old, some Novocain from the dentist and getting drunk once at a high school party. But in Scientology, spiritual salvation is a one-size-fits-all proposition and everyone does all the services on the Bridge to Total Freedom. This is the step-by-step series of services every single Scientologist does, in sequence, to attain what they call "total spiritual freedom". The services start cheap and quickly escalate in price and in time required to do them. Hubbard built this "Bridge" over the years, promising it was now completely worked out and all we had to do was walk over it. He used a bridge as an analogy of crossing over from the dark, ruined hell which was our existence on Earth to a bright, shiny, wonderful place where our lives were our own and we would be free of the endless cycle of living life after life after life, over and over again in an infinite loop. We could take control over every factor of life and make our own destiny, something he worded as "being at cause".

It was many years before they would start making everyone re-do lower-level services over and over again in a blatant money grab. Back in the mid-80s, it all still had an air of legitimacy and made a bit more sense.

The Purification Rundown takes a few weeks and is done rigorously every single day. I was spending five hours in the sauna sweating out these supposed toxins in my body and after I was done, I would get grabbed up by a wonderful (and very beautiful) woman named Alison who recruited me to join staff at the Santa Barbara organization.

I was 17 years old and Scientology had actually cured me of a great deal of my shyness and introversion. Now I was making an even bigger fool of myself socially, but at least I wasn't shy about doing it. I still wasn't getting dates, I wasn't particularly any more popular and I had just as much of a hard time studying as I did before. However, because I felt better about myself, I was able to convince myself I was a better person because of Scientology.

The beginning services in Scientology do have some very workable common sense principles, almost all of which Hubbard ripped off from other sources and claimed as his own "discoveries". However, I still had no real idea of how things worked in the real world and all the promises of good pay and joining a "winning team" appealed to me, especially since they were being delivered by a beautiful blonde who said she really admired me and how obviously intelligent and "good-hearted" a man I was.

I couldn't sign the staff contract fast enough.

My parents were good Scientologists but they had their own horrifying experiences as staff members back in Pasadena and were not enthusiastic about my new career choice. After three days of haranguing and arguing back and forth, they finally relented and they signed the contract too so I could go off and join before my 18th birthday. As a minor, I needed their signatures on the contract.

Just to clarify what I mean by the staff contract: when anyone joins staff in a Scientology church, they sign a legal document which states they are volunteer staff members at that organization for a period of either 2.5 years or five years. If you are going to be sent off for full-time training for a particular staff position (such as being a counsellor or a course supervisor) then you have to do the five-year stint. That's what I signed up for.

The contract is worded to ensure Scientology gets everything (your time, your loyalty and your promise to never talk about what goes on behind closed doors in the churches) and you get nothing. Not unlike the Terms of Service agreements you sign when installing new software, new recruits rarely actually read the fine print and simply join up based on the verbal agreements and promises made by their recruiters.

Scientology staff members, because they are classified as religious volunteers by law, are not entitled to any compensation of any kind. They are promised free Scientology auditing and training services and some even manage to work their schedule in such a way to get some free services, but only after putting in a full work day. Because most staff are paid something on the order of $20 – $40 a week maximum, they cannot afford the time to take the free services because they have to get a real job to subsidize their Scientology employment. The entire eight years I spent in Santa Barbara, I worked 80-hour weeks (a regular full time job and 40 hours as a staff member) in order to afford the "privilege" of being a Scientology staff member.

The Life of a Scientology Staff Member

Now as bad as it might sound to be a staff member with what I've said above, the truth is I agreed to join up because I felt it was a kind of "higher calling" and I learned to accept any sacrifices I had to make along the way as part of the difficult road we travelled to "clear the planet" (Scientology's euphemistic catch-phrase for taking over the world by making everyone into Scientologists). I knew I was suffering as a staff member and I didn't enjoy it but I felt part of a cause and there is nothing more energetic or more dangerous to the world at large then a young person who is deluded into thinking they are saving the world.

I accepted two very important beliefs in my journey into Scientology: (1) Scientology's promises were real and it worked 100% of the time on anyone it was applied to so long as they did it exactly according to Hubbard's directions; (2) Scientology was the answer to every single one of Mankind's problems.

You can take any religious principle, political stance or even social agenda and plug it in for Scientology in the last paragraph and you have the definition of a zealot. There were a lot of struggles and a lot of sacrifice, more than I can easily tell in a book five times this size. To try to tell the entire story of all the craziness which happened when I was on staff would take us beyond the scope of this book, much less this beginning chapter. I will merely summarize by saying I was always struggling financially, intimate relationships were few and far between and every one of them was a disaster because of Scientology (a fact I did not recognize at the time). It was also during this time I started developing some very serious long-term emotional issues due to a rule enforced on Scientology staff called "no case on post". This last point I will elaborate on briefly because it's important.

In Scientology, "case" refers to your personal issues, the things you have going on in your mind which you consider are non-optimum and want to handle with Scientology. This basically amounts to the sum total of bad things which have happened to you in your life and which have created emotional or spiritual trauma. Scientology promises to resolve these issues fully with their auditing procedures. I'll explain more about how later in this book. For now, let's just say I took it on faith my "case" would be fully resolved eventually, all my spiritual problems and upsets would no longer exist, I'd be in a vast spiritual state of awareness and ability which they call "Operating Thetan" and I'd be at "cause over life".

However, regardless of my own unresolved case, one of Hubbard's dictums for staff and Sea Org members is they are not to "dramatize

8

their case on post" meaning they are basically to pretend those problems don't exist and to put on a happy face and always put their best foot forward when dealing with other staff or Scientologists.

On a short term basis, this is perfectly acceptable. I'm sure if you went to McDonald's, you wouldn't want your server to start crying and telling you how their mother died that day and how upset they are about it. If they did, they'd be having "case on post" and it would reflect badly on McDonalds. Of course, the difference is, in the real world, if someone's mother died and they couldn't deal with it, they wouldn't be made to go to work that day! Or the next or the next. They'd be given time to actually grieve and be with family and get themselves back together so they could continue on with their life.

Not so when you are a staff member in Scientology. Your girlfriend left you and you're down in the dumps? You just lost your regular job and don't know what you're going to do for income since the Church is paying you next to nothing? Your kid's in the hospital and you think you can't show up to post? Forget all that. No case on post! You put on a happy face and you do your job! You drown your sorrows in helping other people.

If you do this for enough years, without any other outlet or help and certainly without being able to avail yourself of any Scientology auditing (because there's never time for that), and you'll find yourself with some pretty serious emotional problems. You get into such a habit of not being able to feel how you actually feel, after a while you don't know how to even express real emotions anymore. You literally forget what it feels like to feel.

My emotions were so repressed and on such lockdown it took me almost a year after I got out of the Sea Organization before I even started to suspect there might possibly be something wrong with my ability to express how I felt.

So getting back to my narrative, after eight years of blood, sweat and tears as a staff member in Santa Barbara, I was in the frame of mind the reason the organization was not thriving, expanding and wildly successful was because of our shortcomings and our inability as staff to do what L. Ron Hubbard told us to. It never occurred to me, literally never crossed my mind, the real problem might be Hubbard's contradictory policies or his unworkable "mental and spiritual technology". It was constantly drummed into us by Hubbard himself in his written and spoken works the only reason his organizations did not expand and were not taking over the world at a mad rate was because the staff were not doing their jobs the way he directed. That viewpoint was strictly enforced down the line by Scientology managers, who took Hubbard's words as absolute law.

I had no idea at the time this is one of the characteristics of a destructive cult: a central leader or leadership who are infallible and cannot be questioned, while laying the blame for every single thing which ever goes wrong on the individual members and their lack of faith, devotion or skill. This is the hallmark of a destructive cult. Instilling this point of view is a form of mind control which ensures cult members never question anyone but themselves and their own loyalties and actions. The cult leader is always blameless and never means anything but the best for his flock. Therefore, anything which goes wrong is always your own fault. Always.

So I decided if I wanted to see Scientology really make it, I was going to have to be more responsible and do more. I was going to have to join the Sea Organization.

"Moving Up" to the Sea Org

I spent a total of 17 years in the Sea Organization. If I thought my time as a staff member was insane, it was nothing compared to what happened during these years. Again, to detail them all would be impossible in a work of this size and scope. I will simply cover the highlights of my time in and what I did there to fulfill the major purpose of this chapter, which is to give you my Scientology bona fides.

As a staff member in Santa Barbara, I went from being a course supervisor (like a teacher, supervising Scientology classrooms) to being the executive overseeing all class and auditing delivery in the organization. In Scientology, classes and auditing are considered "technology". As the person in charge of that area, I was the "Technical Secretary".

When I joined the Sea Org, I moved down to Los Angeles and took up residence at the Sea Org base in Hollywood, called the Pacifica Base or PAC for short. The Sea Org is paramilitary so I went through a sort of boot camp called the Estates Project Force (EPF). I was now in uniform, called my seniors "Sir" and was working 24/7 for the cause. All my food and berthing was taken care of and I made a maximum of $45 a week pay (called an "allowance" in the SO). Often times the allowance was less and sometimes it was nothing at all depending on how things were going.

While the pay was not always constant, the working hours were. We were up by 7:30 or 8am each day, seven days a week, and worked until 11pm or midnight. Days off were a thing of the past; at best you could hope to have every other Sunday off if your production was acceptable (which it hardly ever was). Lunches and dinners were a half hour and there were no production breaks day or night. Being a Sea Org member means a life of endless dedication and devotion where giving 110% is not only expected, it's never actually enough.

Within a few months of arriving, I met the woman who would end up being my wife for 17 years, the same amount of time I was in the SO. Her name was Sunny, she was absolutely amazing and I really did love her quite a lot. In retrospect, I think she was more in love with the idea of being married and being in love than she was particularly in love with me. I don't hold that against her, I just want to give an idea of why our marriage didn't really work. We had our ups and downs and it didn't end well when I decided to leave the Sea Org because I knew she was not going to leave with me. Her loyalties were most definitely to the Sea Org first and it was definitely a Sea Org marriage, meaning one more of convenience than passion. One rule in the Sea Org which leads people to quick marriage is you cannot have sex or any sexual activity with someone unless you are married. This makes marriage and divorce a very common thing in the SO.

During our time together, I attempted to make it romantic and do things for her but I always felt they were unappreciated, and I'm sure

11

she would say the same for the things she did for me. To be totally honest, there were times when my eyes strayed and in the end, I did cheat on her while we were still married. That doesn't make me a good person and I'm not proud of my infidelity. It happened, I paid the price for it and I most definitely learned enough to know I will never again do that to any future partners. There's more about this later in this chapter, but for now I'll simply say our marriage didn't end well. I'm sure she'd be happy to see me with a stake through my heart now, but I am past all that now and I really do wish her well. I hope someday she comes to see the truth of the disaster she has devoted her life to supporting and she makes it out of there and maybe even has the family she always wanted but the Sea Org denied her.

Getting back to my SO career, my first position was the same technical administration role I had in Santa Barbara, but instead of overseeing one organization, I was now overseeing the entire Western United States. The name of this position was the Assistant Technical Aide for the West US. There were thirty-one regular organizations and three Sea Org organizations under me. By regular organizations I mean local-level, city churches such as those in Santa Barbara, Denver, Minnesota, St Louis, etc. The Sea Org organizations were the next level up, meaning they delivered higher level services than the local city churches and were staffed entirely by Sea Org members. [Note: the entire Scientology organizational hierarchy is explained in Chapter 13].

My role as a manager over West US delivery lasted for eight years. Working in Scientology management is like running in a hamster wheel while being constantly berated for not getting to your destination and occasionally being let off the wheel to go scrub pots and pans in 120 degree temperatures as punishment for not running fast enough. Management personnel are worse than useless to those they manage because their orders are so random and insanely undoable. You never know from one day to the next what "big emergency" is going to need to be solved. I wasn't aware of it at the time, but the entire tone of this activity is set by David Miscavige and the frantic devotion of the Sea Org to comply with his every whim.

After eight years I couldn't take it anymore. I crashed so hard I went AWOL for three days. I returned because (a) I loved my wife and (b) my parents encouraged me to do what I wanted but suggested I not leave loose ends and take responsibility for my agreements. I went back to the Sea Org base and after getting a justice action (called a Committee of Evidence) for the unauthorized leave and making restitution for it, I was transferred to the Advanced Organization of Los Angeles. I was officially done with being in Scientology management and I could not have been happier about it.

AOLA is the Sea Org org in Los Angeles which delivers the first five OT levels. At first I was a Registrar (the Scientology term for a salesman), convincing people how much they needed the OT levels and taking their money, despite the fact I had no clue what the OT levels actually consisted of or what you did on them. I did that for about six months.

Despite not having done the OT Levels themselves, I was very familiar with much of Scientology's technology and how the whole Bridge to Total Freedom worked, and I thought I was selling pearls for pennies. I was motivated to do a good job and I learned how to do sales from the Chief Registrar, Steve Kemper. I started to build up a "client base" and was getting in a steady stream of income each week. My best week ever, near the end of my tenure as a salesman, was when I arranged a package for a couple in Las Vegas who had barely started on the Bridge but whose eyes were all alight by the prospect of making it to "full OT." I worked with them and between all the services and materials, got almost $100,000 from them. That was a banner week for sure.

As happens almost every other week in the Sea Org, some urgent personnel transfer happened and suddenly they needed me to replace an executive in AOLA who was being sent off for advanced auditor training. I had just settled into the idea of being a salesman and now I was being "handled" to go be an executive again. Thus it was I found myself back in the Tech area, running the division responsible for getting people through the setup actions required to do the OT Levels.

13

I was still pretty burned out from my eight years in management and was becoming pretty disillusioned with the Sea Organization. I got myself into some trouble by starting a non-physical but intimate relationship with a married woman. Although we never even kissed, the Sea Org takes a very dim view on any sort of extramarital activity. Of course, I was not happy for having done that either and my wife, correctly so, was furious. I was so caved in over it and felt so bad about the whole thing, I willingly acceded to being assigned to the Rehabilitation Project Force.

The RPF is the Sea Org's prison detail and I spent three years getting through the program of auditing and grueling physical labor they put you through. When you read "RPF" just think "Maoist reconditioning camp" and you'll have the right idea. It's a complex program, too difficult to easily describe here and will probably be the subject of a future book so I have a chance to really explain it in detail. I will simply state when I started it, I was at the lowest low I'd ever felt and I thought I deserved it. The RPF was the single hardest thing I've ever done and was the worst experience of my entire life. I desperately wanted to make up for what I'd done to my wife and I did not want to be kicked out of Scientology. I worked my ass off and I successfully completed the program – something fewer than 50% of Sea Org RPFers accomplish. I look back now and shake my head at the idea of feeling pride over that accomplishment, because the far more sensible thing to do would have been to leave the Sea Org behind me when I was there. On the other hand, like Marine Boot Camp, the RPF is not for wimps and people who can make it through have truly survived an ordeal which made them a stronger person.

After all the reconditioning and having my face rubbed in every single bad thing I ever did in my entire life (and in past lives too), I came out feeling a lot better about myself and a bit better about being a Sea Org member. Don't get me wrong, because I was not a zombie-eyed fanatical Sea Org member again. In fact, after being away so long, I felt like I had a fresh new look at Sea Org life and I didn't really like what I saw.

Having been away from the main group of the Sea Org, I came back to quite a different Sea Org world, where more radical money-making pressures were ramping up into total overdrive. It was 2008 and the idea of selling and delivering services took a back seat; now all Scientology was doing was blatantly grabbing people's money. It's not like Scientology was all that different at its core or some extremists took over. It was just the money-making scam aspect of Scientology was now not so hidden or covert.

Almost every Sea Org member was now spending at least 3 hours a day on the phones calling the public, some of whom had not been anywhere near Scientology in years, and trying to convince them to buy a set of the newly released Basic Books and Lectures. This was a repackaged set of Hubbard's books which Miscavige spent three hours briefing everyone on at a huge international Scientology event, saying it was literally the most important and monumental event to have ever taken place in the history of Scientology. I'd started studying the new books while I was on the RPF and I liked some of the revisions but Miscavige was in some kind of religious ecstasy over them. He demanded every single person who ever had anything to do with Scientology buy a set and study them. So it was the entire body of the Sea Org took a sharp right turn and made this their number one, top priority to somehow, anyhow, contact every single name Scientology had in its files and convince them to buy these books.

Call Centers were established and Sea Org members manned the phones in shifts, spending anywhere from three to twenty-four hours a day frantically trying to reach people. And I do mean frantically. These call centers were run like intense boiler rooms with supervisors patrolling each aisle making sure sales were happening. If a Sea Org member didn't manage to get someone on the phone after about 15-20 minutes, he had to stand up and do 20 jumping jacks or 10 pushups right then and there to "motivate him". If he didn't make any sales that day, he might find himself up into the late hours of the night and next morning scrubbing pots in the galley, cleaning toilets with toothbrushes, scrubbing trashcans or being hosed down as a form of "being thrown overboard from a ship" (a classic Sea Org punishment from when the Sea Org was actually at sea in the 1970s).

This all started while I was on the RPF and I actually thought I had it easier than those poor guys in the Call Center. The insane scheduling and pressure did not let up for months, until even the executives in charge of this insanity started realizing hollow-eyed Sea Org members were falling asleep during the day on their regular posts and many were secretly leaving in the middle of the night, never to be heard from again.

I was lucky. When I got off the RPF, I went to the one area of the Sea Org in Los Angeles exempt from doing any of this Call Center madness. I was put to work at Bridge Publications, making Scientology books at their in-house manufacturing/publishing facility. While I'd dodged a bullet, working at Bridge was the most boring and frustrating thing ever because I was not good at it. I came to find out I am partially color blind, which hampered my ability to do quality control of color printing. This created real trouble for me in creating book covers and my seniors were seeing red at some of the mistakes I was making. I literally could not *see* what the problem was!

Finally, I got myself out of that situation and back to doing something I liked and knew how to do: going out to the local churches and helping them while recruiting new Sea Org members. The Sea Org is always recruiting new members and they often do this by sending SO members out to remote locations (like local Scientology churches) to talk to Scientologists and convince them to come on board. They also replace staff members at those Scientology churches who want to "move up" in the same way I had from Santa Barbara. That is what I specialized in and I was very good at it.

I was out for about a year doing this and got 11 people into the Sea Org and about 25-30 people to join staff at the orgs where I went. I was getting kind of tired of being away from my wife and not getting any study or auditing time so I was making noises about coming back and staying for good. In response, they transferred me to become what they call a Missionaire, meaning someone who goes out and does

16

nothing but special projects, usually away from the Sea Org bases. You really do have to love the irony sometimes.

Okay, Enough Sea Org, Enough!

In the Sea Org, when they send someone out to a remote location to carry out a special project, they call it "going on a mission". I did lots of those and I was always successful at them. I don't say this to brag; it just happened to be something I was very good at because I liked helping people and it was what motivated me to be in the Scientology in the first place.

I travelled around the western United States doing various missions. I worked on missions in Las Vegas, Portland, Seattle, Pasadena, Orange County and eventually spent most of that time at the Church of Scientology in Twin Cities, Minnesota. I worked on recruiting staff and recovering ex-Scientologists who didn't want to do anything with Scientology anymore. The idea was, if we could recover them back into the fold, we could then recruit them to be on staff.

In addition to the whole push to sell Basic Books and Lectures, one of the other big new strategic pushes David Miscavige came up with back in 2004 was to renovate all the existing Scientology church buildings by doing local fundraising. This generated millions of dollars in real estate because most Scientology churches were moved to new, larger buildings and then those buildings were renovated to be "up to the standard of Scientology." These new buildings were called "Ideal Organizations" or "Ideal Orgs" and this became the number one priority for every single church and for Scientology management worldwide.

My final mission was opening up the Twin Cities Ideal Org. This was a massive new 90,000 square foot church building which would end up being empty almost all the time because there are a grand total of about 150 Scientologists in the five-state region around Minnesota. You see, these Ideal Orgs were not needed because it's not like Scientology was overflowing with so many people they outgrew their quarters and needed bigger ones. No, it is just another part of the blatant money grab Scientology has become.

All these missions and being away from the Sea Org base (and the pressures and insanity created there) made me see what Scientology and the Sea Org were doing from a more exterior point of view. I got to drive all over the western United States handling logistics matters and I was in the unique position of being sent off to do these kinds of tasks on my own. Usually Sea Org members are at least paired up to keep an eye on each other and help each other out. Hubbard said it was policy to never send a Sea Org member out on a mission alone because they would always fail. More likely, what he meant by fail is they would more easily come to their senses and just take off!

Going around from one Scientology organization to another also showed me in vivid living color how empty they all were. Totally and completely empty, with maybe something like 10 or 20 public showing up at a time for services. Compared to the hundreds who were shown in videos and promotional pieces, and the millions of members Scientology's publicists claimed, this was a very sorry state of affairs.

At the five or six annual internationally broadcast Scientology events or gatherings, David Miscavige stands on stage and give glossy audio-visual presentations of Ideal Org openings. These are attended by thousands of Scientologists and local city officials, mayors and other key opinion leaders would be enticed to show up and say a few words about the good works Scientology does for their area. Few of these officials have ever heard of Scientology before they were contacted to speak at these events, or they have a peripheral involvement with one or two Scientologists who were doing "PR work" with them such as local street cleanups or passing out The Way to Happiness booklets or something like that.

The purpose of these presentations was to show how big and "booming" Scientology was and how it was nothing but expansion and good news from all over the world. What they didn't show you at the events was most of those Scientologists in those big crowds were flown in from other regions and many of them were, in fact, Sea Org members! The building construction wasn't even fully completed, the contractors who did the work were not even paid... How the staff for these orgs were recruited from other geographical areas because there weren't enough Scientologists around in that area to draw from.

I got to see behind the scenes in setting up these events and getting these staff relocated. I could see the whole thing was a kind of dog and pony show which just served to keep fleecing the rich Scientology public by making them believe in Scientology's success. It was like a vast Ponzi scheme being played out across the world.

Additionally, because I was out and away from Los Angeles so much on these missions, my marriage basically tanked. I knew by December 2011 I wanted to leave the Sea Org and thus leave Sunny as well. It was a gradual process and once I made the decision, I was not really filled with a lot of regret or grief. I loved my wife but we had grown apart and it was clear to me we were not in our marriage on the same terms or with the same desires. The RPF had been my way of trying to come to terms with that by blaming myself for everything which went wrong in our relationship and working for three years to fix myself. I came to find out after the RPF it was not just me who needed fixing and it takes two to make (or break) a relationship. My marriage simply wasn't working out because we just weren't in it for the same reasons and we did not have the same goals, at least not anymore.

My efforts to talk to her about the troubles I was experiencing and troubles we were having also fell on deaf ears. She simply fed right back to me the standard Scientology lines like "you have black PR" and "you just have overts" and "you need to stop nattering" (Scientology speak for complaining). It was abundantly clear to me my wife was not someone who wanted to help or support me as a husband, but instead was treating me like just another Sea Org member. In all fairness to her, that is what the Sea Org does to its members. Nothing is more important than the Sea Org or Scientology's bogus mission to "clear the planet."

Although I decided I wanted to go, I wanted to complete my final mission rather than go straight back to LA to leave the SO. I had nothing but time on my hands and felt I owed it to the staff and public of Twin Cities to finish what I'd started without making a big mess of the whole project. It was for this same reason I did not tell my wife anything about my decision for a divorce. I figured I would handle that at the same time as I was leaving the Sea Org once I eventually returned to LA.

What happened next I did not expect. I started being more friendly with one of the staff there at the org – initially just as friends because we were both kind of geeky people - and when she reciprocated, we quickly fell for each other as more than friends. I'll call her Joan, even though that is not her name, as despite everything which happened, I still respect her right to privacy and don't see any need to call her out by name in this.

This time, I did have a full blown extramarital affair. Yes, this was adultery and yes it was not really cool. This does make me an adulterer and a bad person. This is a fact Scientology has since used against me to tell other Scientologists why they should not ever listen to anything I say, as though adulterers can never be trusted to tell the truth about anything ever. At the time, knowing my marriage was over and I was leaving the Sea Org, I felt I was ending my old life and I wanted to start a new one. It was a bit of a premature start, perhaps, but since I decided to leave the SO, I wanted to start making my life my own in whatever way I could. Given a choice now, I would have done things differently, namely by just leaving Twin Cities when I first wanted to and leaving the Sea Org behind. However, I didn't and so have lived with the consequences of that decision ever since.

Joan and I were very surreptitious and careful and we did not get caught, although there were definitely some close calls. I fell totally head over heels for her and we talked about our future and where things were going. We were clear on the fact we wanted to make a life together, I was leaving the Sea Org and my wife and she was the woman of my dreams. All that was completely true. To this day, even after everything, not one day goes by I don't think about Joan or miss her in my life. She truly was the love of my life and I don't know if I'll ever feel the same about someone again. I can certainly hope.

At first I was still in touch with my wife by texts but after my decision to leave, this became less and less frequent. I was always the one texting her with little sweet messages and notes, sending her presents and cards and whatnot. Now things were different for me and I was definitely not feeling romantic toward her anymore. I finally stopped texting her altogether just because I was curious how long it would take her to notice. Three weeks later, she texted me and asked what was going on and how I was doing. She wasn't sure what was happening but she finally figured something must be since I'd changed my routine with her. I thought it took her long enough to figure that much out. I'd determined I was not going to lie to her and so when the text conversation suddenly veered into asking me if I was thinking about divorcing her, I told her I was. So in May 2012, I was recalled back to Los Angeles because Sunny reported this to my project supervisor.

No one knew I had this new relationship with Joan and she wasn't the reason for the divorce anyway, so I didn't bring her into it. However, Sunny did get upset about the news of the divorce and she wanted me sorted out.

Within an hour of being back in LA, I submitted my "desire to leave" resignation letter to the powers that be and started what would be a nine-month process of leaving the Sea Org. No one saw it coming. I cooperated fully with everything they asked me to do and didn't act up or reveal my impatience despite the months of waiting around.

The process of leaving basically involves a security check (an interrogation using the E-meter as a kind of lie detector to make sure you tell everything). They want to make sure you haven't done anything they don't know about (literally anything – your entire life is under a microscope in a sec check). I got through that easily enough. I had 1,000 hours of rigorous security checking on the RPF so I knew how to get through one. The E-meter doesn't work the way Scientologists think it does and while I did not fully understand it at the time, I did know it was not accurate and I was not under any compulsion to tell them everything on my mind.

Nine months is a long time and I did maintain communication with Joan via a hidden cell phone I'd brought back with me from Twin Cities. I didn't really care whether I was going to get in trouble or not over the whole thing, but I didn't tell anyone in LA about Joan because I didn't want her to get in trouble. I was leaving the SO but she was still a staff member and her whole family was in Scientology and if we'd been caught out, she would have gotten into a lot of trouble for having sex with a married Sea Org member, regardless of the circumstances. Because I was leaving the Sea Org, going back to the RPF was never an option and never something I was afraid of them trying to do to me. And the truth is after you have experienced something like the RPF, there is very little else you can be effectively threatened with.

Most of the waiting during that time was because they didn't have an auditor to do the security check. When someone wants to leave, they are at the bottom of the priority list so it was a lot of waiting around. I spent my time reading, doing some cleaning and other physical labor, grading tests and course room assignments and sneaking off with my laptop to learn more about Photoshop or watch a movie in a storage closet. Eventually I completed all their requirements and they let me go.

Going Down the Rabbit Hole

The last stage of my Scientology story happened, again, in Twin Cities.

When I first left the Sea Org, I landed at my mother's house in California. My parents had since divorced again (back in the early 1990s) and my Dad was living up in Oregon. They both remarried really nice people who never had anything to do with Scientology.

My parents hadn't done any official Scientology services since the early 1990s but it was at this point I found out both my parents were, in fact, totally out of official Scientology and were never going back in. They had been out for many years but were "under the radar" meaning they just quietly faded away, not taking calls from the Church and not being openly antagonistic when any Scientologist did manage to get through to them. Scientology doesn't really care if you fade away; they go ballistic on you when you speak out against them or do anything which the Church considers will damage its glowing reputation in the media. Little did I realize that was what I was about to do. In fact, being a church critic was the last thing I ever wanted to happen.

I wanted to get back to Twin Cities to be with Joan but I needed to do it in such a way as to not get Joan in trouble by immediately just showing up there and openly resuming our relationship. Plus, I successfully got away from the Sea Org but I still wanted to actually do Scientology and get up The Bridge to OT. I still believed in Hubbard's goodness, even though I knew at this point the current leader, David Miscavige, was off-the-rails and was leading Scientology over a cliff through his greed and avarice.

In my time on Sea Org projects, I generally left a good impression where I went and people thought well of me. Nowhere was that more true than Twin Cities. I personally helped many of the staff and public there. Through my recovery work, some of the staff at the org were only there because of me. In retrospect, I wish this hadn't happened of course, but in the context of the bubble world of Scientology, I was a really good guy who did really good things.

It was a bit of a shock to many of them when I got on Facebook and announced I was no longer in the Sea Org, but generally people were excited. I had some phone calls from friends in Twin Cities and whatnot and hinted I might be coming back out that way. Joan arranged to get me a job with a Scientologist out in Twin Cities (without being too obvious about it) and within a month I was on my way back there to start my new life in earnest.

And so it was, Scientology started messing with me yet again in a more direct and harsher way than I'd imagined.

I was driving across the country, somewhere on the road in South Dakota, when I got a phone call from Gavin Kelly, one of the Sea Org members I'd been on my last mission with in Twin Cities. It turns out at some point after I was recalled to Los Angeles back in May, the mission was disbanded and two of the missionaires were put on permanent postings in Twin Cities. When Gavin heard on the grapevine I was not only out of the Sea Org but was on my way back to Twin Cities to live there, he completely freaked out.

23

This could not be! Shelton coming back to Twin Cities? What bad PR for the Sea Org! What would people think? Someone leaves the Sea Org and is happy and gets on with their life successfully? No way is this acceptable! Absolutely not! Gavin felt it was a moral imperative to put a stop to my move through whatever means necessary.

You see, what I totally spaced on was the Sea Org never forgives and never forgets. It hates ex-Sea Org members almost as bad as it hates psychiatrists. People who leave the Sea Org are considered 'degraded beings' who have abandoned their responsibilities and are not worthy of even being a Scientologist until they have crawled through the mud on their hands and knees to beg forgiveness. This come straight from L. Ron Hubbard's lips. He wrote a policy letter about Sea Org members who resign and literally labels them "Degraded Beings" or DBs. Sea Org members are all too happy to follow Hubbard's lead and shower hate and disgust on ex-Sea Org members.

As a Sea Org member, I should have remembered this but I was so enamored with my new-found freedom and my new life, the dark side of Scientology seemed distant and had nothing to do with me.

All this started coming to me in a rush when Gavin called me and told me in no uncertain terms it was unacceptable for me to come out to Minnesota. I'm standing at a gas station in South Dakota listening to this and wondering just what did he think I was going to do? Turn around and go back to California because he felt uncomfortable having me around? It turns out that is exactly what he wanted me to do. I, of course, refused.

Shortly thereafter I got a phone call from Kellen McIntyre in Los Angeles, who also explained to me it was unacceptable and "very senior people" (I never did find out who) were yelling and screaming at her about me daring to show my face in Twin Cities. She made it clear while she couldn't stop me from moving, I was not to go into the org or contact any Scientologists. Basically, I was being temporarily expelled from the Church for an indefinite period until things "cooled down".

It was at this point I saw what was going on and I realized I was going to have to cooperate if I wanted to pull off my new life and make a go of it with Joan, so I tried to go along with these instructions once I arrived in Twin Cities and settled in. The only problem was a couple of the staff in Twin Cities really liked me and they didn't understand what this was all about. It made no sense. Why was I being singled out? Why was I forbidden to come around the org? There was no policy from L. Ron Hubbard saying to do this, yet the Sea Org was doing it!

They too didn't understand the hate and vile Sea Org members feel toward ex-Sea Org members. I sort of conveniently forgot my own natural revulsion toward ex-SO when I was in, how I thought of them as second class citizens and unworthy of being allowed to continue in Scientology for betraying our trust. Now it was happening to me, my eyes started to open to the fact I was part of a sort of caste system for decades, with ex-SO members being below the status of "wogs" (Hubbard's pejorative for people who have never been in Scientology). It seemed perfectly natural when I was in, but now it was happening to me, the situation was taking on a whole new light.

It's quite amazing how things like this have to happen for so many of us to open our eyes to the injustices and prejudices around us. It's not until it happens to us personally do we realize what we were doing to others. I wish I could say I never stooped to that level or talked down to people. I wish I could say I never acted like an arrogant asshole when I was in the Sea Org but those would be lies. I did do those things and more. I tried to be civil, helpful and just when I saw gross injustices occur and I know I didn't get anywhere near as bad as many of my fellow SO members, but that's no excuse for the poor way I treated many people who did not deserve it.

Seeing what was going on, I tried to counsel cooperation and patience to the two staff members who were railing against the orders coming out of Los Angeles. I tried to placate Joan, who also did not understand what was going on or why I could not go into the org or why we could not be more open in at least showing the world we were dating. It was true there was no written policy or justification for what the Sea Org was doing in keeping me "off the lines" of the org, ordering me not to have contact with Scientologists or be friends with anyone. I was lucky I was able to keep my job with a local Scientologist!

To answer the queries from the staff about me, Kellan and others who used to be my friends in Los Angeles, wrote issues describing what a horrible person I was and sent them to the Twin Cities organization to be posted on the notice boards so people would understand why I was *persona non grata*. The information in the issues was just made up or exaggerated claims about all the horrible things I'd done over the 27 years I was in Scientology, painting me as a villain in order to justify why I was not allowed in the org.

This is what Scientology does. It uses people until they are no use to them any longer and then it castigates them as villains so no "good" Scientologists will have anything to do with them, pretending those who sacrificed almost all their time, money and energy toward the good of Scientology have suddenly gone evil and must be destroyed. This is a direct reflection of L. Ron Hubbard's vindictive personality which has been written into the very DNA of Scientology. I will go over this in much more detail in later chapters.

Back when I was in the Sea Org and was doing recovery actions, I used the internet to locate people and in so doing stumbled on some anti-Scientology articles. I knew there were some bad things going on, David Miscavige was reportedly beating up on his juniors and Scientology had a reputation for being a cult of greed. I'd even seen an email from a former member, Debbie Cook, which powerfully used L. Ron Hubbard's own policies to show how the Church was not following them under Miscavige's leadership and was nothing but a greedy money-making operation. I'd acknowledged the truth of some of that but parked the rest of it because I didn't want to get in trouble for being "disaffected". Reading anti-Scientology material on the internet is a very big no-no.

While I understood what was happening, I was also extremely upset over how I was being treated, mainly because it was impacting my ability to be with Joan openly and to continue to get any of the benefits of Scientology. It brought to mind certain things I'd seen from ex-Scientologists in some of those articles I'd perused on the internet and I decided I needed to learn more. So I Googled "Scientology" and that was literally the beginning of the end for me as a Scientologist. I proceeded to fall down a rabbit hole of amazing depth and scope.

I was fascinated by everything I was finding. I was up late almost every night for a couple of months reading more and more stories, blogs, news media and watching videos from former members and media professionals about what Scientology was really all about. At first I was mainly interested in the abuses of the current regime and how Miscavige had undermined Hubbard's intentions and policies and twisted Scientology into his own image in order to aggrandize himself and centralize all the power of Scientology under his control. The more I read, though, the more inescapable it was that Miscavige was not the real problem at all. He was just a reflection of the real source of the trouble: L. Ron Hubbard.

I found out Hubbard lied too, and not just a little bit. I came to see Hubbard's actual war records, school grades, evidence of his multiple marriages and polygamy and pretty clear accounts of his descent into madness during the last half of his years in Scientology before he finally died alone, hiding from the law in Creston, California.

It's impossible for me to relate the depths of betrayal and anger I felt toward L. Ron Hubbard and David Miscavige at this point. One night it just hit me right between the eyes: I'd been taken advantage of, blatantly used like a chess piece, for 25 years. The vast majority of my life had been spent fighting, sacrificing and slaving over a pack of vicious lies which served only one real purpose: to make money for the head of the Church of Scientology.

It was a bitter and hard truth. Even then, when I did see it all for what it was, it still took me two more years to be able to swallow that bitter pill all the way down. Who wants to believe they have thrown away their "best years" and have been used like a puppet, only to be cast into the trash heap when your strings break and you are no longer useful?

There were two straws which finally broke the camel's back, so to speak, and led me to the inescapable conclusion Scientology was not just utter nonsense, but was actually destructive.

The first was seeing Hubbard's confidential directions and policies for the Guardian's Office (GO) operations which led to the Snow White Program in the 1970s, the *largest infiltration of the United States government ever carried out by any group in history.* The GO was Scientology's old legal and investigative division; it is now part of the Sea Organization and is called the Office of Special Affairs. Normal Scientologists and even most people in the Sea Org never see these confidential issues but there they were, leaked on the internet for anyone to read.

It became clear to me in seeing these issues Hubbard was a paranoid conspiracy nut who literally saw aliens and FBI agents coming after him everywhere he looked. Back in the early 1970s he'd been in real trouble with the law in multiple countries and even had an arrest warrant issued for him in France. In order to deal with this, his solution was to send in his most loyal Scientologists (Guardian's Office staffers) in a James Bond-esque operation to find and destroy all the government records which documented his criminal activities. It was a gigantic operation carried out over years and ultimately involved hundreds of Guardian's Office staff (all Scientologists).

The Snow White Program was uncovered by the FBI after a few very big mistakes were made by low-level Guardian's Office staff infiltrating the IRS. It all came to light in a spectacular FBI raid on Scientology facilities in 1977. Twelve Scientologists went to jail including Hubbard's wife, Mary Sue Hubbard. As the nominal head of the Guardian's Office, she was the scapegoat who Hubbard threw to the wolves so he wouldn't have to go to jail himself. In the end Hubbard was not just a liar and con man but a craven coward who could not take responsibility for his own actions and would rather see his closest "loved ones" suffer than face the judgement he so richly deserved.

What I found ironic in learning about all this is in the Twin Cities, I met one of those low-level Guardian's Office staffers! In fact, I met the man who was more directly responsible for the Snow White Program being blown wide open than anyone else: Jerry Wolfe. He was not only still alive and well and doing Scientology services, but was the best friend of Joan's father! I had dinner with him and his wife and even worked with him when I was in the SO to get him on services! Of course, he never breathed a word about Snow White or his history with it, but there it all was in black and white: court documents with his name all over them. This guy went to jail for Scientology for two years and here he was, still praising L. Ron Hubbard and eagerly eating up Miscavige's latest interpretations of Hubbard's works.

Finding out about the Snow White Program didn't convince me; it was seeing Hubbard's explicit instructions to the Guardian's Office about how to carry out covert operations and destroy the "enemies" of Scientology through any means necessary. "Ruin them utterly" he said in a 1955 bulletin, and in the 1970s Hubbard laid out in detail exactly how to do just that. It put Scientology into a whole new light because I knew while the Guardian's Office had been shut down because of the media circus following the Snow White Program, a new Office of Special Affairs (OSA) was founded in the early 1980s to take its place. Many of the Guardian's Office staffers literally just walked right over to OSA and kept working. The operational guidelines and policies used by OSA were just updated Guardian's Office orders and directives. So it was obvious nothing really changed at all and OSA was carrying out the same mandate as the old GO.

The second thing which tipped me over the edge was when I took the plunge and read the confidential, upper level scriptures of Scientology, the vaunted OT Levels. It can't really be easily understood by non-Scientologists how much mystique and awe surround these things within the bubble world of Scientology. Hubbard made claims the material contained in the OT Levels is so powerful, if you are exposed to it before you are ready (by doing all the lower Scientology services leading up to them) you will quite literally die. He wasn't using hyperbole or exaggeration when he made these claims either; Hubbard meant what he said. He told Scientologists the material would kill you if you didn't follow his explicit instructions. Fool that I was, I actually believed him, as do all other Scientologists.

Over the years, the materials on the OT levels have been leaked into the public domain from former members and they are now freely available in a Google search. I'd saved these for last not because I was savoring the anticipation of finding out about them, but because I was truly scared to read them! Even after everything I'd uncovered about Hubbard being a pathological liar and charlatan and how corrupt Scientology actually was, I was still very heavily indoctrinated to believe the OT materials were the most sacred and powerful scriptures in the universe.

So I opened the first PDF file with great trepidation and started reading about OT III, the Xenu story made famous on South Park. I even went and downloaded the episode and watched it too. Then I read the rest of the OT Levels in order, skimming them quickly and then going back and reading them over in more detail. Included in the same pack of issues were the infamous "L Rundowns" which are also confidential auditing procedures which cost Scientologists tens of thousands of dollars to receive and are only available at the Flag Service Org in Clearwater, Florida.

After reading through them, I wondered if I was now going to develop pneumonia and die, like Hubbard said I would. That's how strong the indoctrination of 27 years had been. However, more rationally and much more consciously, I was even more pissed off at Hubbard because the bottom line was this: the OT Levels don't make any damn sense. They are not logically consistent, they do not sensibly lead to the power and abilities OTs were supposed to have, there are gigantic holes of unanswered questions and concerns which are so obvious I can't believe anyone could seriously swallow them and they were contradictory to the lower level, non-confidential materials. In short, I was not just extremely disappointed but angered that *these* were the hidden secrets I'd been slaving to protect for all those years.

For decades, people who had done the OT levels smiled mysteriously at me whenever the subject of the OT levels came up and said things like "Oh, just you wait."

"They contain the secrets of the universe."

"You'll never guess what's on them"

"They are so amazing. I had no idea."

"They are going to blow your mind."

Yeah, they blew my mind right out of Scientology! Reading them was the last nail in the coffin of my belief in L. Ron Hubbard's genius and goodness. I now saw the Man Behind the Curtain, the Wolf in Sheep's Clothing, the illusionist weaving his web of deceit to ensnare the gullible and unsuspecting. In case you're curious, in chapter 11, I break down all the OT material and point up what is wrong with it.

After all this, I had to vent and had no one else I could really talk to about it in person. My mother was a godsend, for sure, and I spoke with her about all this by phone. I couldn't tell Joan. She was a church staff member and had a bit of a delicate disposition. I knew if I just unloaded all this on her at once, she was going to freak out. Her parents and her entire family were heavily involved in Scientology and I was going to have to proceed slowly and with caution.

Yet at the same time, I was boiling over inside and desperately needed an outlet for what I was thinking and feeling. I started posting anonymously on an internet chat board called Ex-Scientologist Message Board or ESMB, a website specifically set up by ex-Scientologists for people in my position who needed someone to talk to and understand what they were going through. This also led me to Tony Ortega's Underground Bunker and I started commenting there. That's how they found me.

Leaving Scientology Forever

The Church of Scientology is one of the most paranoid and crazy organizations in the world. They are so insanely sensitive to what people are saying about them and who their critics are, they monitor in depth all the blogs about them, all the anti-Scientology websites, and all major media outlets every single day. The purpose of the monitoring is to find out who is criticizing them so they can decide what action they need to take to shut those people up.

They keep databases and file cabinets full of all the negative commentary and analyze it for speech and writing patterns. They watch for clues commenters leave as to where they live, what they do for a living and if they were former members (since many critics or commenters never had anything to do with Scientology but start following it out of interest, outrage or morbid curiosity). Even though I was posting using a pseudonym, I carelessly said too much about myself in a few comments and they nailed down who I was.

It took a few months before I found out they knew about me. They knew Joan and I were friends, but they did not know how close we were. She went back to Flag in Clearwater late in 2013 for some staff training and they cornered her and let her know I was posting on the internet and was not someone to be friends with. She was shocked but did not let on to them what was going on between us.

She called me and I had to admit what I was doing and promise to stop. She did not want me to be declared a Suppressive Person, the official designation Scientology gives to someone when they expel them for doing things Scientology finds objectionable (like thinking for themselves, acting on their own accord and that sort of thing). I promised I would do anything I needed to in order to keep that from happening.

Well, soon after, as a "security precaution" they took Joan's phone from her and I didn't hear from her again. I knew the game was up because she and I had been texting like crazy and it was all on her phone. Assuming they knew everything, and with her still in Florida, I contacted the Church authorities and let them know I needed to talk.

They actually flew two people in from Los Angeles, to help me "avail myself of L. Ron Hubbard's policies and handle my situation". This was not a peace mission or an effort to help me in any way. It was an effort to get me back under control and shut the hell up.

Pam Bowen was from OSA. Her eyes were those of a shark and there was no reasoning or even real communication with her. All she did was continue to accuse me of crimes against the Church and repeat to me over and over again my own wrongdoing was the problem, nothing the Church had done or was doing. I attempted to ask her questions about the things I'd seen on the internet, but she refused to answer even one of these questions or even acknowledge I asked them. Instead, every comment was directed right back at me, every question met with "What did you do?" After two hours, I started screaming at her and left the conference room in angry frustration. I'm generally an even-keeled person and it is nearly impossible to drive me to such a state, but Pam succeeded.

Lon Kloeffler, the second person they sent, was from Senior HCO (the justice arm of Scientology) and he was a lot calmer and a bit more rational. I also knew he had never been on the internet, was raised in Scientology (I knew his father quite well) and would not have any answers to any of my questions because he literally never lived life outside the Scientology bubble world. It would have been useless to try to ask him any questions. So instead, I agreed to sit down with him because I knew if I was ever going to see Joan again, I was going to have to cooperate with these people.

He calmed me down and we worked out an agreement. I was motivated to do what they asked because I wanted to maintain my relationship with Joan and her family. I had asked her to marry me at this point and we were actually secretly planning a wedding the following year (once things hopefully "cooled off" and I was going to be allowed to be around again) and were talking about children. I felt this was the woman I wanted to spend the rest of my life with. I endured nine months of waiting, interrogation and grueling work to get out of the Sea Org, and then traveled across the country for her. If I had to jump through some more of Scientology's hoops to make this happen, I was going to do it.

According to Lon, I was not going to be officially declared a Suppressive Person, but I was going to have to follow the steps a Suppressive Person would take to get back in the Church's good graces. These are called the "A to E" steps because they are laid out in that sequence in a Hubbard policy letter.

For interest, I'll lay them out here so you can see what I was agreeing to do. It's all very formal and written in legalese but in the end it really just means you are going to have to do a lot of work and pay a lot of money until they are satisfied you have said "I'm sorry" well enough they will let you back in their good graces. [Note: most of the Scientologese is defined in the Glossary.] Here are what the steps say:

"If a person or a group that has committed a Suppressive Act comes to his, her or their senses and recants, his, her or their only terminal is the International Justice Chief, via the Continental Justice Chief, who:

"A. Tells the person or group to stop committing present time overts and to cease all attacks and suppressions so he, she or they can get a case gain.

"B. Requires a public announcement to the effect that they realize their actions were ignorant and unfounded and stating, where possible, the influences or motivations which caused them to attempt to suppress or attack Scientology; gets it signed before witnesses and published broadly, particularly to persons directly influenced or formerly associated with the former offender or offenders. The letter should be calculated to expose any conspiracy to suppress Scientology or the preclear or Scientologist if such existed.

"B1. Requires that all debts owed to Scientology organizations or missions are paid off.

"B2. May require that, subject to the approval of the International Justice Chief, an Amends Project suitable and commensurate with the severity and extent of the Suppressive Acts committed be completed before further A to E Steps are undertaken. Before any such Amends Project is begun, the person must submit an Amends Project Petition to the International Justice Chief, using full CSW and stating what he proposes to do as amends, and this must be approved by the International Justice Chief to be considered valid. Evidence of genuine ethics change may be required before approval of the Amends Project is given. (Examples of such evidence might be, depending upon the High Crimes committed: the person has obtained an honest job; has paid off all debts owed to others; valid contributions have been made to the community; the person has totally ceased those actions for which he was declared, etc.)

"It is also within the power of the International Justice Chief, when approving an Amends Project Petition, to require, as a protector of the Church and its tenets and membership, that such Amends Project be carried out entirely off any Scientology organization, mission or network lines, and to require, before the Amends Project may be considered complete, extensive evidence over a protracted period of time that the person has, beyond any doubt, ceased his or her suppressive actions, has created no *problems for the Church or any member of the Church in any way on any line, and has undertaken and completed an action which is clearly and undeniably of benefit to Mankind.*

"C. Requires training beginning at the lowest level of the Bridge at their expense if executives in charge of training will have the person or the group members.

"D. Makes a note of all of the above matters with copies of the statement and files in the Ethics Files of those concerned.

"E. Informs the International Justice Chief and forwards a duplicate of the original statements which show signatures."

I proceeded to do steps A and B right then and there with Lon. He took my write-up back to LA with him along with my promises to be a good boy and not do any more posting or reading on the internet. I maintained email communication with him and the Continental Justice Chief, Richard Valle. Richard was a very confused young man who decided everything Lon had approved was actually totally wrong and the version of my Step B Richard eventually approved said pretty much the exact opposite of what I originally wrote. I found the whole process to be fascinating and frustrating since I was sort of watching the whole thing as a non-Scientologist now. I wanted nothing to do with Scientology anymore but I was determined to get these steps done and do them in earnest because I knew it was going to take a long time to do the amends step and probably cost me a lot of money in the process (nothing says "I'm sorry" in Scientology like cold hard cash).

Because I wasn't officially declared a Suppressive Person, I still held out hope that once Joan got back from Clearwater we could get together and I could explain everything and sort it out with her so she understood what was going on with me. I hadn't given up on us or our future.

By mid-December, I still had not heard anything from Joan, then one day at my place of employment I received a letter from Clearwater with her name on it. I stopped working for that Scientologist many months prior, ostensibly because she couldn't afford to keep me but there may have been other reasons. However, she helped me land a new job with a non-Scientologist couple who were just wonderful and extremely supportive of me. I was working in property management for them and they heard a lot of what I went through in the Scientology world and helped me adjust to life in the real world. I will always owe them a debt of gratitude for that.

The letter from Joan was what is called in Scientology a "disconnection letter". In a nutshell, they raked her over the coals down in Clearwater, she was in a lot of trouble and she was telling me we were completely over and done with forever. It shouldn't have been a surprise (in retrospect none of this should have been a surprise) but it all was at the time I was living it.

I was devastated. This was it. The last thing Scientology could take from me - the only thing that mattered to me at that point - was now gone. There was no interpretation of their own policies allowing for any of what was going on. It was utterly clear to me Scientology was now arbitrarily doing whatever it wanted to hurt or destroy anyone it wanted to, regardless of who they were or what they had done for the organization. It was their way or the highway, a black and white world of them versus everyone else. My 27 years of service, the thousands of hours of hard work and dedication, the hundreds of people I salvaged back into Scientology, the thousands whose lives I touched and helped in some fashion – none of it mattered even a little tiny bit to them. The utterly vindictive and vengeful nature of Scientology is such they cannot live and let live. They have to do everything within their power to ruin you utterly and make your life hell if they think you have crossed them in any way.

Losing Joan was the final straw. I emailed Lon and let him know (quite politely, I thought) I was done with the A-E steps and with any further work with Scientology. I managed to not swear, rant or rave in my email, but kept it to the facts. A week later, he called me and let me know I was formally declared a Suppressive Person. I was never going to be allowed to see the official issue naming me as such. They don't give them to declared SPs anymore since what is said in the SP issues would open the Church up to libel suits plus some people have posted theirs on the internet for all the world to see. If there is one thing

Scientology hates, it's for their bullying tactics and disregard for anything like compassion to be exposed to the world.

Losing Joan is still the biggest loss of my entire life. I was right smack in the middle of that loss, but even then, receiving the phone call was liberating. It was like a monkey was off my back and I was finally free to live my life in the great big wide world with no more interference or having to look over my shoulder. I physically felt lighter. It wasn't a happy moment but it was a moment of clarity and renewal. On that day I knew I was leaving the label of "Chris Shelton, Scientologist" behind me forever.

Why Did I Do It?

It's a question asked often: How do intelligent, rational people get involved in a cult, and once they see the abuses and violations of policy and mismanagement and all the rest, why do they stay?

Well, the short answer is, I was convinced what I was doing was bringing real and lasting help to the world. I believed every person I helped, every program I completed, every person I recruited, made a difference to the world at large.

Not only that, but I believed with every fiber of my being we Scientologists were the only ones who were making a difference. This is a particularly important point when recruiting and why people stay. Once you believe Scientology is the most important thing in the whole universe, it's a very small leap in logic to conclude nothing else really matters at all.

One goes into Scientology, and especially onto staff and the Sea Organization, knowing there are going to be sacrifices. You know you are not going to have as much time off, or be free to sit around watching TV or movies. You know while your room and board may be taken care of and you don't have to worry about dental bills, the price is your loyalty and your perseverance to achieve Command Intention (what the executives of Scientology want you to do). You even swear an oath as a Sea Org member to uphold, forward and carry out Command Intention. It becomes a point of personal pride and duty to do so.

There is, as well, the concept from Scientology Ethics of "the greatest good for the greatest number." Unexamined critically, this concept appears to be a truly wonderful idea. If you help others when you can, then you think, of course, help is going to be returned to you when you need it. If you bring spiritual freedom and eternal survival to others, then of course it will be revisited back upon you. One finds this is not true at all. The "greatest good" depends on the eye of the beholder and whose "good" is being served. There are people who are more than happy to use the "greatest good" to work people to the bone and make them feel guilty for not doing even more. L. Ron Hubbard was one such person; David Miscavige is another. They have perfected this sort of guilt-oriented motivation to an exact science.

Once the foolishness and lunacy become so great a person can't ignore them, there is still a decision to be made about what to do. It was very easy for me to forgive; if someone yells at you, screams at you or even hits you, well, everyone is under a lot of stress and there are intense targets to meet and we're all on the same team, right? Win or die in the attempt, isn't that what we all agreed to?

In addition, after giving years of oneself to a cause, a true *esprit de corps* is established with your teammates. Even if you don't like them all personally, even if you wouldn't want to sit down and eat with them or go to a movie with them, they are your brothers-in-arms. To consider leaving them behind would be to court disaster. Who's going to carry the torch if you fall down or drop it?

Finally, who wants to think all those years were for naught? I didn't want to just give up, not if there was a possibility, no matter how slim, our goals could be achieved and we could "clear the planet." After all that time and all that work, it would be a complete fail to just walk away. No, better to persist and carry on and keep fighting the fight. Our programs may not have been perfect but they were better than nothing!

Despite all these reasons, once I started to see the almost insatiable fixation with getting straight donations out of people (meaning money donated for no expected return of any kind), it became clear to me something was really wrong. Long-trusted and well-respected Int

Management personnel disappeared from Scientology's big yearly event gatherings and soon we never heard anything from them at all. You couldn't even write them a letter or an internal dispatch. They just disappeared and it became all Miscavige's show. The Ideal Orgs were empty despite all the promises of "getting in policy" and "booming like never before." I saw the stats, the empty course rooms, and the idle auditors. The Ideal Orgs were not expanding after they were opened, and despite all the rhetoric coming from the top, making auditors was something we hadn't done in any real volume since the early 1990s. It was no longer the Scientology I had joined and it was not the Scientology described by Hubbard in tech and policy.

The final breaking point for me was when I realized I spent my life working to make other people happy and yet I myself was not happy. My marriage disintegrated after I spent three years on the RPF and an additional four years away from my wife on projects and missions. I made no Bridge progress as a Sea Org member, and I wasn't the only one. In all my years, I saw many Sea Org members grow old and even die in the Sea Org, barely up through a few Grades or maybe Clear. It grated on me this was allowed to happen.

I was spending all my time being a martyr for the cause, and it hit me one day: I could spend the rest of my life that way and no one was going to do anything about it. No one was ever going to stop sending me out on missions. No one was going to take me aside and say, "Hey, Chris, you've salvaged hundreds, maybe thousands of people, and you know what? Now it's your turn. Let's get you up The Bridge." It's all well and good to talk about clearing the planet and salvaging everyone in this sector of the universe, but wouldn't that start with the very people who are supposed to be doing the salvaging? When do they get to partake in all this goodness? When does someone see to it their needs are fulfilled and they are actually happy? If I had stayed, I'm quite sure I'd still be waiting for answers to those questions.

Now I'm out of that life and have had time to decompress and get free of the pressure-cooker mentality, my life has changed enormously for the better. The freedom and happiness Scientologists seek actually does exist. It exists out here in the real world, not inside the bubble. I have experienced more "self-determinism", more honesty, more integrity and more personal certainty in the short time since I stepped out of the bubble than in all the previous years combined.

My life is my own. I am happy. I have reconnected with and made real friends who don't care about me because of my production statistics or because of how much money I can raise. They just like me for who I am. Those are real friends.

So that was my journey. And now you know all that about me, you'll know why I can speak with experience and authority about everything else in this book.

2. Bitter, Defrocked Apostates (or Why Customer Reviews Matter)

What is an Apostate?

One thing the Church of Scientology absolutely hates is when ex-members speak out publicly against it. It really drives them over the bend when someone who was once in the inner circle spills the beans on what really goes on behind the closed doors of the Church. How they have chosen to counter ex-member statements and testimonials is interesting in itself and worth commenting on.

The word chosen by the Church of Scientology to refer to any ex-member critical of it is "apostate." It's an odd word, not something you will hear thrown around in a normal conversation at the bar or even in a regular classroom. Scientology repeatedly refers to former high-ranking members who speak out as "bitter, defrocked apostates on the fringes of the internet" as a way to cast them in a negative light.

If you were to consult a dictionary, you would find "apostate" comes from *apostasy* which means "renunciation of a religious faith"[1]. Delve more deeply into its derivation and you get to the Greek root *apostasia* meaning "a defection or revolt."

This word was not chosen by accident. It has a purposefully negative, derogatory connotation. It is used by Scientology in the same exaggerated way the US media portrays people who fight against repressive, dictatorial regimes. If the dictator those men are fighting against happens to be a US ally, they are "terrorists". Yet those same men are "freedom fighters" if their fight is allied with US interests. Language is powerful and is a method of controlling thought and emotion all by itself. This is a well-established fact, was almost the entire basis of George Orwell's *1984* and is something any public relations specialist or journalist worth their salt knows and uses every day.

Scientology has paid good money to have the argument made for them that apostates are not to be trusted. For example, one religious studies professor has said:

"The apostate must always be regarded as an individual who is predisposed to render a biased account of the religious beliefs and practices of his or her former religious associations and activities....There is no denying that these dedicated and diehard opponents of the new religions present a distorted view of the new religions to the public, the academy, and the courts by virtue of their ready availability and eagerness to testify against their former religious associations and activities. Such apostates always act out of a scenario that vindicates themselves by shifting responsibility for their actions to the religious group." - Lonnie D. Kliever, Professor of Religious Studies, Southern Methodist University, January 24, 1995

This is a blame-the-victim approach to invalidating whistleblowers and former members by calling them out for not taking responsibility for their own actions. It simply assumes anyone who has something critical to say about their past experiences or allegiances is acting out of nothing more than self-interest to justify their own wrongdoing (a view perfectly aligned with L. Ron Hubbard's teachings about those whom he felt wronged him). It doesn't happen to be any more true than the idea rape victims were asking for it by the way they dressed or children who are abused must have done something to antagonize their parents into beating them senseless.

While I'm sure Dr. Kliever was an expert on religious studies, he made no claims to expertise regarding psychology. When it comes to analyzing and evaluating destructive cults, Dr. Kliever was out of his depth and had no business making any such blame-the-victim statements, or assuming anything about why apostates would speak out against their former religious groups. I seriously doubt Dr. Kliever ever spoke to or interviewed any "apostates" to find out why they were doing what they were doing.

Undue Influence

There is something called *undue influence* which is a legal and business term meaning "mental, moral, or physical domination (even if natural or right) that deprives a person of independent judgement and substitutes another person's objectives in place of his or her own."[2] There is extensive discussion of this by psychologist Steve Hassan in his book *Combatting Cult Mind Control.*

I was lied to and actively deceived from the very first day I walked into a Scientology organization. I was threatened with bodily harm and assaulted on numerous occasions as a Sea Org member. I was treated with contempt, scorn and ridicule and made to feel an enormous burden of guilt for the most inconsequential acts if they violated Hubbard's dicta while at the same time cajoled into breaking the law in order to carry out Command Intention and "clear the planet". These things happened, and they happened over and over again. The only reason I bring them up is because context matters and what I did was done under undue influence.

Despite that, I don't blame anyone but myself for the actions I carried out while I was in Scientology and nothing I say in this book is an effort to shift responsibility to anyone else for things I did.

Why Criticize Scientology?

When I was a part of the Church of Scientology and in the Sea Org, I always used to wonder about people who attacked Scientology. I wondered what motivated them: why did they seem so passionate about what they were doing? Why couldn't they just leave well enough alone? Wasn't it enough they didn't like it and they then left? Couldn't they just leave us Scientologists alone to practice our religion in peace? Why did they have to spend so much time and effort going out of their way to write articles, be interviewed by the press, write books and even make whole movies about how bad the Scientology experience was? In other words, why couldn't they just live and let live?

Lots of explanations were fed us about "Church attackers," mainly out of the mouths of OSA staff. In 2008, they carefully explained how Anonymous, for example, were a bunch of no-good criminal hackers and listless, bored teenagers who didn't have anything better to do but make trouble for Scientology. They told us, between bouts of masturbating to internet child porn in their basements and doing drugs, they were being funded by some nameless, mysterious ringleader who organized their efforts in each city and paid them with pizza and $10-20 an hour to go dance around in front of the orgs with signs reading "Ask me about Xenu" and "Scientology is a trap". We were told these mysterious ringleaders were being paid lots of money by Big Pharma to do away with Scientology because we (the Sea Org) were so effectively cutting into the profits from psychiatric drugging of children, profits which run into the billions of dollars per year. It's ironic now, knowing how much money the Church is hoarding in its off-shore IAS bank accounts, how condemnatory they always were toward psychiatry and Big Pharma's "billions in blood money." I've never seen a better example of the pot calling the kettle black.

The Church tells its members that I and other critics are suppressive people who want nothing less than the utter destruction of all Mankind. They say we are so critical of the Church of Scientology because of our own wrong-doings. Apparently in their eyes Scientology is the only organization in the history of the world that can do no wrong and above criticism of any kind. L. Ron Hubbard and David Miscavige are incapable of making any mistakes and are the most selfless, dedicated and altruistic human beings who have ever lived. This may sound like hyperbole but I'm actually not exaggerating the case. This is how Scientologists think of Hubbard and Miscavige. Of course, this defies all logic and reason. The truth about both of these men is far uglier.

It was no easy task to make me into an enemy of Scientology. Even after I left the Sea Org, I was still dedicated to doing Scientology and making it to OT. The Church's injustice machinery worked overtime to turn me to the "dark side." I can only thank them for that now, but at the time it was a journey much like Dante travelling to the lowest levels of Hell. I could never have taken such a life-altering journey without stumbling over some jaw-dropping milestones, the kind which change your outlook forever.

For example, I now know:

- The Church of Scientology is exclusively dedicated to just one thing: making money. Whatever purposes or aims it was founded upon, and no matter how it used to be run, this is its state now. It is actually a for-profit corporation hiding behind a cloak of religious authority, which gives it rights and privileges which no corporation should have. As a recognized religion in the US, Scientology can and does freely engage in stalking, harassment, emotional and psychological blackmail, human trafficking and slavery, all protected by the First Amendment right to the free practice of religion. It should not have this right. If any for-profit business tried to get away with the activities the Church of Scientology engages in on a daily basis, they would be shut down by at least four government agencies within a few days of the first reports of abuse being filed.
- L. Ron Hubbard died a sick, insane man. He was a self-admitted failure, running from the law and wanted for tax evasion and fraud, as well as being an unindicted co-conspirator in the Snow White Program. He did not "go off to research upper OT levels" and "leave his body peacefully" as was falsely claimed by David Miscavige in 1986.
- David Miscavige was among those who took advantage of Hubbard's deteriorating mental state in his final years, feeding him false reports so as to isolate Hubbard further from what was really going on with Scientology. Miscavige did this primarily to create a condition where it was easy for him to grab the reins of power once Hubbard was gone. Indeed, Miscavige already effectively had control of Scientology and according to one ex-Scientology senior official, was freely spending millions of dollars in parishioner monies on his own excesses before Hubbard was even dead.[3] According to numerous reports from those he victimized, Miscavige physically abuses his own staff

45

and has single-handedly managed to decimate International Scientology management beyond repair.⁴ Based on my observations, his greatest skill is his ability to seamlessly and effortlessly lie through his teeth to fool the few remaining Scientologists into thinking he is a great spiritual leader who is somehow the only person ensuring Scientology's future. Ironically, the exact opposite is true, something those remaining Scientologists will be shocked to one day find out.

- In the late 1960s through to the end of the 1970s, Hubbard created, organized and operated a Gestapo-like intelligence operation known as the Guardian's Office. Such an apparatus is simply begging to be abused and that is exactly what happened. Hubbard's wife, Mary Sue played no small part in running the Guardian's Office under Hubbard's direct supervision, ruthlessly attacking anyone who dared to speak critically of the church so as to "ruin them utterly" according to Hubbard's written policies. When the Guardian's Office went too far and was rightfully busted for illegal actions taken directly against agencies of the U.S. government, it was nominally disbanded. In fact its policies and operations were just transferred *en masse* to the newly created Office of Special Affairs under the direction of the Sea Organization. OSA continues to operate in the tradition of the Guardian's Office, practicing the policy of "Fair Game" against anyone the Church's leaders deem an enemy. To this day they overtly and covertly carry out terror campaigns against church critics for doing nothing more than exercising their First Amendment right to speak their minds.

- The Church has amassed literally *billions* of dollars in assets and liquid funds, yet disperses little to none of this money for any of its supposed humanitarian purposes or "key strategies for planetary clearing" such as Ideal Orgs. It doesn't need to collect one more dime from any parishioners in order to achieve its ends. According to the 990T tax forms Scientology is required to file with the IRS and which are public record, the international Church coffers hold enough money to outright buy and renovate every current Church building in the world and build as many new ones as they want.[5] There is enough money to easily produce millions of copies of L. Ron Hubbard's booklet *The Way to Happiness* and mail or even airdrop them all over the Middle East, Southeast Asia, North Korea and any other suppressed or war-torn region of the planet. It can afford to build and staff any number of Narconon drug rehabilitation centers or Applied Scholastics schools all over the world. Planeloads of Volunteer Ministers could be sent to any trauma center or disaster zone at a moment's notice. Yet Church money is hardly ever used for any of these purposes and when it is disbursed, it pays only enough to cover a tiny fraction of what is required or it merely covers the travel costs of the cameramen Scientology sends to film the work Scientologists are paying out of their pocket to perform. Every single time one of the actions I've listed are needed, Scientology parishioners are told they need to pay for it immediately because the Church doesn't have the money. This is probably one of the most bald-faced lies Scientology uses, giving its parishioners the impression it is doing all this humanitarian work around the world while in reality it is doing almost nothing. The only thing all this money is really going toward is to satisfy the material needs of David Miscavige, who never wants for a single thing and is waited upon by numerous full-time support staff literally 24 hours a day. It's not really about the money, though. It's about satisfying an insatiable desire for power. That is what drove L. Ron Hubbard and it appears to drive David Miscavige as well.

Now having learned about all these things in grim detail (and plenty more), I decided I should do something to expose the truth. I'm not alone in this. There are organizations with hundreds or even thousands of members who work full-time to expose these same kinds of abuses, such as the American Civil Liberties Union and Amnesty International. I'm not comparing myself or other Scientology critics to these organizations in terms of the volume of good we do, but I can safely say we are working for the same purpose: to do our best to make the world a better place by exposing corruption, abuse, avarice and financial mis-dealings.

No matter how or why you leave the Church of Scientology, when you find out what is really going on with and in it, you want to do something about it. You want those who are still inside, being blatantly deceived, cheated and abused, to no longer be stuck in that horrific situation. You want disconnected families to be reunited with their loved ones. You want real justice for those who have been so wronged by Church leaders, and you want to see those who are responsible for these abuses held accountable.

That is why I am speaking out and I believe that is the motivating force behind most of the other critics as well. That is why we don't have a "live and let live" philosophy when it comes to leaving Scientology alone. No organization carrying out these kinds of abuses every day deserves to keep operating. They deserve to be punished within the full extent of the law. It is time for the Church of Scientology to end. That is why I speak out and why I hope, through my work, I can convince others to do the same.

3. How Scientology Presents Itself to the World

What Scientology Really is All About

I have had some amusing conversations since I left Scientology with people who were never in it and regard it (rightly so) with suspicion or mystery. They usually go something like this:

Person: Oh, you were a Scientologist? Tell me, what is Scientology?

Me: A money-making scam which uses religious cloaking to hide its true nature but which is designed to enrich just one man with power and money and give him 100% protection from the law so he can continue to scam people without any fear of punishment in the courts.

Person: Well sure, ok, but what *is* Scientology?

Me: What I just told you. That *is* Scientology.

Person: Yeah but what do they believe? What do they tell people?

Me: Oh, you want to know what the scam is and what they say to fool people? Well that's a whole different thing to what it actually is.

I'm not trying to be a jerk when I say stuff like this although I'm sure people could think so. I'm trying to be very precise in answering the question because I want to make it clear right up front it's a scam and nothing but a scam. Otherwise you could start listening to the pseudo-scientific and metaphysical prattle Hubbard put together and start falling for it or giving it legitimacy it does not deserve.

Scientology is a con. All the metaphysical garbage they throw at you is not true and does not work out to be true in the real world. Why do I say this with such certainty? Because if the con were real and Hubbard's explanations of the metaphysical world were accurate, then there would be some kind of tangible results from applying Scientology.

I'm not talking about making people feel a little better or experience less emotional stress when they think about their mother. That is an amazingly easy result to produce and there are many methods in routine psychology and psychiatry which work on a lot of people to make them feel better in their day-to-day life. These methods do not necessarily cure anything or make one's worries go away forever, but they do provide some relief. Unfortunately, all a charlatan like Hubbard needs to do is tell people, "there is so much more to come," and they fall for it and believe everything he says.

When I say Scientology doesn't produce tangible results, I'm talking about producing the *big* gains and results Hubbard promised from the very first day he announced his "discoveries" back in 1950 with the publication of *Dianetics: The Modern Science of Mental Health*. Things like the states of Clear and Operating Thetan and being able to cure physical ailments like cancer and arthritis, and prevent future ones from occurring. I'm not engaging in hyperbole when I say Hubbard promised the moon and the stars to his followers. In the end, he never even got off the ground.

Now, having made that clear, I'll lay out how Dianetics and Scientology explain themselves so the rest of this book will have context.

Dianetics: The Modern Science of Mental Health

Dianetics was originally touted as the "modern science of mental health" with no spiritual aspect to it of any kind. Before Scientology came along, Dianetics was a strictly secular activity wherein Hubbard claimed to have developed a brand new, easy-to-use psychotherapy which treated aberrant behavior caused by moments of pain and unconsciousness in the past. These memories, called *engrams*, were stored in a newly discovered part of the human mind called the *reactive mind*. Application of the Dianetics technique was a kind of regression therapy where the patient would mentally return to these traumatic engrams and recount them to the counsellor (called an *auditor* in Dianetics, meaning one who listens) as though they were living through the engram again.

After going over and over the incident, recounting what happened in detail, if this did not relieve the trauma or produce any emotional discharge, the patient was told to find an earlier time of similar circumstances to the original engram and go back and recount it over and over again. By doing this again and again, finding earlier and earlier engrams, a patient would eventually get to the bottom of that series or chain to the first time it happened, called the *basic*. By recounting it over and over, the whole series of engrams would erase from the reactive mind and the person would be alleviated of the psychological, emotional and physical trauma connected with those incidents.

Hubbard claimed by doing this again and again, eventually erasing all the engrams a person had accumulated, they would achieve a new state of mental and physical well being known as a Clear, meaning a person who had completely erased their entire reactive mind. The engrams would be re-filed in their conscious or *analytical* mind and they could remember them with ease and without any more trauma or upset. They would no longer be engrams but instead just memories.

Originally, Hubbard said Dianetics was *"a precision science. It stems from the study and codification of survival."*[1] He also takes care to separate his work from other similar works in *Dianetics: The Modern Science of Mental Health* when he emphatically stated *"it is not psychoanalysis. It is not psychology. It is not personal relations. It is not hypnotism. It is a science of mind."*[2]

Among other things, a Dianetic Clear is supposed to have the following abilities and attributes according to the text of Dianetics:

"A clear can be tested for any and all psychoses, neuroses, compulsions and repressions (all aberrations) and can be examined for any autogenic (self-generated) diseases referred to as psycho-somatic ills. These tests confirm the clear to be entirely without such ills or aberrations. Additional tests of his intelligence indicate it to be high above the current norm. Observation

of his activity demonstrates that he pursues existence with vigor and satisfaction."

"...has complete recall of everything which ever happened to him, or anything he ever studied. He does mental computations, such as those in chess, for example, which a normal would do in half an hour, in ten or fifteen seconds."

"Clears do not get colds."

"One of the incidental things which happen to a clear is that his eyesight, if it had been bad as an aberree, generally improves markedly, and with some slight attention will recover optimum perception in time."

While fronting his new subject as a science of invariable results, Hubbard made extraordinary claims such as those above but utterly failed to fulfill one of the most wonderful guidelines of skepticism: extraordinary claims require extraordinary proof. In other words, almost from day one, all Hubbard could do was make people feel a bit better or relieve some physical symptoms. The longer-term and bigger results were utterly lacking in this new "science" and so the claims were toned down over the years to much more subjective or indefinite, unprovable results.

Notice how almost none of the claims made now (which come from Scientology's website definition of a Clear) would be things you could measure or define with any accuracy:

- Freed from active or potential psychosomatic illness or aberration
- Self-determined
- Vigorous and persistent
- Unrepressed
- Able to perceive, recall, imagine, create and compute at a level high above the norm
- Stable mentally
- Free with his emotion
- Able to enjoy life
- Freer from accidents
- Healthier

- Able to reason swiftly
- Able to react quickly

Scientology: The Applied Religious Philosophy

Scientology's history and evolution is fascinating. As far as I've been able to determine, the word *Scientology* was first used publicly by Hubbard in the book *Handbook for Preclears* in late 1951. The context is odd and this section has been revised and rewritten in the newer editions of this book but both feature the word *Scientology* to describe the field of research Hubbard says he was engaged in for most of his life and which included the entire field of Dianetics.

Of course, up until 1949, Hubbard was not doing any spiritual or mental research of any kind, unless you count his time practicing occult Magick under the tutelage of Jack Parsons as spiritual research. I don't. His claims in *Handbook for Preclears* were just more lies and in fact, it was at this time Hubbard was rapidly re-writing his own history. He was now claiming his entire life was an intense and directed search for the answers to life and resolving the problems of Man. In hindsight, it's easy to see how he was preparing for the end of Dianetics as a movement (since it went bankrupt once and was on its way to doing so again) and paving the way to start up a new religious movement in its stead.

The word *Scientology* was first spoken of in public in the first lecture in a series he gave on March 3, 1952 in Wichita, Kansas where he stated:

"This is a course in Scientology. That word might seem a little strange to you at the moment. It's a very beautiful combination of Greek and Latin, I am told, but then so is psychology. And I trust that Dianetics will get just a little further than some of its forebears, and it has already gotten into the field of Scientology.

"Scientology would be the study of science, or the study of knowledge, rather than the small segment of therapy which has been, up to this time, Dianetics. Scientology actually embraces these axioms and embraces the various activities of man."[3]

Historically speaking, *Scientology* as a word was not coined first by Hubbard but he did come up with his own system of philosophy and thought which was uniquely his own and it's probable this was a case of independent development rather than plagiarism.

Dr. Anastasius Nordenholz, an Argentine philosopher, actually wrote a whole work around the study of knowledge and science in 1934 which he described as "Scientologie". It's unlikely Hubbard was aware of this since he did not speak or read German, a necessity to read Nordenholz since the doctor was German-educated and wrote in that language.

Hubbard said he coined the word *Scientology* from Latin, *scio-*, meaning "knowing in the fullest sense of the word" and *-ology*, which of course means "study of" or more specifically, "outward form by which the inward thought is expressed and made known" or "reason itself". Hubbard said Scientology was the "science of knowledge".

It is an applied religious philosophy because it is a system of practices addressing themselves to a person as a spiritual being rather than as a body or a mind. He also stated Scientology *"...is the one thing senior to life because it handles all factors of life."*[4] Not one to think small, Hubbard repeatedly inculcated the belief in his followers that Scientology *is* life.

The combined works of Scientology comprise something on the order of 3,000+ lectures, 18 books, many thousands of bulletins and policy letters as well as thousands more internal guidelines and issues of varying types. These cover everything from the essential beliefs/philosophy, the administration of Scientology counselling and organizations, the conduct of the Sea Organization, how to make films and other miscellaneous directives. Hubbard was nothing if not prolific.

The modern description of Scientology according to the Church's website, is *"...a religion that offers a precise path leading to a complete and certain understanding of one's true spiritual nature and one's relationship to self, family, groups, Mankind, all life forms, the material universe, the spiritual universe and the Supreme Being.*

"Scientology comprises a body of knowledge which extends from certain fundamental truths. Prime among these are:

"Man is an immortal spiritual being.

"His experience extends well beyond a single lifetime.

"His capabilities are unlimited, even if not presently realized.

"Scientology further holds Man to be basically good, and that his spiritual salvation depends upon himself, his fellows and his attainment of brotherhood with the universe.

"The ultimate goal of Scientology is true spiritual enlightenment and freedom for all."

From this description, one gets a sort of generalized view of Scientology as a kind of McDonalds or Burger King of Spiritual Enlightenment. One size fits all, you can have it your way and we're not going to shove anything down your throat. It's this kind of pleasant language which appeals to a certain percentage of the population and gets them thinking maybe there is something to Scientology after all.

Dianetics is relatively simple in its practice and method. Scientology has many different procedures and forms of practice, so it's impossible to describe its basic therapy in the same way as with Dianetics.

Auditing, the practice of having a counsellor and a patient, is the same insofar as there is a Scientology practitioner who asks questions or gives commands. The patient is referred to as a "preclear" (one who is not yet Clear) or "pre-OT" if they are Clear and progressing through the OT Levels. Other than that, the auditing procedures in Scientology are totally different from those in Dianetics.

For example, one common type of procedure, or *process* as they are called in Scientology, is the repetitive process. There are literally thousands of these using different commands or questions but the procedure is basically the same. A person is asked the same question or given the same command over and over again until he feels better and has a *cognition*, meaning a realization or new understanding about some aspect of his life. An example of a command would be "Recall a time that was really real to you" or "Recall a secret". Sometimes there are a series of two, three or four questions which are asked over and over again in sequence.

There are also repetitive processes which involve physical exercise rather than sitting in a chair recalling things. These are called Objective Processes and involve walking around, touching things or looking at things over and over again. For example, there is a process called Opening Procedure by Duplication which is carried on for at least 25+ hours regardless of what the preclear says or does. The procedure is to walk back and forth between two tables, one of which has a bottle on it and the other has a book on it. The preclear is told:

"Look at that book." (or bottle)

"Walk over to it."

"Pick it up."

"What is its weight?"

"What is its color?"

"What is its temperature?"

"Put it back in exactly the same place."

This exact series of commands is repeated over and over again, making the preclear comply with each command before giving the next. This is usually done for days on end, each session lasting anywhere from two to eight or more hours before calling it a day and picking it up next time.

Whereas it seems rather obvious this kind of procedure being run on anyone for hours on end would produce a hypnotic trance, Hubbard claimed instead this sort of thing runs hypnosis *out* of a person and wakes them up, rather than puts them to sleep. I would beg to differ.

I think after 25 hours of the above procedure, a person would be in a mental and emotional state of willingness to say or believe anything just to make it stop. If that includes convincing themselves they had an out-of-body experience or they now feel better and are "more awake", I'm quite sure they'd say it just so they could stop the auditing.

Scientology has many other aspects to it besides just the auditing procedures. A complete survey of the subject is impossible in such a short chapter as this but briefly, Scientology also includes such things as:

- an entire administrative system to run any size organization according to Hubbard's "management technology" including comprehensive reviews of subjects germane to any organization such as public relations, finance, human resources and overseeing production through the use of statistics.

- a system of ethics and justice which imposes a sort of Orwellian control on Scientology's members. This includes having members write reports to "Ethics Officers" on any infractions or offenses they witness or even just suspect fellow members committing; the administration of internal courts and committees to confront those accused of Scientology infractions, weigh evidence and find on their guilt or innocence; and a formal practice of labelling members who have gone against Scientology leaders or rules as a Suppressive Person (SP), who are then shunned (meaning all Scientologists must completely disconnect from the SP lest they themselves also be labelled as SPs).

- a series of guidelines and rules for how to study, which involves classroom "supervisors" who watch as people study Scientology materials and make sure they don't disagree with anything Hubbard says. These supervisors also help students clarify any questions they have in such a way as to always end up agreeing with everything Hubbard said or wrote.

- ceremonies for marriages, funerals, naming newborn babies and the like.

There are Churches of Scientology all over the world but as their true nature and abusive practices are exposed, their numbers are becoming fewer and fewer. If Scientology delivered what it actually promised, or even part of what it promised, the world would be beating down its doors demanding it deliver Scientology to all levels of society.

Instead, the end result of Scientology is an empty bank account, credit card debt beyond imagination and, in many cases, broken families and broken lives.

4. Scientology: Bona Fide Religion or Destructive Cult?

In the last chapter, I gave a summary of what Dianetics and Scientology are and some examples of how their "therapy" works. Now let's take a look at this in more detail and see, in depth, what is going on.

Scientology is not a religion in the sense most people understand the term or how religion is practiced. However, this is tricky because Scientology *appears* to be a religion: it has religious trappings and language, it can dress its auditors up in minister outfits and put on Sunday Services and its followers even believe they are part of a religious movement. They are being deceived, as is anyone who listens to Scientology officials when they describe Scientology as a religion.

By the way, this deception very much extends to religious scholars and non-Scientology apologists, including many in the field of cult studies who should know better. There are some who have described Scientology as a "new religious movement" in an attempt to appear less derogatory because the word "cult" has such bad connotations. I do not have any such compunction because I know what Scientology is and what goes on every day behind its closed doors where they don't allow the religious scholars and non-members to go.

The truth is, the humanitarian and religious façade Scientology officials present to the world is just a front. It's a public relations sham to comply with IRS tax codes and ensure they maintain tax-exempt status so they can enjoy all the legal and financial advantages afforded to religions.

Plainly put, Scientology is a for-profit business which uses religious cloaking to hide its true purposes. In fact, it is not just a business in the sense of a McDonalds or Microsoft, which seek to sell a service or product and make a steady stream of income to enrich its shareholders or owners. Scientology is much worse. It is a money-making scheme with two simple purposes: (1) to enrich its Founder, L. Ron Hubbard, and keep him in power at any cost (a mantle which shifted to David Miscavige in the early 1980s); (2) to "slam Hubbard's name into history"[1] by preserving Hubbard's written and spoken works on nearly indestructible materials which will survive any natural or man-made catastrophe though the ages, thereby giving Hubbard a sort of immortality. Those two things are all Scientology is actually doing. Anything else occurring because of Scientology is simply a side effect, a fringe benefit to keep the flock happy and give them a reason to keep handing over their hard-earned money. And yes, I do mean all the auditing and all the training and all the activities of its front groups. All that, in the end, is not what Scientology is really about.

This is so easily provable, it's hardly even worth considering, but people get confused because so many Scientologists spend so much time auditing and training and whatnot. The run-of-the-mill Scientologist or even "independent Scientologists" (people who leave official Scientology but continue to practice Hubbard's techniques on their own) would argue with me about this all day long. They misguidedly believe Hubbard did what he did because he wanted to help people. They think Hubbard actually discovered things. They think because they have a few subjective "wins", Scientology as a spiritual philosophy is valid and credible and Hubbard, for all his flaws, was really a great humanitarian or at least a great scientist. Unfortunately, they literally have no idea what they are talking about.

It's not that people don't have gains or feel helped at all. I'm not trying to blanketly invalidate every gain anyone made practicing Scientology. I'm talking about the broad purposes and activities of this group and why it exists in the first place. All the auditing and classwork and everything else is just busy work and is never what motivated the leaders of Scientology, past and present, to do what they are doing.

This is a hard and bitter pill to swallow, especially for ex-Scientologists who want to hold on to some positive experience from Scientology. It was not something I could accept until fairly recently myself. This is not a condemnation of anyone's subjective gains or happiness. It's a condemnation of destructive cults.

So why do they go to all the trouble of putting up crosses, training ministers, holding Sunday Services and all the rest? Why all the religious cloaking? The simple answer is it's a survival point for the organization. Without the benefits and rights they enjoy from their religious status under law, Scientology would have been torn apart legally many years ago.

Let's look at how this came about.

A Little History

Hubbard published *Dianetics: The Modern Science of Mental Health* on May 9, 1950. He called it a science for a reason. The religion angle was not yet a part of what he was pushing. Hubbard wrote scientific-sounding axioms and used big bold capital letters to describe some of the pseudo-scientific principles he espoused so uninformed readers would think they were seeing something very advanced and well researched.

In *Dianetics*, Hubbard refers to such lofty sounding things as the "Dynamic Principle of Existence" and "Laws of Returning" which he claimed to have discovered through research. Of course, none of his research papers, experiments or notes were ever made available to the public, much less to any other scientists who wanted to actually validate his findings. The concepts of real scientific validation and peer review were foreign ideas to Hubbard because as far as he was concerned, he was the only person in history who was capable of discovering real truth. His own son even noted his "research" usually consisted of a series of one – either himself or someone he talked to – and he then wrote voluminous treatises on how everyone responded and behaved according to the principles Hubbard just dreamed up as he went along.[2]

Hubbard setup a "Dianetics Research Foundation" and talked about its work with testing and experimentation in lectures he gave back in 1950. While this may have given the appearance of trying to be a legitimate science, Hubbard constantly derided this group for not doing its work properly and being incapable of doing proper research. This served as a nice cover for him so he could continue to be the only one who could "discover" any of the important principles. Years later he glibly stated in a policy letter called Keeping Scientology Working, "We will not speculate here on...how I came to rise above the bank"[3] but merely claimed he was the only one who was somehow brilliant enough to be able to pierce the mysterious veil of the mind and give Mankind the answers no one else ever could. That's not how science works and any freshman in high school knows it. Science was not one of Hubbard's strong points in school, though, as shown by his routinely poor grades.

Science doesn't just believe someone because he looks good or sounds good. There has to be evidence or proof and the findings of a science have to be reproducible to others. Every attempt made by independent research groups I could locate found Dianetics and Scientology to be lacking on every front.

Dianetics was initially a runaway best seller and Hubbard rode a wave of positive repute and an electrified public who were keenly interested in improving themselves mentally with this new "science". However, the fame was short-lived because the results were just not there.

Medical claims Hubbard made about Dianetics created real trouble in the form of FDA investigations and bad press from the American Psychology Association. Hubbard was claiming to literally be able to cure cancer, leukemia, bad eyesight and a host of other "psychosomatic" ills. Were there any reality to these claims, Dianetics would right now be practiced worldwide in every hospital in the world. Instead, the last place you will ever find a Dianeticist is in a hospital using this "miraculous technology" to cure the invalid or dying. It's the same thing as why no psychics ever win the lottery. Ask any

Scientologist today why they aren't in hospitals doing this and you'll get nothing but evasive answers and they'll beat a hasty retreat.

Soon the trouble from these false claims was landing squarely on Hubbard's plate because he was the one making the claims and he was facing potential criminal charges. He knew he needed to act, and fast.

If he were protected with a religious status, suddenly all these medical claims would be a matter of faith rather than scientific fact. No scientific validation or proof would be needed. Those who weren't cured could simply be blamed for not having enough faith or belief in the processes. He could dream up other reasons to hold the procedures faultless and would instead blame the person who wasn't cured. This would ensure the rest of the believers would continue to have faith and, more importantly, would continue to pay hundreds and thousands of dollars to benefit from its miraculous curative promises.

When Dianetics went bankrupt in 1953 due not only to lawsuits for false medical claims but also for gross malfeasance and financial mismanagement, it was nothing at all for Hubbard to take the handful of followers he had left and convert them over to religious adherents by founding the Church of Scientology in Camden, New Jersey in December, 1953.

What Scientology Has Become

The point of this chapter is not to give a history lesson on Scientology, but more to analyze what it is today and what is wrong with it so people will stay as far away from it as possible. Instead of documenting what happened with L. Ron Hubbard and Scientology from the 1950s forward to today, let's jump ahead to what Scientology has become now.

If you look up Scientology in media reports, books or on the internet, you are going to find it described in a lot of places as a *cult*. I'm sure most Scientologists find this term offensive, but the truth is they probably don't understand what it actually means, so I thought I would make an effort to clear this up.

Is it really fair to classify Scientology within the same category as James Jones' Peoples Temple or the Branch Davidians or Westboro Baptists? Well, in a word, yes.

The word *cult* goes back to the Latin term *cultus* which referred to the care owed to the gods and their temples and churches. It goes back to an earlier Latin word *colere* which meant to take care of, as in cultivating land or practicing agriculture.

The word *cult* came into English in 1617 through the French word *culte* which meant worship.

By the 19th century, it started to take on the idea of "excessive devotion" and by the late 1930s was being used by Christian groups to describe Satanic societies and heretical activities.

I use the term "destructive cult" rather than the more general term "cult" because it makes it much more clear such a group is engaged in harmful activities against its members and society in general. Language is liquid and evolving and the word "cult" as a pejorative has gone into disfavor in some circles because of its prejudicial history. When the term "destructive cult" is used, there is no question we are discussing something different from an accepted mainstream religion which is not subjugating its members.

Any group or culture has things about it that define its members as different from other groups or cultures. That's as it should be. Humanity revels in its differences across the planet and there's nothing wrong with that. We should celebrate our differences in dress, food, thought and even ideas of worship.

One of the biggest problems with a destructive cult is it takes those inherent differences to a whole new level. It takes the natural diversity of life and vilifies anyone who doesn't come to agree with the way the cult leaders say things should be.

There are a lot of different groups out there with a lot of different beliefs. All of them claim to have a monopoly on the truth. To determine if a group is a cult or not, you have to look at what they do, not what they believe.

Why Scientology is a Destructive Cult

Early on in my education on cults and mass movements, I came across a paper written by Janja Lalich, Ph.D. and Michael D. Langone, Ph.D. titled "Characteristics Associated with Cultic Groups" which is available through the International Cultic Studies Association website. Let's look at 5 specific characteristics of cults and where Scientology fits into these. Just to be clear, there are many other characteristics we could examine, but these will make the point.

1. THE GROUP DISPLAYS EXCESSIVELY ZEALOUS AND UNQUESTIONING COMMITMENT TO ITS LEADER (WHETHER ALIVE OR DEAD) AND TREATS ITS BELIEF SYSTEM AND PRACTICES AS ABSOLUTE TRUTH. QUESTIONING, DOUBT OR DISSENT ARE DISCOURAGED OR EVEN PUNISHED.

One of the first things any visitor to a Church of Scientology will notice is the many photographs of L. Ron Hubbard throughout the building. Almost every room is decorated with some portrait of him, something Hubbard insisted be done in his policies.

He's been dead for over 25 years yet every Church also keeps an office for him, complete with desk and books and stocked up with supplies so if Hubbard were to miraculously walk in, he could get right to work. I don't know of any other organization or Church which does this.

L. Ron Hubbard referred to himself as Source, and made it clear he alone was the single source of all Scientology's teachings. Any issues or writings on Scientology which were not written by him have since either been destroyed or they were changed to put his name on the signatory even though someone else actually wrote it. This actually happened with *far* more issues than most Scientologists think, but unless you have a long memory or access to those earlier works, you wouldn't know this now.

The most important policy in Scientology is titled "Keeping Scientology Working."

In it, Hubbard states in no uncertain terms how Scientology is the most important discovery in all history and quite literally every single person's life depends on becoming a Scientologist. He also asserts any disagreements anyone may feel about Scientology come strictly out of their mental aberrations (a term he adopted which means to not think straight or clearly).[4]

Scientologists are forced to accept all this as Truth.

While studying Scientology or receiving its counselling methods, if Hubbard is questioned in any way, the standard response is to ask "What do your materials state?" and continue to go over and over what Hubbard said until the person says they agree whatever Hubbard was talking about is true, whether they really agree with it or not. Some Scientologists get very good at convincing themselves they truly understand materials which actually don't make any sense at all, just because Hubbard wrote it.

Hubbard's mantle of infallibility has now passed to David Miscavige. He has overseen massive revisions and changes to Hubbard's works over the past 30 years, all under the guise of "making it the way Ron intended."

No one in Scientology dares to question Miscavige, unless they want to get into a great deal of trouble and potentially get kicked out of the church altogether. Back in 1993, when I was a staff member at the Santa Barbara branch of the Church, I sent a written query to one of Miscavige's orders. The response came within two days.

Two Sea Org members from the Religious Technology Center showed up in Santa Barbara to interrogate me on an E-meter to find out why I would dare to presume to question an order from Miscavige. I quickly learned to toe the line and not ask any more such questions.

And just so you see how far this unquestioning commitment has gone, the very first thing Tom Cruise did when he received the highest award in Scientology – the Freedom Medal of Valor – was to praise David Miscavige in terms which defy all reason. Cruise stated unequivocally he had met world leaders, even the "Leaders of Leaders," and none of them could hold a candle to Miscavige.

This was shown to the world in 2008 in a famously leaked video of Cruise ranting about how great he is and how Scientology has made him that way. Scientology's efforts to get the video taken down created a worldwide Anonymous protest and ended up exposing so many of Scientology's secrets to the world at large. They have never recovered since.

2. THE GROUP IS ELITIST, CLAIMING A SPECIAL, EXALTED STATUS FOR ITSELF, ITS LEADERSHIP AND MEMBERS.

Throughout his writings, Hubbard comments repeatedly as to the special and superior nature of anyone who is in Scientology. After being indoctrinated in Hubbard's writings, Scientologists come to believe that to be a fact. They begin to think of themselves as being more ethical, more intelligent and, in a word, more righteous, than anyone else. For example, in the policy I mentioned earlier, Keeping Scientology Working, Hubbard wrote:

"For that matter, look how we ourselves are attacked by 'public opinion' media. Yet there is no more ethical group on this planet than ourselves."[5]

When writing about auditors, Hubbard said *"It is my opinion and knowledge that auditors are amongst the upper tenth of the upper twentieth of intelligent human beings. Their will to do, their motives, their ability to grasp and to use are superior to that of any other profession."* He later said, *"Scientologists are the best people on each of the five continents and that's all there is to it."*[6]

There's certainly nothing wrong with giving any group's members a pep talk or making them feel good for being part of one's group. But to say Scientologists are in the "upper tenth of the upper twentieth of intelligent human beings" is a bit much, especially if Scientologists are compared to people who have made real forward strides and substantial gains for all mankind in the time since Scientology has been around such as Dr. Martin Luther King or Mahatma Gandhi.

3. THE GROUP HAS A POLARIZED US-VERSUS-THEM MENTALITY, WHICH MAY CAUSE CONFLICT WITH THE WIDER SOCIETY.

Because Scientologists are told and believe they are unique and are better than other human beings because of the special spiritual states they supposedly attain, it's very easy for them to artificially create differences between themselves and the rest of the world, where no such actual differences exist.

The spiritual states Scientology offers are wholly subjective with no real proof ever having been offered these "higher states" even exist, much less that they create more powerful, more able or more "causative" human beings.

But that doesn't stop Scientologists, even those who haven't even been put through these advanced spiritual procedures, from thinking they are superior to non-Scientologists. Hubbard even coined terms for non-Scientologists, calling them "wogs" or "raw meat."[7]

This us vs them mentality goes so far as to bring about the separation of families and friends, when those who are not Scientologists express concern or distress over what the Scientologist is involved in. Rather than engage in rational discourse free from any agenda, Scientologists instead are made to do carefully orchestrated PR "handlings" on their relatives, friends or associates. If this doesn't work, then the Scientologist must permanently separate, otherwise they won't be allowed to do Scientology anymore. This is called "disconnection".

There is no such thing as religious tolerance or "live and let live" in Scientology. If you don't agree Scientology is the best thing to ever happen, you quickly will find Scientologists very reluctant to have anything to do with you.

4. THE GROUP TEACHES OR IMPLIES ITS SUPPOSEDLY EXALTED ENDS JUSTIFY WHATEVER MEANS IT DEEMS NECESSARY. THIS MAY RESULT IN MEMBERS PARTICIPATING IN BEHAVIORS OR ACTIVITIES THEY WOULD HAVE CONSIDERED REPREHENSIBLE OR UNETHICAL BEFORE JOINING THE GROUP.

Once someone is involved deeply enough with Scientology, he or she will find themselves justifying all sorts of behavior they never would have considered acceptable when they first got involved.

To pay for their next Scientology services, or just to donate to the "future good" of Scientology, members have cashed in their children's trust funds or retirement accounts, taken out double or triple mortgages on their homes, or taken on more and more burdensome debt to the point of having to declare bankruptcy. This happens far more often than you might think, and is actually the least of the morally reprehensible things Scientology pushes its members to do.

Scientology plays fast and loose with the concept of truth, especially when it comes to public relations. For instance, Hubbard wrote about the concept of an "acceptable truth".

"Handling truth is a touchy business also. You don't have to tell everything you know.... Tell an acceptable truth. Agreement with one's message is what PR is seeking to achieve.... So PR becomes the technique of communicating an acceptable truth - and which will attain the desirable result."[8]

It's all about communicating whatever will create the effect they are trying to achieve. If that means not telling the whole story, leaving out important bits or, through inference or deception, creating an impression which is just not true – it's all good. This is a common tactic when they are trying to avoid difficult topics like how families are broken up with disconnection or where all the money they collect actually goes or how they can claim to have millions of members worldwide yet have empty church buildings all around the world. These are questions most Scientologists can't answer. When they are caught flat-footed, they are indoctrinated into always putting a happy face on things rather than even imply something might be seriously wrong with Scientology.

However, their "end justifies the means" mentality goes far beyond just telling some fibs. It's well-documented that core members of Scientology, both Sea Org, regular church staff and even certain trusted public Scientologists, engage in what the Church calls Fair Game activities.

In a nutshell, this is where Church members execute Hubbard's directions to "ruin utterly" anyone who they perceive is an enemy of the Church. The lengths the old Guardian's Office and now the Office of Special Affairs have been known to go to carry out Hubbard's directions have almost no limits.

Right now the Church is fighting in court to defend its supposed right to harass and stalk its critics and ex-members, but these activities are actually amongst some of the more tame examples of what Scientology is willing to do to someone when it decides that person is an enemy of the Church.

The fact is, they don't just hire private investigators to follow people around. They have successfully gotten people fired from their jobs, infiltrated people's personal and business lives in order to break up relationships and business partnerships, engaged in breaking and entering and committed cyber crimes like hacking into people's computers, email accounts, etc. This is in addition to purposefully and with malice aforethought, tearing apart families, friendships and businesses in order to keep Scientologists from learning the truth about what Scientology is up to.

They will go to any length they feel is necessary to find whatever they want to know about their perceived enemies. They then use that information against those enemies to disrupt their lives permanently. Another kind of Fair Game activity is taking ex-Scientologists and critics to court, not for any real purpose other than to harass the person into stopping whatever the Church disagrees with.

Hubbard's policy bluntly states "*The purpose of the suit is to harass and discourage rather than to win. The law can be used very easily to harass, and enough harassment on somebody who is simply on the thin edge anyway...will generally be sufficient to cause his professional decease. If possible, of course, ruin him utterly.*"[9]

Now to be clear, not all Scientologists engage in this Fair Gaming to such an extent. Many of them don't even know this kind of thing goes on. They get hints about it or read something which maybe indicates this kind of behavior is okay with the Church and they turn a blind eye to it. Scientologists need to take their blinders off.

They do these things without remorse, feeling entirely justified in their criminal behavior because they think they are saving the world.

When someone first signs up for Scientology, they never imagine they will get involved in any of these kinds of activities – financial mismanagement, deception and even breaking the law. It's done gradually, step by step, kind of like Walter White in the TV show *Breaking Bad,* each decision gradually worse and worse until they find themselves in circumstances where they are committing actual crimes, hurting people and thinking they have no other choice.

5. THE GROUP IS PREOCCUPIED WITH MAKING MONEY.

Anyone who has ever been involved with Scientology knows, despite any hype or PR about how you can do Scientology for little to no money, the truth is Scientology courses and counseling cost money. To get all the way to the top, we are talking about a lot of money.

The Church's website states *"In the Church of Scientology, parishioners make donations for auditing or training they wish to receive. These contributions are the primary source of financial support for the Church and fund all Church-sponsored religious and social betterment activities. Scientologists are not required to tithe or make other donations."*

As any Scientologist knows, these statements are not true. Yes, Scientologists do donate for the courses and counselling, but a tremendous amount of church income comes from a different kind of donation. We'll call these straight donations, made by parishioners who are talked into giving the money for no exchange of any kind. In other words, they aren't buying anything for their money.

These are donations made to either the International Association of Scientologists Religious Trust or to building fundraising. The church is making millions upon millions of dollars on these kinds of donations and there is no accountability or transparency of any kind on this. The fact is, parishioners have absolutely no idea where those straight donations go or how much the church spends on what. They simply trust the Scientology executives to wisely invest in whatever will forward or enhance Scientology.

Considering the only thing Scientology really has to show for itself these days are big empty church buildings, it doesn't seem like all these hundreds of millions of dollars in straight donations are actually being spent on anything.

There are certainly no broad dissemination or promotional campaigns being carried out, as the church has a negative PR value in the media and its very name is used as a punchline by talk show comedians.

There's no tangible evidence of Scientology carrying out any of its stated purposes to rid society of drugs, illiteracy, crime or insanity. Every claim ever made by the church on this cannot be substantiated by any other media source and fact checking routinely shows what the church says they are doing, is not in fact, what they did.

That doesn't stop David Miscavige or the International Association of Scientology fundraisers from continuing to push parishioners hard for more and more of their hard-earned money, no matter what the cost to the church members personally.

Let's Put this in Perspective

Scientology is a system of belief which enforces mental and spiritual control under the guise of giving its members "total spiritual freedom."

If you are in Scientology, I want you to honestly look at the points I've covered here. Look at where you are now compared to what your life was like before Scientology. Now let me ask you some questions about your freedoms.

- Are you really free to think for yourself? If you don't agree with L. Ron Hubbard or David Miscavige about something, do you feel safe in talking about your disagreements openly or would there be bad consequences if you spoke up?
- Are you free to ask where the money you donate is actually going? Do you have any idea what it's really being spent on? Could you get an accounting of it if you asked for one?
- Are you free to look at anything you want to on the internet?

- Are you free to read anything you want about Scientology itself, even materials not written by L. Ron Hubbard?
- Are you free to talk to anyone you want, regardless of what they think about Scientology?
- Do you freely tell anyone and everyone you are a Scientologist, or are there some circumstances where you feel it's just better to not bring it up? Why do you think that is?
- And finally, are you really better off spiritually? Financially? Physically?

In the end, there really is no question about it. Scientology is a destructive cult, a money-making scam dressed up as a bona fide religion which abuses its members for as long as they will allow it to before it casts them aside, taking as much of their time, money and energy as it can get away with.

5. Why Scientology is Imploding

Destruction is in its DNA

The Church of Scientology is imploding at what any outside spectator would call an alarming rate. While its leader, David Miscavige, stands before enthralled devotees several times a year claiming highest-ever membership and off-the-top production figures, the truth from inside is quite the opposite.

Since the late 1960s, Scientology has claimed membership in the millions. Yet those un-named millions have never been tallied from any official membership rolls nor validated in any way. In fact, it's been reported by those who were actually there the reports of "millions of members" were literally created out of thin air as nothing but PR fluff to satisfy some demanding senior Scientology executive who wouldn't settle for anything less.[1]

While the Church may lie to its public and the world in general, inside the organization they keep tight tally every single week of how many parishioners are actually attending services in every one of their organizations as well as how many attendees they have at their yearly event gatherings. For example, in 2009, I saw international event attendance was at 50,000 and that included all staff and Sea Org members. Since then, insiders have reported these figures are an ever-dwindling spiral, now down to as low as 30 - 35,000 worldwide. Since these include the staff and Sea Org, public membership could be as low as 25,000. Even if the membership figures were ten times this amount, it's still not even close to a million members, much less tens of millions.

L. Ron Hubbard wrote many volumes of policies governing the purposes and activities of every single part of the organization, from its highest management echelons down to how cleaning personnel are to wash windows. No matter was too small for his personal attention. Within the Scientology world, Hubbard's word is law, so there is no real doubt as to where these policies originated but every time things have gone wildly wrong in the execution of these policies, blame is shifted to those who carried out the orders or even to its intended victims. Hubbard himself clearly and repeatedly stated the source of all Scientology was Hubbard himself and that remains church doctrine today, no matter how corrupted or altered Hubbard's writings have become.

The belief system of Scientology, what its adherents call "the technology" is not the problem I'm referring to here. Like any other religion or cult, Scientology has its own unique set of ideas as to where the universe comes from, what Man's relationship is with God and life, and its own codes and rules for happy living. None of these beliefs are really so very different from other belief systems, certainly not enough to call Scientology's adherents crazy just for believing in them. Very few get away with calling Catholics insane for believing they are imbibing the blood and flesh of Jesus Christ in Mass, and so it is with the Scientologists and their beliefs in the galactic ruler Xenu, Invader Forces conquering our solar system over the past many millennia and spiritual entities called thetans being the single source of all life anywhere. There are lots of things wrong with how Scientology is practiced and there are mind control techniques written into its methodologies, but in the end the belief system of Scientology has nothing whatsoever to do with why it is imploding. That doesn't mean the beliefs are logical or could stand up to even a casual application of critical thinking. They are completely irrational. They just aren't the *cause* of the implosion.

Instead, a review of Scientology's *policies* and *activities* shows why this worldwide implosion is occurring. While this gives the answers as to what the organization must do if it is to survive into any kind of realistic future, it also shows why the Church will never execute the needed changes. The truth is the Church is its own worst enemy.

Here are the five aspects of Scientology's organizational policies and activities which it must change to survive. These changes are never going to occur, since it is part of its very DNA to continue these practices until the very end.

Incessant demands for money with no accountability or exchange

Because Scientology is currently classified as a religion and not a for-profit business, it thrives and survives on the "donations" of its parishioners. While Hubbard himself categorically stated these donations were only to be accepted for actual services rendered and materials delivered, beginning in the late 1970s donations started being sought for non-service and material-related activities. Initially this was for legal defense when many of the Church's highest members found themselves behind bars as part of the infamous Snow White Program.

Finding this defense fundraising lucrative, this practice was ramped up enormously with the founding of the International Association of Scientologists (IAS) in 1984, ostensibly a membership fund with different classes of membership awarded to donors dependent upon how much money was donated. Many millions of dollars have been collected over the years from Scientologists, claiming this money was needed for the IAS "war chest" to fund legal defenses and grant monies for special Scientology projects. This has been such a lucrative activity for the Church, they established continental offices for the IAS with full-time solicitors who do nothing but spread tales of doom and gloom to alarm Scientologists and convince them their hard-earned monies are needed immediately to avert some deadly crisis, a crisis which only Scientology can handle.

Never is any proof given as to where any of these IAS funds actually go. If Scientologists were to ask about this, or for any degree of financial transparency at all, they would be hounded by the Church's Ethics Officers (people who enforce Church discipline and its justice actions) over their lack of faith in the organization and its highest executives. The internal membership rolls of the IAS, listing its actual number of current and expired memberships, are among the most closely guarded secrets in all of Scientology.

Since about 2004, additional fundraising efforts have been made out to the tune of many hundreds of millions of dollars to purchase and renovate new church buildings. These fundraising activities are carried out with a fervor and vehemence not often seen anywhere else, with parishioners cashing out trust funds and IRAs, giving up their children's college funds and borrowing money from each other to give even more. All so the Church can buy unnecessarily large quarters for each church building in the world and then renovate them at vastly unnecessary costs. This program is referred to as the "Ideal Org Program" and it is going on to this day.

The end result is church buildings which stand nearly empty all around the world. Again, the Church provides zero transparency or accountability as to where the collected funds were actually spent. There is plenty of evidence parishioner funds are being misused, and there was even a legal case of fraud brought against the Church in Florida over this kind of abuse. Like so many other cases brought against Scientology, they managed to wiggle out of it through legal chicanery and contract law. Scientology makes its members sign contracts giving away all their rights before they are allowed to do any services including their right to not be defrauded.[2]

In many cases, non-Scientology contractors have gone unpaid for months or even years after these buildings were opened, dunning the local church for the unpaid bills incurred by the international Church headquarters which arranged for these contractors to actually do their work. I witnessed this firsthand in Las Vegas and again in Twin Cities, Minnesota.

The IAS and building fundraising activities have far exceeded the amount of money the Church's local organizations raise for actual services delivered and materials purchased. So basically, the Church is making a great deal of money and delivering absolutely nothing in return. This practice has been going on for so many years it is expected and routine for IAS fundraisers to visit local churches every one to two months to dish out a new round of bad news and then demand the parishioners give more to solve the trumped-up crises.

No world catastrophe or incident is beyond the reach of the IAS fundraising vultures. If there is a typhoon in Malaysia, funds are needed to supposedly send Scientology Volunteer Ministers to provide relief. If there is war in the Ukraine, funds are needed to allegedly print pamphlet-sized booklets that will somehow be distributed in the region and magically create an aura of calm and goodwill. Whether these Volunteer Ministers ever arrive or whether these books are ever distributed is rarely reported on.

The Church of Scientology is a church, but it is definitely not a charity. The lack of accountability and transparency is a very large red flag in regard to its finances. Its incessant demand for more and more money with no exchange to its parishioners is causing ripple effects throughout its membership, who are more and more dissatisfied with the lack of any actual results despite the fundraising propaganda. Empty churches, a shrinking membership and no change in society as a result of Scientology's efforts are not what these parishioners have been donating toward for all these years, but it is what they are seeing.

A complete failure to acknowledge or correct its errors

Fundamental to Scientology's core beliefs is its inherent infallibility. The first line of the all-important "Keeping Scientology Working" policy letter states *"We have sometimes since passed the point of achieving uniformly workable technology."* Hubbard then goes on to describe in some detail how Scientology is a methodology which produces results 100% of the time on 100% of the people to whom it is applied (Chapter 9 contains a complete breakdown of this policy letter).

This claim is absurd from the outset, as easily proven by the numerous and varied reports (from all around the world) of Scientology not being able to produce the promised results no matter who is applying it or under what conditions. However, within the Scientology world, this claim of uniform workability is considered to be an absolute truth.

Interestingly, just two months after writing "Keeping Scientology Working" in 1965, Hubbard quietly backpedaled and wrote some more policies to explain why there are some people Scientology just doesn't work on. Rather than admit Scientology might not be for everyone, or some people are just harder to handle with his brand of psychotherapy, instead he wrote this:

"Does their [the parishioner's] *history of routine auditing reveal any gains? If the answer is NO then there is your Suppressive Person....one only uses this one fact – no case gain by routine auditing over a longish period."*

"One hears a whine about 'process didn't work' or sees an alter-is [illegal change] *of tech. Go look. You'll find it now and then leads to a Suppressive Person inside or outside the org."*[13]

Auditing not working on you? Well, it's because you are a Suppressive Person (SP). What does this mean exactly? This is defined as *"a person who seeks to suppress, or squash, any betterment activity or group. A suppressive person suppresses other people in his vicinity. This is the person whose behavior is calculated to be disastrous."* Hubbard went on to write quite a bit about Suppressive People. Basically, they are evil-intentioned psychopaths who are actively engaged in criminal activities on a daily basis.

It is a key principle of Scientology dogma that if you don't want auditing or if you try it and it doesn't seem to work on you, the only possible reason for that is because you are a psychopathic criminal.

Knowing this makes it easier to understand why Scientology executives have little to no compassion nor understanding for its critics, and why absolutely no effort is ever made to change or adjust Scientology itself if someone is dissatisfied with its results.

It also makes it easy to see why getting a refund of services or membership fees is all but impossible, when the organization responsible for returning your money thinks you are an undeserving criminal psycho. Those who have asked for refunds have compared their experience to being treated like criminals, and this is why.

For these reasons, Scientology executives and leaders will never contemplate the idea they or their organization could be doing something wrong and will therefore never seek to make operational changes or adjustments. As history has consistently proven, any group which cannot change or improve itself is a group not long for this world.

Suppressing free speech and expelling members for discontent

If nothing else, Scientology is an interesting study in dichotomies (opposites). Its policies, technology and history are replete with contradictions.

At one end, the Creed of the Church states *"That all men have inalienable rights to think freely, to talk freely, to write freely their own opinions and to counter or utter or write upon the opinions of others....and that no agency less than God has the power to suspend or set aside these rights, overtly or covertly."* Note this Creed clearly states "all men" and does not differentiate between Scientologists and non-Scientologists. Everyone is supposed to have free speech and free thought, according to one of the most fundamental documents of Church doctrine.

At the other end of the spectrum, the Church has a proven track record of repeatedly and consistently expelling members who openly voice disagreements with the Church's management or its policies. If a Scientologist is caught even looking at anything anti-Scientology on the Internet, he risks being declared a "Suppressive Person" which will result in his immediate expulsion from the Church and disconnection from all other Scientologists.

In Scientology, freedom of speech is encouraged only so long as you don't try to direct that freedom toward the Church itself.

Very early in Scientology's development, Hubbard wrote about the importance of communication, asserting it is *the* key component of life and is extremely important to every person's success. In numerous ways he repeatedly stated communication will resolve any difficulties or entanglements and if someone is having a personal issue with another, only through communication can those issues can be resolved. In fact, Hubbard went so far as to state it is communication alone which permits a person to get better at all.

So it's somewhat surprising (or maybe it isn't) Hubbard would then turn around and write policies requiring a parishioner be expelled for communicating their disagreements or upsets with Scientology, its founder or its executives. Yet that is exactly what he did. Rather than use communication to resolve those issues and bring the person back into the fold, the Church finds it more convenient to simply kick the "troublemaker" out entirely. As more and more pressure has been exerted on Scientology from the outside through critics and media stories, Scientology has doubled down on this policy, tightening their grip harder and harder to keep parishioners in line and giving them the boot if they even appear to be allied with or connected to anyone critical of Scientology.

On the internet, there is a list thousands long of people who have left Scientology and then spoke out publicly against it.[4] Almost everyone on that list was unable to have their claims or problems impartially evaluated when they were still active members. Most had no desire to be expelled and did not leave the Church of their own volition, but were just kicked to the curb by the Church's internal "justice" system. Many were trying to bring about some kind of reform or change from within, whether it be trying to reverse some injustice or correct a senior executive who was wrongly applying Hubbard's policies. Very few of these thousands ever wanted to leave the Church and be a whistleblower, but the Church's unreasonable policy to silence all critics left them no choice.

Before the rise of the Internet, Scientology's ability to control the flow of information about itself was relatively easy. Suppressing media at a local newspaper level or stopping a few television reports with threats of legal action were easy enough to arrange. The Office of Special Affairs liked to flex their muscles and did so often to silence public criticism through harassing lawsuits whose only purpose was to waste the time and money of their targets and ruin them personally and/or financially. Hubbard himself wrote the Church policies demanding they engage in these costly legal battles, all to wear down the Church's opponents and leave them in the financial gutter. "Ruin them utterly" Hubbard said.[5] It's hard for me to understand how some ex-Church members can actually continue to support Hubbard when presented with evidence he personally gave directions like this for how to deal with Church critics.

Like many fascist and dictatorial governments are finding in this modern age, controlling the flow of information since the 1990s has been harder and harder, and now is a near impossibility. So it is no coincidence Scientology's membership has been steadily decreasing since then.

In 2007, the internet social justice collective known as Anonymous decided to go head-to-head with Scientology. Almost overnight, the abuses and actual crimes being perpetrated by the Office of Special Affairs and the Church's management were suddenly known the world over. Information exploded all over the cybersphere and Scientology's public image went from a mysterious and somewhat kooky fringe religion to something actually dangerous and was ripping apart families. Their practices of expulsion and disconnection were now easily proven to be true, as more and more stories began to surface with real people coming forward and telling their stories. Stories of actual physical abuse being perpetrated by the head of the religion were too numerous to be easily explained away or shrugged off.

So it's no wonder the Church's members, who may not be entirely candid with Church officials about how much they are reading on the Internet, are quietly leaving in higher numbers than ever before.

Hubbard died in 1986 and despite all his vaunted knowledge of intergalactic civilizations over the past many millennia, he somehow never envisioned the World Wide Web. Using entirely antiquated and inadequate policies, Church officials continue to try to squelch the free flow of information to their parishioners with ever-increasing draconian control measures over their thoughts and actions. The tighter they draw the noose, the more members are slipping through and quietly exiting out the back door.

Active harassment and persecution of ex-members and critics (Fair Game policy)

There is something very unique to the Church of Scientology setting it apart from other religions and even most other destructive cults. Many Scientologists have no idea this goes on and would categorically deny their church does anything like this. However, there is ample proof of this activity and the church even admits to it. What I'm talking about, of course, is the policy of Fair Game.

Hubbard said much about the subject of justice before Scientology even existed, after publishing *Dianetics: The Modern Science of Mental Health* in 1950. There's a whole section in this book about Judiciary Dianetics. His first real codification of how to go about administering justice was in a now-obscure reference called the *HCO Manual of Justice*. It was published in 1959 but you won't find it in any Church policy volumes because it's a confidential reference.

This manual is not very long but it contains the roots of much of what is wrong with Scientology today.[6] I highly recommend you read it if you are interested in how Scientology justice personnel are trained. I'm not an expert on covert intelligence operations, but my take on this manual is it is a fascinating study in paranoia and how to make illogical conclusions almost 100% of the time.

In the introduction, Hubbard wrote:

"People attack Scientology; I never forget it, always even the score.

"People attack auditors, or staff, or organisations, or me. I never forget until the slate is clear."

He then goes on to say:

"When things go wrong and we don't know why already by intelligence, we resort to investigation.

"When we need somebody haunted we investigate...

"When we investigate we do so noisily always. And usually mere investigation damps out the trouble even when we discover no really pertinent facts. Remember that - by investigation alone we can curb pushes and crush wildcat people and unethical 'Dianetics and Scientology' organizations."

Now in anyone else's estimation, what Hubbard is talking about here is stalking and harassment. I mean, what else could *"when we want somebody haunted"* mean? He calls it "investigation" and so we see a classic example of re-defining words to hide criminal activities in plain sight.

He goes on to describe how people can be interrogated on an E-meter, which he recommends be used as a lie detector, even though he said in many other lectures an E-meter cannot be used for such a purpose as it is inaccurate in spotting if someone is actually lying.

Later in the manual, he recommends using private investigators:

"Overt investigation of someone or something attacking us by an outside detective agency should be done more often and hang the expense. It's very effective. Often investigation by a private detective has alone closed up an entheta [bad] source or a squirrel organisation. In fact at this writing I can't remember a time when it hasn't!

"The reason for this is simple. Of twenty-one persons found attacking Dianetics and Scientology with rumours and entheta, eighteen of them under investigation were found to be members of the Communist Party or criminals, usually both. The smell of police or private detectives caused them to fly, to close down, to confess.

"Hire them and damn the cost when you need to."

So you see, all the way back to 1959 Hubbard had it nailed that only evil Communists and criminals would ever dare speak out against Scientology. According to his logic and what he instills in his followers, if you publicly disagree with Scientology and say so, you must be a Communist or a criminal or both. Feel free to peruse the full list of the types of people he says to suspect in the *Manual of Justice*.

Amazingly, if a Church attacker actually *is* a criminal, Hubbard's direction is not to turn the guy in, but instead to use the data to blackmail him into silence! I find this fascinating. If you got the goods on someone and you really wanted to stop them from continuing to speak out, wouldn't you turn them in to the authorities so they could go to jail? Isn't that actually what real justice is all about?

Now with this background in mind, flash forward eight years to the very beginning of the Sea Organization and Hubbard's release of the

85

now infamous policy called "Penalties for Lower Conditions" on October 18, 1967.

In it, Hubbard first uses the term "Fair Game" as the penalty for being an enemy. He says the consequences of being an enemy and being "Fair Game" are *May be deprived of property or injured by any means by any Scientologist without any discipline of the Scientologist. May be tricked, sued or lied to or destroyed.*"

Now if you read this and you remove any filters or rationalizations, what Hubbard is actually describing here is a penalty wherein a person may be beaten, stabbed, shot or even murdered and no discipline of any kind will be enacted on the offender. You can steal his mail, trash his car or burn his house down and the Scientology Ethics Officers won't bat an eye. If you think I'm being extreme, then you don't know the history of the Church of Scientology and how far the Guardian's Office and Office of Special Affairs will go to "protect" it.

About a year after the Fair Game policy was issued there was so much bad PR from this practice, Hubbard was forced to cancel the use of the term "Fair Game" in a policy he issued on October 21, 1968, CANCELLATION OF FAIR GAME. This issue does not cancel the earlier issue which includes the description of Fair Game and Hubbard took care to note this did not cancel any policy on the treatment or handling of a Suppressive Person.

So in effect, this didn't really change or cancel anything, it merely eliminated the offensive wording.

As further proof of this, fast forward to 1984 when you have the Church attorneys in a court of law defending the use of Fair Game policy as a "core practice of Scientology".[7] So if you had any doubts up to now what I'm talking about is somehow old, not practiced anymore or ancient history, the Church's own attorneys can prove you wrong.

Right now in Comal County, Texas the stalking and harassment of ex-Scientologist Marty Rathbun and his wife, Monique (who was never a Scientologist of any kind) is being actively defended under the same arguments by the Church. It is a matter of court records that both Scientologists and hired private investigators carried out extensive surveillance of the Rathbuns for 4-6 *years*.[8]

The Church attorneys argue this practice of Fair Game is a constitutional right guaranteed by the First Amendment as a reflection of their freedom of religion and freedom of speech.

Technically speaking, standing outside someone's house and calling them names all day is protected free speech under the US Constitution. So is standing outside a funeral with signs reading "Thank God for Dead Soldiers" and "Fags Doom Nations" as the infamous Westboro Baptist Church does. Just because it's within the literal interpretation of the law does not make it right or decent or civil. In fact, "disgusting" is more the word which comes to mind.

However, if this were just a free speech issue, I wouldn't be writing any of this. Scientology takes this practice of Fair Game far beyond free speech. In just this most recent case with the Rathbuns, it's again a matter of court record the Rathbuns received threatening anonymous phone calls, were followed everywhere they went when they left their home, information about visitors to their home was published on the internet, Scientologists tried to pick fights with them and antagonized them verbally in person, and they found hidden surveillance cameras pointing to the inside of their home.[9]

They finally got up and moved to get away from the harassment, only to be followed by Church operatives, who continued the surveillance. According to the testimony of one of the Squirrel Busters (the group of high-level Scientologists who were actually harassing them), all this was done specifically to "make their life a living hell", which you'll recall is exactly what Hubbard directed in his *Manual of Justice* back in 1959.[10]

The Scientologists have no shame, no barriers and no limits when it comes to what they think are their "rights" to take out their perceived enemies. They will do anything and everything they feel the need to in order to destroy their opposition.

Thankfully when the church formally attempted to have the Rathbun's suit dismissed the judge on the case shot them down in flames and made many interesting points in his written judgment. Among them was the point that the Church's free speech defense was on very thin ice and did not really hold water given the fact actual physical pain and suffering resulted from the Church's actions.[11]

Freedom of speech ends when real harm to its intended victim begins. This court case is making it clear this activity on the Church's part will not be tolerated any longer.

Pat Broeker is a name from Scientology's history most won't recognize now. He was a top church executive in the 1970s and 80s who worked side-by-side with David Miscavige until shortly after Hubbard's death in 1986. Broeker was ousted when David Miscavige took over the Church since Broeker was Miscavige's only real rival for the top position. Broeker left and it was thought he took the upper OT levels with him. This turned out to be a rumor and it's pretty much agreed-upon any OT levels beyond OT VIII were never actually written.

It was revealed in August of 2013 private investigators Greg Arnold and Paul Marrick were paid somewhere between $10-12 million dollars to follow Pat Broeker for 25 years and report on his every move personally to David Miscavige.[12]

An entire book could be written citing examples of how the Church has inflicted its Fair Game policy on undeserving people over the last fifty years. Incidents are well documented all across the Internet and in many different courtrooms. I've spoken personally with many people who right now have various Fair Game activities directed against them, including attempts to directly stop their business activities and means of income. Many have been subjected to underhanded and even illegal activities to sabotage ex-Scientologists' business ventures. The history of the Church in this matter speaks clearly: careers ruined, relationships shattered, bank accounts gone bust and lives destroyed.

As Hubbard said, it is required you "always even the score." This is a pattern of revenge, not justice. And when you see enemies in every single person who speaks badly about Scientology, I guess you get a very inflated idea of what that "score" adds up to.

It's not a question of "Is the Church of Scientology doing this?" There is no question about that. Just ask anyone in the upper levels of the Office of Special Affairs or the people who are paid to defend the Church.

The money Scientologists give to the Church supports these Fair Game operations. Literally millions of parishioner dollars are used to hire private investigators and lawyers so David Miscavige can defend his right to stalk and harass ex-Church members.

Disconnection/shunning

The most toxic and some would even call *evil* policy of the Church of Scientology is the one known as 'disconnection'. Simply put, this is the equivalent of shunning, where a member is expelled and no other Scientologists in good standing are permitted to speak with or associate with the shunned member ever again.

In terms of religious practice, shunning is an archaic and uncommon practice, but it is not unique to Scientology. It's a weird and creepy thing for any religion to do, but Scientology takes it to a whole new level.

The policy works like this: if Joe is connected to an SP, no matter who that SP is, then Joe is labelled a Potential Trouble Source (PTS). He is denied any further Scientology services until he "handles or disconnects" from the SP. If Joe wants to continue to be connected with the SP (for example, if the SP is Joe's mother), then Joe has to somehow get the SP to recant and stop whatever activity the Church considers suppressive (posting anti-Scientology statements online, telling Joe how bad Scientology is etc). *"Any PTS who fails to either handle or disconnect from the SP who is making him or her a PTS is, by failing to do so, guilty of a Suppressive Act."*[13] So if Joe doesn't disconnect, he is also declared a Suppressive Person.

When asked, Scientology PR officers have vehemently and repeatedly denied there are policies requiring its members to disconnect from apostates (SPs). Other religions which practice shunning are not afraid to admit to the practice.

89

Yet in keeping with their contrary nature, whenever anyone who has been victimized by the disconnection policy goes to the media about it, the Church claims the practice is entirely voluntary.

Outsiders find it difficult to understand why anyone would disconnect, voluntarily or not, from their closest relatives, spouses and friends. The choice Scientology presents is simple: either disconnect from the SP or forget doing any more Scientology forever. For believers this is really no choice at all; not doing any more Scientology means they are giving up their eternal souls, not to mention never seeing their Scientologist family and friends ever again. Scientologists have a peculiar idea of what a "friend" is, because they will easily and immediately disconnect from anyone (even people they have known for decades) if a Scientology Ethics Officer tells them that person is no longer in good standing with the Church. Sometimes it doesn't even take any formal notice; Scientologists have disconnected from people they have known and visited and shared their lives with for decades simply because they were told in a Facebook comment such-and-such person is no longer in good standing. The mere rumor or hint of impropriety. is all it takes these days to destroy relationships in Scientology:

Disconnection policy is ostensibly stated to be for the protection of Scientologists, to keep them from being harmed by vicious antisocial personalities who seek to belittle or demean Scientology or stop people from achieving spiritual freedom. Of course if someone is viciously attacking you every day (whether those attacks are mental or physical) then it is your right to no longer remain in that person's vicinity. That is common sense.

But when an Ethics Officer tells you your mother, son, brother, sister or even grandmother are antisocial because they express concern over you spending your retirement savings on Scientology for no visible return, that is not religious freedom expressing itself. It is a paranoid organization trying to control every aspect of its members' lives so nothing interrupts the flow of money coming into its coffers.

In a Nutshell

The Creed of the Church of Scientology is supposed to guarantee freedom of speech and freedom of thought to everyone, Scientologist or not. However, this is merely a convenient façade, written and promoted only to fool the Church's members and make them believe they are part of a humanitarian organization fighting to bring an end to the hostilities of the world. The truth is, the Church of Scientology does nothing but foment hostilities every chance it gets.

Scientology, like so many other small-time cults which sprang into existence in the 20th century and faded away just as quickly, is not long for this world. Its own policies guarantee it, while a steady stream of ex-members continue to break away on an almost daily basis and blow the whistle on its immoral and even criminal activities.

The seeds of its destruction were sown many years before its current leadership took power, when Hubbard in his delusional paranoia wrote policies to "safeguard the Church" against his imagined enemies and set up a legal affairs division to enforce them. Those policies and the financial greed of the Church's current leadership ensure it will not last much longer.

Those Scientologists who work in the Office of Special Affairs are not just willing, but are actually eager to violate the human rights of anyone who leaves the Church and dares to speak out about their experiences. The only thing holding them in check at present is the fact their criminal activities are being exposed on the Internet and in the courts. This exposure is making it more and more difficult for OSA operatives to get away with the kind of activity they used to routinely engage in: stalking, harassment, trespassing, vandalism, breaking and entering, blackmail and worse.

Whether the Church of Scientology goes out with a bang or a whimper we have yet to see, but its destruction is assured. By its very nature it can't help but continue to destroy itself from within.

While Scientology claimed to be striving for an end to war, criminality and insanity, it ironically brought about those exact things within its own ranks.

The world will be a better place for its passing. It will not be missed.

6. Who was L. Ron Hubbard?

"The evidence portrays a man who has been virtually a pathological liar when it comes to his history, background and achievements. The writings and documents in evidence additionally reflect his egoism, greed, avarice, lust for power, and vindictiveness and aggressiveness against persons perceived by him to be disloyal or hostile. At the same time it appears that his charismatic and highly capable of motivating, organizing, controlling, manipulating and inspiring his adherents. He has been referred to during the trial as a 'genius,' a 'revered person,' a man who was viewed by his followers in awe. Obviously, he is and has been a very complex person and that complexity is further reflected in his alter ego, the Church of Scientology." Judge Paul G. Breckenridge, October 1984

There have been men and women made famous in history for their purpose and vision: great people who were determined to accomplish their goals no matter the cost or the sacrifices necessitated by fate or life. Such are remembered for centuries or even millennia because of their impact on the world: Alexander, Julius Ceasar, Joan of Arc, Lincoln, Newton, Einstein, Gandhi, Tesla, Susan B. Anthony and Martin Luther King Jr are but a few. The names are so indelibly etched into our minds, in most cases we only need refer to them by their surnames to know who we are talking about. The world is truly a different place because of them and our lives are all better for their having lived.

L. Ron Hubbard was not one of those men, but he believed he was. One of the chief differences is while you can say what you want about the character flaws or quibbles of these people, each of them was great because they had a purpose or a dream which reached far beyond themselves. None of the great men and women of history did what they did simply because they were trying to carve their name into the history books.

There is a phenomenon amongst us not-so-great people to tear down our heroes after a time and try to bring them down to our level. With the luxury of hindsight and having gained the benefits of their sacrifices, sometimes gained at the cost of their very lives, we look back on some of these great leaders and criticize their sexual orientation or try to redefine their lives through some petty quarrel with a compatriot or some other such nonsense. The things which made these people great were not their foibles, but the fact they were able to overcome what we cannot and make their dreams come true.

I don't know what drives us to do this and I'm not making the point because I'm criticizing our nature. People are people and it's natural for some to want to tear down idols out of jealousy, pettiness or other base motives. What I'm really trying to do is make it clear this chapter is not my attempt to fulfill that tendency.

I have a weekly Q&A show on YouTube where I answer people's questions, mostly about Scientology. The two most frequently asked questions are along the lines of (1) what is going to happen to David Miscavige and (2) what was going on in L. Ron Hubbard's head when he came up with Scientology in the first place? i.e. did he know it was a con or did he actually believe it was helpful and of benefit to Mankind?

The very nature of these questions makes them nearly impossible to answer with any degree of certainty. As much as we revere greatness, we are also fascinated by psychopaths and sociopaths. We want to know what motivates destructive cult leaders and what kind of bad things these people will get up to next. Did they really mean to do bad? Are they basically evil? Or did they really mean well and just make mistakes?

After reading thousands of pages and listening to hundreds of hours of lecturing by someone, you'd think you'd know them pretty well. I certainly formed a very good idea of who I thought L. Ron Hubbard was when I was in Scientology. I thought he was a rough-and-tumble kind of man who traveled all over the world, saw all sorts of things and had adventures the likes of which I could only dream of experiencing. I thought of him as a hearty and hale type of man who was quick with a joke and a deep laugh, who sniffed at danger and had no fear of death. He told lots of stories during his lectures, tales of combat and rescue, of hypnotizing a roomful of psychiatrists and nurses just for fun, of braving the elements on every sea on earth, and of helping his fellow man wherever he went and whatever else he was doing. If you listened to L. Ron Hubbard talk about himself, you soon got the idea this man was larger than life - someone capable of conquering not just the external world of physical peril, but also the inner world of our psychological torments and traumas.

So it was no small degree of shock and betrayal I felt when I learned Hubbard was not just a master storyteller but was, in fact, a pathological liar. Sure, some of his tall tales seemed a little too tall when I first heard them, but there was no doubt he had a kind of charisma or magnetism about him which made you want to believe what he said. I never met the man in person but the force of his personality and the strength of his convictions certainly came through in his spoken and written words. Many of those who recall meeting him have said as much. If someone of lesser stature or certainty tried to pawn off some of the stories Hubbard so casually threw out as truth, they'd be laughed out of the conversation, but somehow Hubbard had a way about him and he got away with it.

When I was a Scientologist, I made it a point to quiz everyone I ever met who worked with Hubbard and the answers were always the same: he was larger than life, took great care to make you feel special and important and he was the kindest, most gentle and wonderful soul they'd ever encountered. He was special in a way no one else could be. I didn't know what hero worship and infatuation were, beyond the sort of things people experience as kids for their idols, so I didn't realize then what I was hearing was a combination of adulation and blind worship, a not uncommon trait among followers of a cult leader.

Do you know an actor from the roles he plays? Do you know a writer from the stories he tells? We all like to think we do but of course, we really don't at all. You come to find out when you read enough interviews, Robert DeNiro is actually one of the gentlest men you'd ever want to know, someone who is careful on set to never hurt anyone; yet he can portray the most ruthless, domineering mobster or raging maniac on the big screen and he's *very* convincing.

It's quite possible Justin Bieber is a very nice young man in real life. He is the second highest granter of wishes for the Make-A-Wish Foundation and I'm sure he can be funny and warm in his private life. Yet if you listen to the Twitterverse and celebrity gossip rags, Bieber is just one step up from our primitive ape ancestors and should have been deported to Canada years ago. Public perception can be a fickle beast.

L. Ron Hubbard's biography is a story of two very different men depending on which accounts you care to follow. It's impossible for me to know the cold hard truth of what really motivated him, but having researched and studied as much as I have and after nearly three decades of devotion to the man, I think I'm in a place now where I understand what he was about and what went wrong.

I'm going to cover some of Hubbard's life story but the intent of this chapter is not to detail everything he did or all the events of his life. If you are looking for a thorough accounting of Hubbard's life, you need look no further than Russell Miller's *Bare-Faced Messiah* or Jon Atack's *A Piece of Blue Sky*. These are exhaustively researched works which detail every aspect of Hubbard's life and were invaluable resources to me (among many others) in learning what I needed to in order to answer this question.

What I'm looking at here is what motivated L. Ron Hubbard and whether we can answer the question of whether he knowingly, purposefully and with malice aforethought started a con to bilk people out of their money.

Hubbard's Early Life

Hubbard was born in Nebraska in 1911 and one thing I think a lot of modern readers miss when examining him and his history is he was a product of the turn-of-the-century Midwest. His blatant racism and misogyny, while not excusable, are certainly understandable when you look at the context of his upbringing. He was an only child and his family moved around a lot when he was a kid but it doesn't seem like that was really all that unusual for the time. He didn't lack for love or affection from his immediate or extended family and if anything he was coddled and spoiled in his early years.

Whether because of an overinflated ego or a need to impress others, he seems to have developed a very active imagination about his own doings and, like all teenagers, his own puffed-up importance in the world. His imagination served him well as a writer of stories from a young age but his grades and school record clearly show he was not at all interested in following the prescribed path for his life. He wanted to do things his way.

His father forced him into formal college education but Hubbard hated it and dropped out by the time he was 21. His antipathy toward formal schooling came through loud and clear in many of the Scientology lectures he gave years later. In fact, this was used to justify telling many young Scientology and Sea Org recruits they had no need for higher education. They would miss nothing by dropping out, because Hubbard figured out all the answers to life's problems and his words were all the education they would ever need.

Hubbard was much more interested in writing, flying gliders and easy money. A few months before he dropped out of school forever, he even commissioned a ship to go down to the Caribbean, conning fifty other young men to go with him, ostensibly to engage in filming of pirate haunts and collecting old artifacts which could be sold to museums. This may well have been the first time he attempted a kind of con job on a large number of people, since each of the 56 who went had to pony up $250 for the privilege.

Keep in mind this was only two years after the Stock Market Crash of 1929 and the Great Depression was in full swing. Getting a bunch of semi-Ivy League university students in Washington DC to hand over a total of $14,000 must have put big dollar signs in Hubbard's eyes (that's $225,000 today). The trip was, of course, a complete disaster and turned back before it even really got going due to foul weather and very bad planning. Hubbard blamed the captain, the other students, and basically everyone but himself for the trip's failure, but did admit years later, "it was a crazy idea at best, and I knew it, but I went ahead anyway."[1] Whether he made any money on the scheme or not is beside the point (he didn't). The fact is, this is the kind of thing Hubbard thought was a good idea at the time, which speaks volumes about how he approached his life.

The Depression and The One Command

The Church thoroughly supports Hubbard's self-created portrait of himself as a man of vision and purpose, driven from the time he was three years old to help others and discover the single source of Man's travails. Hubbard's life has been recast with him as a Messiah in the making, with everything which happened to him and everything he did hammered into a fictional story about a lifelong plan to become the Savior of Mankind. The sad thing is, I and thousands of other gullible people actually fell for this claptrap.

In reality, Hubbard was no such thing. He wandered from place to place and got into scrape after scrape trying to fake his way through life, basically flying by the seat of his pants. When I think about how Hubbard embellished his entire life story, changing the details over and over again depending on whom he was talking to, I think of the line Stinger gives Maverick in the movie *Top Gun*, "Son, your ego is writing checks your body can't cash." If only someone had gotten in Hubbard's face and gotten that message through, perhaps things would have gone very differently.

As it was, Hubbard's ego went unchecked and his one real talent – telling stories – earned him a living through the Depression despite his shortcomings and misadventures.

Besides the pulps and yarns which paid a penny a word and kept food on the table, there was another work Hubbard wrote in 1938 which is of extreme importance. Originally titled *The One Command,* it was later known as *Excalibur* and rarely as *The Dark Sword.* Its existence has been confirmed by multiple sources although it was never published and has been read by only a small handful of people. Apparently three manuscript copies survive in the vaults of the Church of Scientology.

Hubbard's references to this book are always couched in vague generalities because he claimed the book drove some people mad when they read it (but at least it didn't give them pneumonia and kill them, as Hubbard would later claim the OT III Xenu story would do). In one lecture I recall, Hubbard described the reaction of readers to this book as "going up the pole", comparing it to the idea of a two-dimensional worm reading the book and suddenly discovering there was a third dimension and he had the ability to climb this pole he'd previously been running into but unable to see. Some might react with joy and delight at discovering a hitherto unknown and unperceived dimension while it might make others quite insane to even consider the prospect.

Apparently the genus of this book was a dental surgery in April 1938, during which Hubbard's heart stopped and he had a near-death experience. He imagined seeing a light and a place of wonder and woke up thinking he had been shown the secret of life itself. Although he'd been told by some disembodied voice to forget everything he'd seen, he didn't forget.

Hubbard later embellished this story when he related it to his literary agent, Forrest J. Ackerman, in 1948. In this version, his epiphany happened during the war when he was in surgery for war injuries (which we can wholly write off as fiction because Hubbard never suffered any injuries in the war, certainly none which caused him to undergo surgery). It probably just sounded more dramatic to

Hubbard to lie about it because that's what he liked to do. He lied about everything.

As the story goes, after this dental surgery in 1938, Hubbard holed up in a cabin on Puget Sound and pounded out *The One Command* in a week, eating and drinking very little or nothing. Another account says Hubbard was drinking alcohol the whole time. Nothing is certain about any of this because the only one who would know for sure was Hubbard himself and he changed his stories to fit the audience in order to best create whatever effect he was trying for at the time.

In a 1961 edition of *The Aberee* (an unofficial Scientology newsletter), a fellow by the name of Arthur Burks wrote a short article claiming to have been the first person to have read the manuscript. Burks was another writer of pulps who was not intimate with Ron but considered him an acquaintance. For some reason, Burks was the first person Ron reached out to with this book. Perhaps he was the first one Hubbard could reach on the phone.

The reason this book is important is not so much its content, (still clouded in mystery except for Burke's 1961 description of what he remembered from 23 years before) but because Hubbard felt he had hit on something of singular importance – an explanation or a kind of philosophy of the mind which would enable him to have utter and complete control over other men if he so desired. Hubbard said "he wanted to make changes. He wanted to reach inside people and really work them over..."[2] Thus it was they haggled over titles and eventually Burks came up with *Excalibur* after King Arthur's sword, which Hubbard liked more than his earlier titles.

Burks relates Hubbard was very worked up at the time and Hubbard thought this book was going to revolutionize human behavior. He said it would have a greater impact than The Bible. It's very like Hubbard to think along those lines - he was not someone to ever take the lesser road and he never suffered from anything resembling humility. He seemed to really believe he had something huge and this was going to change human thinking.

Excalibur is sometimes described as a forerunner of *Dianetics: The Modern Science of Mental Health* but Hubbard said it offered no explanation of the reactive mind or therapeutic technique like *Dianetics* did. Instead, it apparently explained Man's behavior in terms of cellular activity and how it all came down to the idea of every cell trying simply and only to *survive*. Of course, this is fairly self-evident but Hubbard elaborated on it in such a way it really drove the point home survival was *the* very overriding principle of life, much more important than anything else such as love, compassion or purpose.

Even more importantly, from Burks' recollection there is a lot more about human motivations and behavior which I think is very telling in terms of how Hubbard viewed the world and the people in it. When philosophers and writers talk about the world at large and other people in it, I think they are often reflecting on themselves and their own views, opinions and ideas, which they project onto the world at large. I think it would take a great deal of insight and understanding to be able to avoid projecting ourselves onto what we see when we study the motivations and behavior of others, and I don't think Hubbard was a man of such insight and understanding. So I think these descriptions from Burks actually give us a window into Hubbard's own soul:

"He'd begin to picture the ocean and the seas and ponds as having the life cells growing on them like scum. These are ourselves, our beginnings, our own beginnings because in the womb we start in this very way.

"Away back then, we began to develop motives for things. Now, it is seldom that what we tell somebody our motive is, is the real one - and this is where you start to squirm. Somebody will say, 'Well, I'd like to do a certain thing,' 'I would like to do this with you,' or something or other, and you look at this person and realize, 'I wonder why he's doing that.' And you look into yourself and think if you were doing that, what would your motive be and whether you would hide it. You think that perhaps he's hiding his real motive and trying to get you to do something because he's giving you to understand that his motive is thus and so because that appeals to your vanity - and of course this makes you look at yourself to see about this business of vanity - and why you're likely to do that. All the time, looking at this other person, you can see squirmy things in him. You can see squirmy things in him that make him look like an entity peering at you

thru gauze, or around a corner. You don't see all of him. He's like the iceberg that's seven-eighths submerged - you can't tell anything about him.

"As these things are pointed out to you by Ron in the first chapter, or thereabouts, you begin to see that the cells in any body that you're looking at are all endowed with this ability to survive - a determination to survive - and with motives to survive that are sometimes extremely questionable. When you look at a person, the lips may say one thing, the eyes may say something else, or nothing, and the flesh may say something entirely different. Literally, your right hand doesn't know what your left hand is doing. You shake hands, and this is a friendly gesture, but behind your back you may be holding a knife to plunge into him and he may be holding one for you. You can't tell just by looking at people. One of the things Ron intended to do with Excalibur was to make it possible to see and look into this.

"Other things I remember is Ron's explanation as to why there is no such thing as a crowd - that a group of people actually still consisted of individuals - but a crowd could get out of hand and do things other people wouldn't. He showed how that could happen by explaining the relationship of people to each other in the same way that he explained the relation of cells to each other before they were people away back when life was developing into different shapes. He would take two persons, for example, and put them side by side, and show how the two of them were both less and more than one person, and yet each one was an individual. Each individual could think of himself as being individual, but being somewhat "crutched", as it were, or held up by the other person. These two people were very wary of each other, like a couple of bantam roosters running around waiting to get in a thrust, but they knew that they needed each other, and each one felt that he needed the other more and that he didn't wish to be taken advantage of, and so there was always this pulling and hauling between two people that kept them at razor's edge all the time.

"Each one, to some extent, gradually - a little bit at a time - gave away some of his sovereignty to the other. In other words, he let the other fellow lean, provided the other fellow would let him lean, and the two people became somewhat less than they would have been if they had stayed apart.

102

The relationship between the two people became something that would really get you."

"Then he moved in with these two people a third person - could be of the same sex - and you still have all the difficulties, all the problems, and all the squirminess - the questioning as to motive and everything, and wondering why, for example, three males would get together, or three women. If you have a person of the other sex come in on two who were together, you begin to see where the problems are. Of course, he went into this business of sexual attraction to a considerable extent in a way that just made you wonder whether or not your attitude toward sex was reasonable or wrong, whether it was a horrible thing or a beautiful thing spiritual or whatever. I think perhaps it would make you think about it to the point where you'd be almost afraid to perpetrate the act of sex, even with someone you loved tremendously."[3]

If you were looking for some kind of idea of what drove Hubbard and why he thought it was a good idea to lie to people and take advantage of their weaknesses for his own aggrandizement and opportunity, I think you'd find your answer in the passages above. To him, people are like individual cells in a great race for survival, a dog-eat-dog mentality where only the strong or clever survive, often at the expense of those around them.

There is certainly a degree of truth in some of what is said above, but to believe that's all there is driving life forward is quite a cynical and calloused view of people and what makes them tick. I don't share those views but knowing what I know about Hubbard, what he did with his life and how he treated his family, friends and followers, I have no doubt Hubbard took all those words to heart and felt very strongly if he didn't step on other people to get where he wanted to go, they were going to step on him.

The really wild thing to me is despite this, Hubbard also apparently believed this material was going to actually help people and would pave the way to his personal fame and fortune. According to a letter Hubbard sent to his wife Polly in October 1938:

"Sooner or later Excalibur will be published and I may have a chance to get some name recognition out of it so as to pave the way to articles and

comments which are my ideas of writing heaven ... Foolishly perhaps, but determined none the less, I have high hopes of smashing my name into history so violently that it will take a legendary form even if all books are destroyed. That goal is the real goal as far as I am concerned."[4]

When "The Book" did not get sold off immediately to the publishers Hubbard was shopping it to, meaning no one wanted to publish it, he packed it up and went back to Washington and nothing more was heard about it for many years. Burks said Hubbard was considerably disappointed the book wasn't published. I think that is very true and as we'll see, this work was something Hubbard would later return to with Dianetics and Scientology.

You're in the Navy Now

Shortly after all this, Hubbard ended up joining the Navy. World War II was still months away from being declared but it was fairly obvious at the time America would get actively involved at some point soon. I doubt Hubbard was interested in actually participating in combat, but he did seem to have a kind of interest in military life and especially working in military intelligence. Hubbard was not only raised by a Navy father but was also in the National Guard and later the Marine Corps Reserve in college, so he had some history with this himself. On the other hand, he may well have enlisted just to get away from the responsibilities of his first wife and the two children she bore him, a pattern of abandonment he would repeat many times in the future. Hubbard was never a good father or husband, cheating on his first wife routinely while on writing trips to New York, and he excelled at running away from his obligations.

One thing certain from the amount of work he put into getting enlisted is Hubbard wanted to work in Naval Intelligence and likely fancied himself as a spy in the making. Unfortunately for him, his skills and abilities were not well suited for anything like Intelligence and regardless of Scientology's later claims he was an undercover operative throughout the war, no such thing actually happened.

104

Things didn't work out nearly as well as Hubbard planned, with one disaster after another plaguing his naval record, all of his own making.

For example, he spectacularly claimed to have taken out a Japanese sub (or two) off the coast of Oregon literally within hours of setting forth on his first command of a sub-chasing destroyer. No evidence of this sinking could be found anywhere and the commander of the Northwest Sea Frontier rejected this claim after a full investigation of the incident. Within just a couple of months, Hubbard's command was taken away after he engaged in unauthorized shelling of an island in Mexican territorial waters.

Hubbard was never injured in combat because he never saw combat. That didn't stop him from later claiming because of his his war wounds, he was laid up for a year at the Oakland Naval Base in California and tricked his way into the medical library to study physiology and endocrinology. He claimed to use this newfound knowledge of the endocrine system as well as his vast knowledge of Freudian psychotherapy to develop mental therapy techniques which baffled the doctors at the hospital because he was curing fellow patients of physical ailments the doctors themselves had no remedies for. He later claimed all this is what eventually evolved into Dianetics techniques.

However, every bit of this story about research and healing people at the hospital was just made-up nonsense. None of that ever happened. What was true is Hubbard did strenuously and repeatedly claim he was suffering from physical problems: ulcers, deteriorating eyesight and bursitis, amongst other things. Being the charlatan he was, and trying desperately to get more and more pension to make up for lack of steady income through anything as honest as real work, Hubbard made up more and more physical troubles in his persisting applications to the VA.

He was still considered physically fit for shore duty and did stay in the Navy through 1945 in California until he was transferred to inactive duty in February 1946. His pestering for increased pension finally came through when they upped it to $55 a month (which is about $725 in today's value). Not a bad con for someone with nothing seriously wrong who just gamed the system.

Conning Jack Parsons

Far from being laid up in Oakland's Naval Hospital for a year, Hubbard was actually out and about meeting people. Before Hubbard was discharged from the Navy, he made the acquaintance of Jack Parsons in Pasadena through mutual friends in the sci-fi community. Jack was a rocket scientist at the Army's Jet Propulsion Laboratory by day and a devil-worshiper by night. He owned a mansion in the Orange Grove region of Pasadena which he opened as a sort of boarding house for strange and unusual types, who mooched off Jack's fascination with the occult and paranormal.[5]

Hubbard ingratiated himself to Parsons with his larger-than-life presence and tall tales of adventure from his world travels and the war. None of it was true, of course, but in that environment who was anyone to call someone else out for letting their imagination run wild?

Parsons was quite taken by Hubbard and it appeared they struck up a kind of friendship, but it's my opinion this friendship was one-sided as I don't think Hubbard had any good intentions regarding their relationship.

Parsons had a hidden temple built into his mansion and held Thelemic black magic rituals there, under the tutelage of Aleister Crowley. He kept up regular correspondence with Crowley (who lived in England) and was a primary financial supporter of Crowley's Order of the Golden Dawn through his generous donations.

Hubbard was still married but his wife and children were still up in Bremerton, Washington. Polly refused to relocate herself or the children and Hubbard didn't want to go back to Washington to be a family man. He found a home in Parsons' mansion and convinced Jack he wanted to be more than a small part of his branch of the Ordo Templi Orientis and help him in his efforts to conceive a "moon child".

Much has been made of Hubbard's and Parson's involvement in the occult and its influence on Hubbard's development of Scientology terminology and philosophy. Hubbard was a plagiarist and stole as much from Crowley's Magick symbolism and occult practices as he did from other sources when he formulated Dianetics and especially when he put Scientology together.

There is definite evidence, which we'll get to shortly, Hubbard did come to believe Magick was real and felt he had a Guardian Spirit watching over him to guide him in his life. It's unclear from what I have read and studied whether Hubbard had an earlier connection with black magic or the occult before meeting Parsons, but he certainly embraced it wholeheartedly during this time period.

From what I can tell, Hubbard was not in a good or happy place after the war and was looking for something to help him regain what he felt he had lost – personal power, physical well-being and the ability to create positive change in his life through the force of his will. It seems he thought Crowley's Magick would give him these things.

Perhaps at the time, Hubbard was pretending or perhaps he really did believe. There's no way to know for sure one way or the other, but evidence suggests he was a True Believer. Regardless of his spiritual or black magic beliefs, though, there is no doubt Hubbard was putting one over on Parsons.

Within just two months of taking up residence in Parsons' own house, Hubbard stole Parsons' 21-year-old girlfriend, Sara Northrup. Parsons tried to take the high road and claim he was above petty jealousies but it was apparent Sara's changing loyalty grated on him. However, not so much for him to end his friendship with Hubbard and they all three began a grand investment scheme to sell yachts from Florida to businessmen in California. Parsons invested most of his substantial savings in a joint company with the other two, while Hubbard invested very little and Sara invested nothing.

It was Aleister Crowley who saw through the scheme all the way from England (he never met Hubbard personally) and advised Parsons to stop Hubbard before it was too late. Hubbard went off to Florida with Sara, ostensibly to purchase their first boat and sail it to LA for resale, but in actuality to live the high life on Parsons' money. Hubbard and Sara had no intention of returning to California or getting any of Parsons' money back to him. Parsons travelled to Florida, succeeded in getting an injunction and dissolved the company they'd formed as part of the con, but couldn't recover his money and eventually ended up having to sell his Pasadena mansion to stay afloat.

By July 1946, Hubbard gave Parsons a promissory note to repay some of what he stole but otherwise got away with it scot-free. However, he had nothing left from the money he'd conned out of Parsons because of his pathological tendency to squander any cash he got his hands on. This was a recurring problem with Hubbard – his financial insolvency was almost entirely caused by his total inability to be responsible with the money he made. He spent it as fast as he got it and had a very carefree attitude about making more, always sure "something would come up".

Broke again, he sold the boat he had purchased with Parson's money just so he and Sara could eat. In order to stay afloat, he put renewed energy into conning the Veterans Administration into increasing his pension again.

The Crazy Starts Coming Out

With money from the boat sale, Ron and Sara looked like they could make a fresh start and, in August 1946, they went by train to Maryland and got married. Now Hubbard could add "bigamist" to his long list of dubious accomplishments. Neither of his wives knew of the existence of the other and wouldn't for almost another year.

The newly married couple settled in Laguna Beach, California and for the next three months Hubbard proceeded in earnest to convince the VA to increase his pension, but to no avail. They were soon poor, getting by only with the help of family. It appears during this time, Hubbard worked himself over with a kind of self-hypnosis, and this gives us our next big reveal into what was going on in his head.

The Affirmations are a series of written statements Hubbard made, perhaps inspired by Crowley's Magick or by hypnotism (which

Hubbard was practiced in). He probably played them back to himself using a Dictaphone-type setup as a form of self-hypnosis to allay his fears and insecurities.

These Affirmations are the most damning extant evidence of Hubbard's mental state a few years before he penned *Dianetics: The Modern Science of Mental Health* and started down the road to self-aggrandizement through cult leadership. They were never meant to be seen by anyone else. The fact he even kept them around and within reach of others is factually amazing to me, though they weren't uncovered until the early 1980s, decades after they were first written.

The Affirmations are literally a window into Hubbard's psyche and it's not a pretty picture. I think anyone who is human is liable at any stage of life to feel overwhelmed, fearful about the present or future and regret the past. There isn't anyone who doesn't wish they could undo or re-live some part of their life, or want to be stronger, faster, smarter or more appealing to the opposite sex. None of us are perfect and it would be folly to claim we don't all have our moments of weakness and trouble.

However, what the Affirmations show is a man who was not only trying to deal with a host of emotional and mental issues, but also someone who wanted dominion over his fellow man, who literally worked to convince himself "men were his slaves." They show a personality completely narcissistic and consumed by personal power yet also filled with self-loathing and distrust of anyone else.

To anyone familiar with Scientology techniques, so many of the psychological and emotional issues Hubbard claimed to have solved were issues he was struggling with himself. It is so obvious after reading these Affirmations that Hubbard projected his problems and views on every other person he encountered. I suspect over the years he developed Scientology, he really was looking to find ways to resolve his own major psychological problems. Considering how things worked out in the end, I don't think he ever succeeded.

In Appendix 2 I've re-printed The Affirmations in full for you to see for yourself the extent of what he wrote and judge for yourself the man's mental state when he did so.

Excalibur Redux

And so we come to the advent of Dianetics and Scientology. There have been some very well-written critical analyses of Dianetics which take it apart scientifically much more thoroughly and completely than I could. In keeping with the purpose of this chapter, I'm only going to cover enough of this material to make my case for Hubbard's intentions in regards to Dianetics, rather than critiquing the subject itself and everything wrong with it.

There are two main points to be made about Dianetics. The first is Hubbard's intention when he began working out Dianetics in early 1949 and the second has to do with the actual methodology of Dianetics counselling, which I'll cover in the next section. For the first part, let's start with a confidential letter Hubbard wrote to his literary agent, Forrest Ackerman (whom he refers to as "4E"). In the letter, Hubbard alludes to *Excalibur*, calling it also the *Dark Sword*, and it quickly becomes apparent he was inspired to again haul out this work and try to get it published. Instead of a purely philosophic work or a dissertation on cellular life and how it relates to Man's behavior, he reimagined it as a form of therapy.

Hubbard's desire to smash his name into history (and his determination to make a fortune doing it) had not died out over the intervening years but simply sat brewing in the back of his mind. I think the letter speaks for itself and makes it clear Hubbard had other things on his mind than salvaging Man when he contemplated what this new science of the mind would do for him. Note the letter is reproduced exactly as it was written, misspellings and all.

Box 1796
Savanah, Georgia
Jan. 13, 1949
Dear 4E:
I have been meaning to back up the last note of Sara's but didn't, been powerful busy trying to nail down a stack of copy. Been using an old dictaphone arangement which was on the verge of driving me stark staring. Finally today managed to get my big paws on a new Audiograph setup.

They were used by the airforce in planes in the war and transcribe or record in any position with a minimum of breakdown. They use a half hour per side vynolile plateing which means an hour of dictation per record. The stuff is clear and the transcribing is very easy and simple. They are very light and streamlined. Been out for two or three years now in commercial work. Rather high priced so I really have to grind now to support my writing.

Have a nice office. Had another one but didn't take to [the] noise. Present one is in the same apt. building, very neat and very quiet, with its own silk and gilt. Could become a den of vice very easily, I fear, so I only allow women over 16 in there.

Wanted to tell you that Sara is beating out her wits on fiction and is having to do this DARK SWORD -cause and cure of nervous tension – properly – THE SCIENCE OF MIND, really EXCALIBUR – in fits, so far, however she has recovered easily from each fit. It will be considerably delayed because of this. Good as my word, however, I shall ship it along just as soon as decent. Then you can rape women without their knowing it, communicate suicide messages to your enemies as they sleep, sell the Arroyo Seco parkway to the mayor for cash, evolve the best way of protecting or destroying communism, and other handy household hints. If you go crazy, remember you were warned.

Good publishing trick, by the way, is to have the bookseller make the buyer sign a release releasing the author of all responsibilities if the reader goes nuts.

Scanning it to insert a few case histories I'd come across here and there, I got interested again and have not decided whether to destroy the Catholic church or merely start a new one. And I grow restless when I think of all the charming ladies and young boys who walk around without the slightest taste for LIFE.

Thought of some interesting publicity angles on it. I might post a ten thousand dollar bond to be paid to anyone who can attain equal results with any known field of knowledge. A reprint of the preface, however, is about all one needs to bring in orders like a snow storm. This has more selling and publicity angles than any book of which I have ever heard, I think, and may very well be able to support them without much effort.

Looking over its project, I find a son of a luckless millionaire here has taken to drink and the millionaire wants him cured bad. Might undertake it for ten grand some afternoon.

Don't know why I suddenly got the nerve to go into this again and let it loose. It's probably either a great love or an enormous hatred of humanity. Just a few months ago I would now and then decide [to] use it and start right in to apply and I would lose my nerve. But lo! courage rose and the book is going out before it sinks again.

So here you have the dope.

Looking at all the fantasy movies, how about you contacting Laura Wilck in poisonally and making her scout around when we go in hard covers.

So far what'd Bill Crawford do about assembling the TRITION. Did he like MAN EATS MONSTER?

Best regards my friend, don't Kroshak the little kids in the neighborhood.

Love and Kisses,

Ron

P.S. This here epistle is confidential, pard.

Dianetics - the Modern Science without the Science

Before getting into what Hubbard did to invent and popularize Dianetics, I first have to get into an aspect of Dianetics counselling which is not broadly recognized or understood. That aspect is hypnotism.

Very few ex-Scientologists actually bother to avail themselves of the materials of Freud or study hypnotism in general. Thus, they continue to ignorantly repeat Hubbard's mantras about these two subjects. I don't use the word *ignorantly* as an insult but in its exact dictionary definition. They literally don't know any better and so even years after leaving Scientology behind them, they still believe what Hubbard told them about Freud and about hypnotism because they have no other information with which to compare it.

When I first came out of Scientology and started finding out for myself what it was all about, I would sometimes run into this assertion that all Dianetics and Scientology counselling were a form of hypnotism and we were all induced to enter trance states in our auditing. I could not have disagreed more with this, since I felt like I knew what hypnotism was all about. I had an almost knee-jerk reaction against the idea of hypnotism, that I was ever hypnotized in auditing. Nor did I hypnotize others when I was auditing them. I actually held on to this idea up until fairly recently.

It was while researching this book I realized everything I thought I knew about hypnotism came from one source: L. Ron Hubbard. Needless to say, that source can be suspected of telling one or two fibs about this subject to his followers.

After learning more about this from sources other than Hubbard, I can safely say anyone who thinks they know anything about hypnotism because of what L. Ron Hubbard told them is simply dead wrong.

Hypnosis is a word which gets bandied about very readily and without a very clear idea of what it actually is. It can seem difficult to nail down because there is very little hard science on the subject. Hypnosis has been portrayed in our culture and entertainment as a sort of mystic practice which relies on the artful skill of the hypnotist and the gullibility or suggestibility of the person being put into a trance.

After looking into this to determine its relationship with Dianetics and Scientology counselling for myself, I found hypnotism's mystical and mysterious reputation wholly undeserved. It's quite understandable, even if its practice and effects are so varied amongst the individuals upon whom it is used.

I don't intend for this section to become a full treatise on hypnotism. It's not my point here to prove whether hypnotism does or does not work, nor to give a history of its origins or practices. I'm going to cover just enough to make clear its relation to Dianetics.

Basically, in a hypnotic state your conscious, thinking mind sort of takes a break (to a greater or lesser degree), making your "subconscious" mind susceptible to directions or suggestions from external sources. Another way of putting it is the hypnotist takes over the thinking of the subject and by so doing he can suggest ideas which bypass the rational process and take on extra weight or importance. In some cases, a hypnotist can even implant ideas the subject would not have thought of on their own at all.

In many people, hypnotic states are not difficult to induce. We even do this to ourselves when we are tightly focused on something such as watching TV, driving or doing repetitive work, such as on a factory production line. There are countless stories of entertainers, speakers and salesmen who induce hypnotic states in their audiences and then "force" them to do embarrassing things or blatantly fool them, even when they warned the audience beforehand what they were going to do.

It's a myth that *anyone* can be hypnotized by simply walking up and snapping your fingers in their face or waving a watch in front of their eyes. That works on some people, but not everyone. Depending on the method used, it may happen quickly or it may take a while. It's also not true at all a person has to first agree to be hypnotized in order to induce a hypnotic state where a person can be influenced by a hypnotist or external source. In fact, people induce hypnotic trances in others all the time without even meaning to. For example, go into a grade school classroom sometime and look around at the kids. You will see some of them are in a light trance state brought about by the boring subject matter and droning teacher's voice. The teacher in no way is trying to hypnotize his students or give them any suggestions. It's simply the reaction some students occasionally have to the monotonous or repetitive nature of the way the teacher talks and subject matter they barely understand.

Trance states can be classified as light or deep. The whole "close your eyes, you feel sleepy" until the person literally nods off is a pretty deep trance, whereas someone put into a condition where they are just staring off into space, thinking fixedly about one particular thing to the exclusion of everything else, would be a fairly light trance.

As I mentioned in Chapter 3 when I described Dianetics and Scientology auditing procedures, there is no question Hubbard's procedures can induce trance states. As it was first described in

Dianetics: The Modern Science of Mental Health, Hubbard gave his readers instructions on how to do exactly this:

"The patient sits in a comfortable chair, with arms, or lies on a couch in a quiet room where perceptic distractions are minimal. The auditor tells him to look at the ceiling. The auditor says: 'When I count from one to seven your eyes will close.' The auditor then counts from one to seven and keeps counting quietly and pleasantly until the patient closes his eyes. A tremble of the lashes will be noticed in optimum reverie."[6]

Hubbard went to great lengths throughout his works to say what he was doing was something different than hypnosis and even claimed hypnosis was a way to damage the mind. It was a pattern he would repeat many times over the years - badmouth any other practice, therapy or science even when he himself was doing exactly what he said not to do. In this case, the blatantly hypnotic trance state he says to induce he renamed as "reverie".

Hubbard's books, especially those having to do with Dianetics materials, are rife with claims and contradictory statements about hypnotism. Jon Atack wrote a very good article about this called "Never Believe a Hypnotist" where he documents the numerous statements Hubbard made both for and against hypnotism and explains how it was used as a tool in developing Dianetics.[7] What is crystal clear throughout is when it came to the subject of hypnotism, Hubbard understood perfectly what it was, how to do it and how to use it extensively in the practice of Dianetics. Anyone who understands hypnosis and has read *Dianetics: The Modern Science of Mental Health* can attest to this.

The point is, with Dianetics Hubbard was inducing trance states and then giving people post-hypnotic suggestions to believe they were better because they received auditing.

While Hubbard made exaggerated mention throughout Dianetics to explicitly forbid the planting of suggestions in the mind of a patient in reverie, his own auditing demonstrations from 1950 (and later) clearly show him doing exactly that. One can find examples of this in transcripts and audio recordings of his demonstrations.

It was a constant source of confusion to me when I was involved in Scientology how Hubbard could write an Auditor's Code clearly stating to never evaluate for or invalidate a preclear undergoing counselling, yet in every one of his auditing demonstrations, Hubbard did exactly that. He constantly badgered them, told them what he thought of how they were doing, interpreted the meanings of their mental image pictures etc. The contradiction was so obvious and yet I couldn't grasp the simple truth of Hubbard's duplicity. What he was actually doing with auditing was not at all what he said he was doing.

Another important factor with Dianetics therapy, and all Scientology to this day, is a lot of pre-therapy indoctrination to ensure the patient understands what the auditor is doing and, more importantly, what results the preclear is expected to achieve from the auditing. The expected responses and end results are all setup in the preclear's mind before the auditing even begins.

While it's fine for the auditor to want the preclear to understand what is expected of him during the procedure, this pre-indoctrination is actually quite time consuming and goes far beyond just a few educational steps. In science, this is called setting up a confirmation bias. This ensures everything a preclear experiences in an auditing session is then compared to what he thinks is supposed to happen, and he will then modify his own thoughts, emotional responses and "cognitions" to fit what he thinks he ought to be achieving. There are certainly no shortage of psychological experiments which show both the power of confirmation bias and the remarkable tendency of people to do exactly what I'm describing, even with subjects or issues much less important than their own psychotherapy.

Once he worked all this out, it was clear to Hubbard he could fool people into believing they experienced something special and unique and were on their way to a new state of existence, which he called a Clear. If he'd stopped at just relieving his subjects' stress or emotional trauma, that would have been fine, but he didn't. He instead made up a whole new form of therapy which promised brand new states of existence far beyond anything Man had ever before experienced, in the bargain also attempting to do away with all psychology and psychiatry. As I've mentioned before, Hubbard liked to aim high.

Hubbard never provided research notes or documents from any laboratory experiments. Indeed, no such notes exist because no verifiable experiments were ever performed. Instead of designing experiments, documenting case studies or engaging in any real scientific work, he glibly used scientific jargon which, to the layman, sounds very convincing but in fact is just pseudoscience. For example, he claimed the axioms of Dianetics "are laws which can be subjected to the most vigorous laboratory and clinical tests." He claimed the idea Man is basically good "is now an established *scientific fact*, not an opinion"[8] (emphasis his). Dianetics is peppered with these kinds of claims, yet when anyone attempted to apply actual scientific method to the axioms and methods of Dianetics, one by one they came up short of any actual results. Hubbard never presented any evidence for any of his claims; his word alone was supposed to be all the proof anyone would ever need.

I think because Hubbard had very little understanding of how actual science worked, he thought he could pass off Dianetics as a science. Hubbard was a layman who flunked out of college and had a very poor understanding of how science was conducted. He knew some scientists through his science fiction writing, and based on these acquaintances he probably thought the whole field was rife with fraud and conjecture. In a scientific environment like the one he imagined, he would be able to muddle his way through presenting a new science to the world and things would "just work out", especially since he was so adept at talking his way out of almost anything. After all, that had been his modus operandi for most of his life and he'd gone from one mess to another relatively unscathed.

I don't think he expected as much scrutiny or as many demands for results as came his way when he popularized his new "science". He thought he had come up with a foolproof method of conning people by having them hypnotize each other and, through positive suggestion, "cure" each other's ailments and worries. For a great number of people, this seemed to produce positive results and as a result they believed what he said. Wasn't this anecdotal evidence proof enough?

117

In the world of real science, anecdotal evidence is one step up from no evidence at all. There are so many variables to the human psyche, if you are going to present a mental science which claims invarible results on 100% of the people upon whom it is practiced, you had better have a whole lot of case studies and evidence to back up your claims.

Having none of that, and absolutely no organizational or administrative skills sufficient to the task of running a national organization of mental healing, Dianetics tanked within just a year. That was not just because Dianetics wasn't what it claimed it was, but because Hubbard had a singular knack for not being able to organize his way out of wet paper sack and no small skill for alienating those who wanted to help him succeed. Even with the saving grace of a bailout from Wichita millionaire Don Purcell in April 1951, Hubbard still managed to ruin what could have been a perfectly good pseudoscientific scam which might have grown as popular as homeopathy or quantum healing.

Completely bankrupt and without even the rights to the name "Dianetics" or any of its materials, Hubbard should have been finished. Dianetics was a flash-in-the-pan, a fad which took America by storm like the Cabbage Patch Kids and Pac Man. Everyone heard about it, some loved it while others saw through Hubbard's shenanigans right away. Eventually, its utter failure to fulfill its claims ensured its demise.

However, Hubbard had one more card to play and it ended up giving him the winning hand.

The Religion Angle

The final element of this equation is what Hubbard called "the religion angle" which led to the creation of Scientology as a religious organization.

According to Miller's biography and interviews with those who knew Hubbard, he had been saying for years if you wanted to make a lot of money, the easiest way was to start a religion.

The earliest record of him saying this was to roommate Nelson Himmel during the fall of 1945, when Hubbard was first staying at

Jack Parsons' house.[9] It's entirely possible Hubbard observed the rate at which Parsons sent money to Crowley in England and thought to himself this would be pretty easy money.

According to other biographies and affidavits, Hubbard repeated this idea to others, both individually and in groups, throughout the remainder of the 1940s.

Having unwisely tried to resurrect the philosophy in *Excalibur* as a science, and having squandered his chance at fame and fortune in doing so, Hubbard finally decided to try his hand at being a cult leader.

Professor Stephen Kent of the University of Alberta suggests in a paper entitled "The Creation of 'Religious' Scientology" part of the impetus for this career change lay in groundwork Hubbard was setting about past lives. In *Science of Survival,* Hubbard's second book on Dianetics, written in early 1951 but not published until August of that year, Hubbard claimed:

"Evidence is growing — good evidence of a highly scientific nature on a much more practical level than parapsychology — that the human soul does exist in fact."

Professor Kent says:

"That discussion, however, already had become commonplace among Dianeticists, many of whom nonetheless had become disappointed with their ideology's techniques and results. Hubbard's eventual translation of allegedly past life recall into an ideology of the soul allowed him to make claims about the superiority of Scientology over Dianetics as part of his efforts to regain 'control over the Dianetics community' It also allowed him to reach out to new members of the public who were outside of science fiction fandom."[10]

There were many other factors at play also motivating Hubbard, other than just transitioning skeptical Dianeticists into fervent Scientologists. He was all about making money, lots of it, and securing his future with an unending source of new money.

By the end of 1951, Hubbard was running full force with the concept of past lives. He spent the entire year of 1952 laying down a spirit-based science, first by introducing the concept of Scientology as an umbrella philosophy which contained all of Dianetics within it and a whole lot more. He started working out a 'whole track' cosmology of incidents which he claimed took place millions of years in the past and were supposedly still having profound traumatic effect on all the people of Earth. These were documented in *Scientology: A History of Man.*

In December 1952 in Philadelphia, Hubbard gave an intensive series of lectures describing the exact nature and abilities of Man as a spiritual being and revealed his "discovery" of the new state of Operating Thetan (OT). This was something far superior to the Clear described in Dianetics. An Operating Thetan was not just able to think faster than a regular human and avoid sickness; an OT was "cause over matter, energy, space, time, life and form". In short, Hubbard was talking about a kind of personal apotheosis.

What do you do when the stated goal of going Clear is unobtainable with your Dianetics techniques and you are losing followers? You create a whole new goal and you get everyone excited and talking about that instead. That's what Operating Thetan was all about and it was a goal so grand and so amazing, the possibility of achieving it kept people following Hubbard for decades.

Scientology was not originally presented as a religious concept. It was the "science of certainty" and took a sort of middle-of-the-road approach as a deep scientific philosophy with religious overtones.[11] However, with Dianetics tanked financially and the well pretty much dried up, by April 1953 Hubbard was thinking in earnest about finally starting the cult he'd been talking about eight years prior.

Hubbard went to London after his Philadelphia lecture series to get a foothold established in England. Perhaps he was even considering setting up shop there if things didn't work out in the US. Back in Philadelphia, he had Helen O'Brien and her husband working tirelessly (and, in the end, thanklessly) as franchise holders for Scientology. They basically ran the entire Scientology apparatus in the US during Hubbard's extended absence in Europe, through much of 1953.

Here are the key excerpts from one of the many letters Hubbard sent to Helen O'Brien regarding his keen attention to getting money. He wanted to offer professional auditing in specially set up clinics and also turn Scientology into a religious institution rather than continue it as a form of psychotherapy.

"If we were to run there the United States Central Processing Office or whatever, we'd be able to count on ten to fifteen preclears per week at $500 for 24 hours of processing. That's real money. I have seen it happen before. We'd get more preclears at $850 per week's intensive. Charge enough and we'd be swamped. We need that money. We should not long plan to have it siphoned away. The HAS [Hubbard Association of Scientologists] *is the cause of that inflow and it is granting the favor in providing preclears and income. From that income I would like to see go into a general fund for general operating expenses from here – press, communications, stenos – at least $2,500 per month. If I had that much to operate with you couldn't see over the amount of business we'd get or the number of dead bodies piled up before trial. You get the idea. But it takes money, lots of it. The clinic, as I see it, is the most eligible bet to provide that money. For one reason, 24 hours of processing now is 500 old style. I have here a short, quick package, carefully saved. I can raise the dead, which is, of course what I mean when I say 'dead bodies piled up.' Resurrection would so influence public opinion."*

A bit later in the letter he says:

"We don't want a clinic. We want one in operation but not in name. Perhaps we could call it a Spiritual Guidance Center. Think up its name, will you. And we could put in nice desks and our boys in neat blue with diplomas on the walls and 1. knock psychotherapy into history and 2. make enough money to shine up my operating scope and 3. keep the HAS solvent. It is a problem of practical business.

"I await your reaction on the religion angle. In my opinion, we couldn't get worse public opinion than we have had or have less customers with what we've got to sell. A religious charter would be necessary in Pennsylvania or NJ to make it stick. But I sure could make it stick. We're treating the present time beingness, psychotherapy treats the past and the brain. And brother, that's religion, not mental science."

It appears this was the decision point because shortly afterward, at the end of April 1953, Hubbard published *The Factors* in the Journal of Scientology. These Factors, generalized statements about how spiritual

121

existence began and what it is doing to create life, read like Biblical passages. For example, here are the first two:

Before the beginning was a Cause and the entire purpose of the Cause was the creation of effect.

In the beginning and forever is the decision and the decision is TO BE.

The rest of 1953 was spent not-so-subtly morphing the "science" of Dianetics into the religion of Scientology. By December 1953, he took the plunge and incorporated three new churches in New Jersey. These were the Church of American Science (the umbrella church for the other two), the Church of Scientology and the Church of Spiritual Engineering. Yes, he really started a church called "spiritual engineering".

Finally in February 1954 on the west coast, Scientologist J. Burton Farber incorporated what would eventually become the real mother church for Scientology for many years to come: the Church of Scientology of California. This fact would be used by Hubbard in the future to disavow his personal hand in the creation of the Church, stating it was the work of others and he'd just gone along with it because it's what everyone else wanted.

Incorporating as a church and starting his own cult not only turned out to be the single most lucrative move Hubbard ever made, but solved almost all his legal troubles overnight. Claims of healing, for example, were now matters of faith no longer subject to oversight by the FDA or AMA. There would be no more fear of lawsuits due to practicing medicine without a license. And as a religion, Scientology now opened the door to possible tax exemption through 501(c)3 "nonprofit, charitable organizations" status under the IRS tax codes. The religion angle was a total win.

Hubbard managed to amass a small fortune over the next few years and built a worldwide religious empire on the backs of his loyal followers and adherents, all of whom foolishly believed he meant it when he talked about raising them up to become like gods. After all, what price is too high to attain certain immortality and "cause over life"?

The rest, as they say, is history.

Complex People are Complex

I've made a case here that Hubbard was a con man who, knowingly and with malice aforethought, fooled tens of thousands of people for the purposes of self-aggrandizement and profit. However, like every person who ever walked the earth, he was a complex man who had multiple motivations and methods to his madness. There was a lot going on in his head and easily tossed-off labels like "megalomaniac" or "profiteer" do not explain everything there is to know about him.

There is evidence Hubbard suffered from physical ailments he wanted to eliminate, though we know he did exaggerate how bad off his condition actually was. He used self-hypnosis to address some of these and when that wasn't effective for the others, he may well have thought the "treatment" methods he came up with in Dianetics (and later Scientology) would actually work. He had terrible eyesight, for example, which he hid from the world at large and wanted to cure. His claims of a Scientological cure for poor eyes became so exaggerated, Hubbard bragged of a barrel of old eyeglasses preclears dropped off after auditing cured them. Yet somehow Hubbard never benefited from those gains.

Whether or not Hubbard actually believed what he was doing was helpful, or whether it would cure his own problems, there is no question whatsoever it was not this purpose and vision which drove him, but a vision of self-aggrandizement, money and power. All the correspondence I've cited and statements he made in his private writings indicate he was obsessed with his personal fortune and glory, not with helping other people.

There is certainly no question that in the later years of his life, I believe starting in the early 1960s in fact, he fully bought into the mythology of Scientology himself and basically fell for his own con. For example, he engaged in solo auditing almost daily, a practice of sitting in a room by himself with an E-meter thinking about things and imagining he was ridding himself of mental and spiritual trauma. Activity like that makes no sense whatsoever unless he thought he was actually doing something productive and helpful for himself.

There is also the testimony of Steve Pfauth, one of the last people to ever have real conversations and interactions with Hubbard at his ranch in Creston up until his death in 1986. Pfauth related Hubbard was desperate to get rid of his body thetans and continued in that vein right up until he died.[12] I have no doubt we are looking at the ravings of a madman at that point. Through all the years of conning others, excessive use of drugs and alcohol and working to destroy all those who ever had anything contrary to say about him, Hubbard finally succumbed fully to the madness always lurking in the back of his mind.

Rather than a shining example of the powers of his spiritual technology and greatness, Hubbard died in a self-created exile from all his family and friends, hiding from the law and snapping at demons. A truly pathetic figure who deserves none of the adulation and worship showered on him by the few remaining Scientologists in the world.

7. An Important Aspect of the Brainwashing

The Certainty Trap

When you start to look at the main things wrong with dangerous cults, or any kind of mass movement in general, you quickly find your attention going to the nature of belief itself and what is real versus what is fantasy. What I'm about to discuss doesn't just apply to religion, though it's one of the easiest examples for most people to see. This also shows up in politics, economics, consumerism and even civil rights and gender issues.

How many times have you been caught out trying to fake knowing all about something which you really knew very little or nothing of? How many times in life do we pretend in order to impress, to try to entertain or at least not appear foolish? It happens all the time. We delight in catching people out when they do this, but hate it when we meet someone smarter or more experienced than we are or who can just see through our shenanigans.

Now imagine behaving this way every waking moment of every day of your life. Habitually pretending you know everything about everything - especially all the "important" things like the meaning of life, why everyone acts the way they do, where we all came from and where we are all going with our lives. If you live under this pretense long enough, you forget any questions you had and develop a certainty you have all the answers to everything that matters.

That is what life is like in a dangerous cult like Scientology. To one degree or another, that can also apply to any mass movement.

The Psychology of Certainty

Certainty. Decisiveness. Conviction. Positivity.

These are traits we look for and appreciate in leaders in any field including politicians, teachers, ministers, news reporters, parents and even our boss at work. When the chips are down and things are looking grim, it is natural for people to look for someone who knows what they are doing to lead them to safety, security and a longer life. No one wants to follow or even listen to wishy-washy, uncertain people who are constantly second-guessing themselves. Our natural tendency is to look down on such individuals, so it's not for nothing we value certainty and emulate those who have it. You could say certainty is one of the defining characteristics of a leader.

Yet, after living life in the big wide world for a few years and learning how vast and complex it is, most of us realize we are never going to know everything we'd like. We learn very early in our childhood that people who reveal their foolishness (or at least ignorance) get laughed at, ridiculed or worse. So we learn to hide our uncertainties and fake our way through.

Given it is part of our makeup to do this, is it really so surprising something like Scientology would have appeal? Not only does it promise happiness, success and spiritual freedom but above all else, its founder L. Ron Hubbard actually defined the word Scientology as *knowing how to know* and described it as the *Science of Certainty*. Those are buttons which hit every human being at a gut level.

But let's face it: the promise of certainty is an illusion. The truth is, after millions of years of existence, and at least six thousand years of civilization recorded to one degree or another, there is hardly anything we are truly certain of about ourselves, our planet and the universe. Endless debates rage daily on social forums about almost any social, scientific or political issue. We can't even get everyone to agree the Earth is round or we actually put men on the Moon. It seems to me the only thing we could all agree on is we are never going to *all* agree about anything!

So where does that leave us when it comes to sorting out what is true and what isn't?

Science and Reason

When you are a follower of a mass movement, by definition you are convinced of the veracity of your position and believe you have found some form of Absolute Truth. Thus we have almost all religions, political pundits, fanatical terrorists, etc. It's easy to see this in the extreme forms of religious, political and social intolerances which splash across media headlines every day. Yet don't we all have shades of this to one degree or another? It's in our nature.

When our personal truths are shattered for whatever reason, we are left adrift and often will search for new truths to cling to. This happened to me when my certainty about Scientology was broken. Once I started unraveling the lies inherent in much of Scientology's teachings and availed myself of all the resources available on the subject, it was painfully obvious I was deceived and manipulated for decades. That was a hard truth to accept and a very bitter pill to swallow.

I was so sure I had all the answers. For years, I assured others they could have the same certainty I had if they would just learn and practice Scientology. Never mind all the things which didn't quite make sense or the gray areas we all didn't talk about. We just brushed those little questions aside. If something in Scientology didn't seem to work, it was my fault, never the subject itself.

Once a core belief like that is cracked, it's only natural to start looking for new truths and new ideas to hold onto which will give some kind of life support. It was clear to me I was going to have to re-evaluate everything I'd been taught. I was going to have to look at all my personal beliefs and see if they were based on what I truly knew from my own experience and knowledge, or were just based on what I was told to believe.

The one thing I did not want to do was swap one cult for another, one totalitarian thought control system for another. I wanted to be able

127

to examine evidence and facts and, in short, live in the real world and not some cult leader's fantasy.

I was lucky at that moment to hit upon science and critical thinking. Specifically, these two concepts totally rocked my world:

"...Science is not about certainty. Science is about finding the most reliable way of thinking at the present level of knowledge. Science is extremely reliable; it's not certain. In fact, not only is it not certain, but it's the lack of certainty that grounds it. Scientific ideas are credible not because they are sure but because they're the ones that have survived all the possible past critiques and they're the most credible because they were put on the table for everybody's criticism.

"The very expression 'scientifically proven' is a contradiction in terms. There's nothing that is scientifically proven. The core of science is the deep awareness that we have wrong ideas, we have prejudices. We have ingrained prejudices. In our conceptual structure for grasping reality, there might be something not appropriate, something we may have to revise to understand better. So at any moment we have a vision of reality that is effective, it's good, it's the best we have found so far." - Carlo Rovelli (Italian theoretical physicist)[1]

"Science is a way of thinking much more than it is a body of knowledge." - Carl Sagan (US astrophysicist and author)[2]

I thought science was all about sure and absolute knowledge of us and the world. I could not have been more wrong and learning how I was wrong really convinced me critical thinking was the key to a happy life.

The Certainty Lie

A key principle in critical thinking is to not make assumptions or jump to conclusions before you conduct the experiment. Good science is founded on observation, research, experimentation and using the knowledge gained to then come to a conclusion, from which more testing and more evidence-gathering is then done. It's a never-ending process.

A scientist does not start with a conclusion and then try to prove it. He starts with an educated guess which he thinks may explain something. This guess is called a hypothesis. A hypothesis is only valid or useful if it can be subjected to testing. If you can't test something then you aren't dealing with science, you are dealing with faith and belief. That's the difference between fact and fantasy and the primary difference between science and religion.

You can believe anything you want, but you don't get to say those beliefs are the same as facts or truths because that's not what they are. They are just ideas you have about how things might be. If you can't test or prove them, then you have no business obnoxiously insisting other people accept them as true, and you certainly don't have any right to go committing violence or killing anyone else because of your beliefs. That's about as irrational as you can possibly get.

No scientific principle is guaranteed to be 100% Absolute Truth, no matter how many times it's been tested. It may be there are exceptions to any of the scientific principles we are all familiar with, like gravity or Einstein's famous $E=mc^2$, but those exceptions just haven't been discovered yet. In fact, Einstein himself said *"No amount of experimentation can ever prove me right; a single experiment can prove me wrong."*

In good science and in rational thinking, there is always an element of uncertainty or doubt. No matter how farfetched or inconceivable an idea may be, it might just turn out to be true. To dismiss it out of hand, with no evidence or facts to support your dismissal, is not critical thinking but arrogance. For example, there may well be UFOs visiting Earth on a regular basis and Atlantis may really have sunk under the ocean three millennia ago. We can always keep our eyes and ears open for evidence of these things. If such should appear, then we are that much closer to understanding more about the world in which we live.

Of course, as Carl Sagan advised: *"It pays to keep an open mind, but not so open your brains fall out."* Once an idea has been disproven, it's silly to continue to cling to it. A person has to be willing to change their mind and a critical thinker will do so when the evidence is clearly not supporting his position.

To a cult member or someone in a mass movement, they cannot afford to be uncertain. They build up walls in their thinking and won't let facts or evidence get through to challenge any of those certainties. By doing so they limit their *own* thinking and, really, close themselves off to a lot of what the world has to offer. You don't have to be a member of a dangerous cult to fall into this pattern. We all can do it and it is a wise person who can not only accept new information but also admit he's been wrong and change his mind.

Knowing How to Not Know

The certainty groups like Scientology offer is not just an illusion but is actually a kind of trap. It's a way of shutting out observation and closing off thinking. There is not one subject known to Man which can offer total certainty of life, the universe and everything. That level of knowledge simply doesn't exist.

There's nothing wrong with knowing things. Anyone can have well-founded ideas, can form new opinions from them and get by in the world. We all do just that every day.

What we often don't do and what would be a beneficial change for everyone is to adopt the idea it's just as important to know what you don't know, and to be okay with that too. In fact, the recognition one does not know, and beginning the quest to learn, is actually the point where all wisdom begins.

I'd like to see a lot more of *that* on social media and in the news. Maybe then the world wouldn't seem like such a crazy place.

8. Is There Anything Good in Scientology?

People have asked me many times about whether there is anything good in Scientology or whether there was anything worthwhile I got out of it. My easy answer has been, "Well of course there was good in it" because no one would stay involved in something like that for so long if there wasn't. However, the real answer isn't quite that simple.

You see, one of the biggest lies Hubbard perpetrated on his followers and gets away with to this day, even in the ex-Scientology community, is he was the single source of Scientology. He drummed this in so hard, people in Scientology actually call him Source, saying this with a kind of worship and reverence Hubbard completely does not deserve.

It took me quite a while after I got out to realize Hubbard was not only a pathological liar about himself and his own history, but he also lied through his teeth about having "discovered" Dianetics and Scientology. He used words like "research" and "discover" to give himself a legitimacy not earned through hard work or real scientific research. Instead, he literally ripped off the work of others and pretended it came from him, or he just made things up out of whole cloth and expected people to believe it because it sounded so good.

For anyone familiar with Dianetics and Scientology teachings, I'm not talking about a few suggestions people might have thrown Hubbard's way over the years. I'm talking about the very fundamentals of the subject: things such as Dianetics procedure, which comes straight out of hypnotism and original Freudian practice; the idea the basic unit of the universe is two, not one, comes from Buckminster Fuller, a contemporary of Hubbard's who was cited in a few of his writings but only credited once; the much-vaunted Study Technology was not Hubbard's discovery - he flat out lied about this in the mid-1960s after two English teachers, who were also Scientologists, presented it to him at Saint Hill in England; then there's the E-meter, the original version of which Hubbard tried to rip off from Volney Matheson in the early 1950s. When that didn't work, Hubbard told Scientologists they were unnecessary for auditing and there were no E-meters in use from 1954 to 1957. That changed when another Scientologist loyal to Hubbard figured out how to make them using transistors. Then Hubbard slapped his name on them and suddenly they were his invention.

When you look at the stark truth of this, you start to see a lot of the "good" Scientology provides is not really Scientology at all but is plagiarized work from another source. So to answer the question of whether there is anything good to be gotten from Scientology, you first have to look at whether you are actually doing Scientology or you are doing something else entirely.

What is real Scientology anyway? What parts of it did Hubbard actually invent or "discover" himself? Well, there's the totalitarian ethics and justice system he developed in the mid-1960s which demands total compliance with Hubbard's every word lest you be labeled a Suppressive Person and cast out of the Church forever. There's the whole system of disconnection, one of the harshest forms of shunning which exists among any religious group in the world. Families, friendships and whole businesses have been torn apart through exact application of Hubbard's directions.

It doesn't end there. Hubbard also developed the Guardian's Office, which was responsible for carrying out his orders to "ruin people utterly", Scientologist or not, if they dared speak one critical word against him or Scientology. They call this practice Fair Gaming because they think anyone who speaks against the Church basically deserves anything to come at them and it's the Scientologists' responsibility to make sure that person suffers as much as possible.

This is so well documented, it's not even a question whether it happens nor that Hubbard was directly responsible for ordering it in the first place. The Guardian's Office was caught breaking the law in one of the largest criminal conspiracies ever documented against the US government, but did they learn their lesson and stop? No, of course they didn't.

Hubbard simply morphed the Guardian's Office into the Office of Special Affairs, which continues to carry on the tradition of Fair Gaming to this day. These campaigns of hate and harassment against Scientology critics include those against the people featured in Alex Gibney's landmark documentary, appropriately titled *Going Clear: Scientology and the Prison of Belief.* Even Church leader David Miscavige's own father is not exempt from harassment and stalking since he left the Church's employment a few years ago.

Any good Scientology has managed to do over the 60 years of its existence has been completely eclipsed by the lies, fraud and tangible harm it has brought to far more people than it ever helped.

People are amazing and they are capable of helping their fellow man in the most adverse of conditions, under the most distressing of circumstances. The people who have done good things in Scientology did so because of *their* greatness, not Scientology's workability. The help which came to people in Scientology was done *despite* Scientology, not because of it.

In the end, Scientology has been and continues to be about one thing and one thing only: generating money and power for one man. At first that man was L. Ron Hubbard. Now it's David Miscavige. Everything else is window dressing, designed to entrap and ruin the very people it is claiming to save. And *that* is Scientology.

9. The KSW Mind Trap

L. Ron Hubbard is like the Wizard of Oz, presenting an image of greatness and wisdom, revered by thousands who believe every word he utters is a divine commandment of truth. Yet in reality, he is a wizened little man who hides behind a curtain, manipulating the gears and levers of a fake persona who never really existed. In this chapter, let's look into the deepest and most important part of Scientology and exactly how Hubbard convinced his followers Scientology is the most important thing in the world: more important than their job, their money or even their friends and family. Let's take a look behind the curtain.

Hubbard was a prolific writer, not only writing books and giving lectures, but also issuing thousands of bulletins and policy letters which laid out the rules and guidelines for the Scientology religion. Here I want to critically analyze what Scientologists consider to be the single most important issue he wrote, entitled "Keeping Scientology Working".

This issue does not lay out the belief system of Scientology nor tell people how to do Scientology methods or procedures. It was issued as a policy letter, meaning it was meant to be an operating guide for the conduct and activities of Scientology as an organization and how the individual Scientologists were to conduct themselves.

He wrote this issue in February of 1965, a time when Scientology had become a well-established and going concern worldwide. It had grown far beyond any of Hubbard's initial hopes and dreams.

Organizations were answering up to him each week with their progress through a state of the art (for the time) Telex communication system and were directed by Hubbard and his aides on what to do. Royalties and fees were being sent to Saint Hill, and Hubbard was pocketing a lot of money (tens of thousands of dollars every week). In short, he was drunk on power and convinced by this time of his own messianic powers and superiority over all other humans.

Hubbard decided it was time to lay down the law and get his followers into a very dedicated frame of mind about Scientology. It wasn't just a self-help group now, but something Hubbard thought of as a life-or-death matter.

He would later refer to this policy letter as the single most important matter in all Scientology. To this day, this policy is cited over and over again throughout the Scientology world, quoted from extensively and used as a core teaching of the Scientology religion. Every Scientologist is familiar with it and many can recite whole passages from it verbatim.

David Miscavige, the current leader of Scientology, has stated his most important role as Chairman of the Board of Religious Technology Center or RTC, indeed the very purpose of RTC as an organization, is to see to it this one issue is enforced throughout Scientology.

If all that isn't enough, Hubbard specified it be placed at the beginning of every single major Scientology course. This doesn't include the beginning courses done by those fresh off the street. No, I mean this issue shows up on what they call the "major" courses, once a person has moved past the beginning services. In other words, once someone gets their foot in the door and starts on "the real stuff," they begin the real cult indoctrination with this issue. Like any cult's indoctrination, it only works through repetition.

At 6½ pages, this issue clocks in as a hefty one. Hubbard has a lot of indoctrinating to do. I've broken it down into sections and I'm not going to reproduce the whole thing here. Instead, we'll walk through the sections one at a time and I'll highlight the important passages.

Section 1: The Setup

First, there is the introduction or setup. It begins with

"We have sometime since passed the point of achieving uniformly workable technology."

Hubbard refers to Scientology here as "technology" which I'll talk about in more detail a bit later. Here he is saying Scientology is supposed to work on everyone all the time. There are some Scientology apologists who might try to wheedle out of this by arguing the definition of "workable" and the absolutist claim here, so let's take a closer look at this.

Hubbard uses the word "uniformly" which means "something done in a consistent or identical manner."

Workable means "capable of producing the desired effect or result".

So there is no question Hubbard is using language implying Scientology will produce the desired result when it is used per instructions and it will do this all the time. There really isn't any other way of interpreting "uniformly workable".

Yet if you look at this from a modern perspective, this claim of uniform workability doesn't make sense. Hubbard made a lot of changes after 1965 to Scientology's methods and practices. If everything were utterly workable and perfect at that point, then why did Hubbard have to:

- Invent the OT levels
- Invent all the ethics and justice policies
- Invent the Suppressive Person and everything which goes along with it
- Revise Dianetics procedure with Standard Dianetics in 1969
- Clarify and revise fundamental basics like how to read an E-meter
- Completely revise how to do Scientology confessionals ("sec checks")
- Do a full correction and revision of all aspects of Scientology methodology in 1975

137

- Revise Dianetics procedure *again* in 1978 with New Era Dianetics
- Write hundreds more bulletins and policy letters

I'm just skimming the surface here, based on my casual recall of what Hubbard ordered done from 1965 until he died in 1986.

Since 1986, there have been no less than five MAJOR overhauls of Scientology's methods and materials. Not just repackaging of the materials but full revisions of all the books and course materials to ensure "it was in full compliance with Ron's wishes".

Knowing all that, does it sound like Hubbard really had it nailed in 1965? Or even 1970 when he had this policy letter re-issued? Or again in 1980 when he had it reissued again?

Let's face it - the most important issue in all Scientology starts off with a bald faced lie.

He goes on to say if Scientology organizations, called orgs, get bad results or can't get results at all, they are going to have upset people on their hands. That's true enough with any customer service business. Of course, such a thing isn't true of many religions, because I think it's safe to say religion is not a results-oriented activity. You either believe or you don't believe, but you don't see too many people beating down a cardinal's door because they didn't get tangible results from their prayers. This is not a major point, but I thought it worth mentioning how Hubbard is clearly approaching Scientology with a business attitude.

He then says:

"Attacks from governments or monopolies occur only where there are 'no results' or 'bad results'"

This is also interesting because here Hubbard is planting the seed of an idea which he developed over the next few years into an elaborate international plot he claimed existed to destroy Scientology. He said newspaper chains, psychiatric groups and even government officials were owned and controlled by a select few international bankers and these puppet masters were making the governments and monopolies attack Scientology. It's a kind of weird logic here, because wouldn't such attacks only come if Scientology actually *worked* and *were*

138

producing results? Why would attacks come from these bad guys if Scientology weren't producing any results? Well of course they wouldn't, because no one would care. Now we know that's actually the case anyway, but I'm just analyzing the backwards logic of Hubbard's claim here. What he's saying actually makes no sense.

Section 2: Scientology is the Only Correct Technology

Hubbard states the only way to deal with this is to get Scientology applied. Instead of saying "Scientology," he refers to it instead as "the technology" which is very much done on purpose. Technology is a more generalized term which refers to the methods or applications of a body of science. It's kind of a loaded word because it carries all sorts of connotations and meanings with it, different from just the word "Scientology".

In a relatively new Scientologist's mind, freshly reading this, he might disagree if the word Scientology were repeated at him over and over again. Since "technology" is a regular English word, is already perfectly acceptable and reminds the reader of other exact sciences like engineering, physics and computer programming. It makes everything Hubbard is about to say about Scientology more agreeable.

So what does Hubbard say? He lays out a series of ten steps necessary to get Scientology (or "the technology") into correct use. The steps are:

One: Having the correct technology.
Two: Knowing the technology.
Three: Knowing it is correct.
Four: Teaching correctly the correct technology.
Five: Applying the technology.
Six: Seeing that the technology is correctly applied.
Seven: Hammering out of existence incorrect technology.
Eight: Knocking out incorrect applications.
Nine: Closing the door on any possibility of incorrect technology.
Ten: Closing the door on incorrect application.

See what he's done here? He's actually written a road map to a state of mind of fanatical devotion.

Hubbard is using the word "technology" and giving it the double duty of carrying a more generalized meaning. When he says "hammering out of existence incorrect technology" and "closing the door on any possibility of incorrect technology" he's not just referring to Scientology technology but any technology. For example, Hubbard despised both psychology and psychiatry, and he never missed an opportunity to bash them in his lectures and writings.

It's no stretch of the imagination for someone to think after reading these points Hubbard would demand such "incorrect technologies" be hammered out of existence. Look at what Scientology tries to do to psychiatry right now with their Citizens Commission on Human Rights. This group has no other reason to exist except to eradicate psychiatry. I'm quite sure anyone in that group would be proud to say they are following the steps of Keeping Scientology Working by doing so.

So here's the thing: according to steps 7, 8, 9 and 10, the only way Scientology is supposed to work is if you literally destroy anything else not Scientology! This is *very* important. It is the foundation upon which the rest of Scientology doctrine rests. Once a person accepts these steps as true, they have started down a very slippery slope which ends up with them believing nothing in the world matters except what L. Ron Hubbard says.

Now lest you think I'm exaggerating, let's see how Hubbard follows this up. He says:

"Seven is done by a few but is a weak point. Eight is not worked on hard enough. Nine is impeded by the 'reasonable' attitude of the not-quite-bright. Ten is seldom done with enough ferocity. Seven, Eight, Nine and Ten are the only places Scientology can bog down in any area."

"Reasonable" is a bad word in Scientology. In Scientology, Hubbard actually redefines the word "reasonable" to mean "faulty explanations" or "accepting reasons why something can't be done" or even "dreaming up false reasons or justifications for something." It's no accident "being reasonable" in Scientology is a very bad thing, because the last thing

140

Hubbard wanted any Scientologists to do was apply logic or reason. So here he is saying if you don't close the door on any possibility of incorrect technology, you are illogical and actually destructive.

Getting back to the text, you see right off the bat he's using insulting language to say no one is actually doing these steps ferociously enough and Scientologists' failure to destroy all things other than Scientology is the only reason Scientology doesn't succeed. I couldn't make any of this up.

The next paragraph is more of the same. The passage is full of Scientologese:

"The reasons for this are not hard to find. (a) A weak certainty that it works in Three above can lead to weakness in Seven, Eight, Nine and Ten. (b) Further, the not-too-bright have a bad point on the button Self-Importance. (c) The lower the IQ, the more the individual is shut off from the fruits of observation. (d) The service facs of people make them defend themselves against anything they confront, good or bad, and seek to make it wrong. (e) The bank seeks to knock out the good and perpetuate the bad."

So the fast translation for this is people who don't do these things are self-important and stupid, they literally have a low IQ and can't observe and their mental problems make them so crazy they want to destroy good things and keep bad things going.

Right here is the exact place where Hubbard sets up an *us-versus-them* mentality. Anyone who is not ferociously on the side of Scientology is stupid, self-important or somewhat psychotic. No one wants to be any of those things, so of course they want to be on the side of Scientology, where the good people are getting results and making the world a better place.

He ends this section by saying:

"Thus, we as Scientologists and as an organization must be very alert to Seven, Eight, Nine and Ten."

It is a vital part of any destructive cult to establish that kind of us-versus-them thinking to ensure loyalty and get a person into a frame of mind where they will defend 'us' and attack 'them'.

141

Section 3: Hubbard is the Only True Savior of Mankind

In the third part, Hubbard switches gears and starts talking about himself and how important he has been to Scientology.

One of the defining characteristics of a destructive cult is having a centralized leadership, usually a single person, who holds all the answers and demands unquestioning loyalty and commitment. When you're not in a cult and look at those who are, you can easily think they are just a bunch of idiots and you would never blindly follow anyone like they do. It might make you feel more comfortable or superior to think that, but statistically speaking you're probably wrong. It's not just religious cults people fall for either. Look at the fanaticism which exists in politics, sports or social issues.

So how do people like Hubbard get their followers thinking so fanatically? Well, let's take a look at what he says in this next section. It starts with this:

"In all the years I have been engaged in research I have kept my comm[unication] *lines wide open for research data. I once had the idea that a group could evolve truth. A third of a century has thoroughly disabused me of that idea. Willing as I was to accept suggestions and data, only a handful of suggestions (less than twenty) had long-run value and none were major or basic; and when I did accept major or basic suggestions and used them, we went astray and I repented and eventually had to 'eat crow'".*

Eat crow is an old term for admitting you are very wrong, the idea being you were humiliated and now have to eat crow, which tastes really bad, to make up for what you did.

Here we have Hubbard starting to assert this idea he is the only one who could come up with truth and everyone else was just making things worse when they were trying to help. What's actually kind of amazing about this statement is how insulting it is. He's literally saying no one else said anything constructive or could add to his "research". This, of course, flies in the face of every great discovery made in Mankind's history because no one, not one person in history, has ever made any discovery all by themselves which wasn't improved upon by

142

someone later. Popular media makes it easy to believe in lone heroes who make great advances with no help, but a cursory study of history reveals collaboration at every level of human endeavor. Hubbard's claims to sole ownership of any idea are ridiculous.

Beyond that, not only did Hubbard not come up with this subject all on his own, he actually plagiarized other people's material and called it his through the whole history of Dianetics and Scientology (a few specific examples of this were given in the previous chapter). I'm talking about very major and basic parts of the technology, not what Hubbard describes as incidental and unimportant things. Hubbard got away with this for years but only in 1965 did he make it a point of Church policy to say it had always been just him.

He goes on to say:

"On the other hand there have been thousands and thousands of suggestions and writings which, if accepted and acted upon, would have resulted in the complete destruction of all our work as well as the sanity of pcs. So I know what a group of people will do and how insane they will go in accepting unworkable "technology". By actual record the percentages are about twenty to 100,000 that a group of human beings will dream up bad technology to destroy good technology. As we could have gotten along without suggestions, then, we had better steel ourselves to continue to do so now that we have made it."

If he actually received 100,000 suggestions over the course of 15 years, that means he was getting 18 a day every single day of the week. Now we are supposed to believe out of all those suggestions and tips, only 20 of them were actually of any use and all the others were not just unhelpful but actually destructive and would result in people being worse? These numbers are simply unbelievable no matter what statistical metric is used.

The only way to buy this would be to raise Hubbard up on a pedestal of greatness and, at the same time, reduce everyone else to the status of very dangerous morons. Maybe they mean well, but they just can't help their destructive nature. Believe me when I say this is exactly what Scientologists think of non-Scientologists. He then justifies this mental shift by saying:

143

"This point will, of course, be attacked as 'unpopular,' 'egotistical' and "undemocratic.' It very well may be. But it is also a survival point. And I don't see that popular measures, self-abnegation and democracy have done anything for man but push him further into the mud. Currently, popularity endorses degraded novels, self-abnegation has filled the Southeast Asian jungles with stone idols and corpses, and democracy has given us inflation and income tax."

Here he is pretty bluntly describing how bad the world is when people are allowed to think for themselves and how awful the combined works of Man actually are. This not only helps justify the us-vs-them mentality Hubbard instigated earlier, but it's the sort of thinking which gets Scientologists to support the idea of people not having rights in the first place.

Here's what I mean: Hubbard says democracy has given people income tax and inflation. Democracy also gave people like Hubbard the constitutional right to freely utter his destructive tripe without fear of prosecution or consequences. Not just here in the United States, but if you look at any country where Scientology exists, you'll find the kind of democratic system where people are afforded the rights to speak and think freely. So here Hubbard is lambasting and ridiculing democracy but the fact is, Scientology couldn't exist without it.

Of course, it is this kind of thinking which allows Scientologists to justify why people like me, a critic of Scientology, shouldn't be afforded these same rights, even when they are written into the Creed of the Church of Scientology. The irony here is so thick you could cut it with a knife.

He ends off this section by bringing it back to those ten points of KSW and the language he uses is pretty interesting:

"So realize that we have climbed out of the mud by whatever good luck and good sense, and refuse to sink back into it again. See that Seven, Eight, Nine and Ten above are ruthlessly followed and we will never be stopped. Relax them, get reasonable about it and we will perish."

Notice how he uses "we" in this section three times. He's spent all this time throwing everyone except himself under the bus, but now he's kindly including the reader - the Scientologist - into this tight knit conspiracy of people who have the special miracle information to save the world, and implores them to ruthlessly destroy anything not Scientology. Otherwise everyone, themselves included, will all perish. None of this wording or language is used on accident.

So you can see here Hubbard is faithfully following the cult leader's playbook step by step, instilling in his followers the exact beliefs needed to put them in a frame of mind where they will follow his word as law, negate any other beliefs or subjects and view the world through an us-vs-them filter.

Section 4: The Group is All, the Individual is Nothing

Hubbard starts the next section talking about keeping Scientology technology straight and ensuring no one be allowed to alter it. He says

"I have not failed on Seven, Eight, Nine and Ten in areas I could supervise closely. But it's not good enough for just myself and a few others to work at this."

That sounds sensible enough for any service organization, but then check out this contradictory statement in the very next paragraph:

"Whenever this control as per Seven, Eight, Nine and Ten has been relaxed the whole organizational area has failed. Witness Elizabeth, N.J., Wichita, the early organizations and groups. They crashed only because I no longer did Seven, Eight, Nine and Ten. Then, when they were all messed up, you saw the obvious 'reasons' for failure. But ahead of that they ceased to deliver and that involved them in other reasons."

So which is it? Has he never failed on Seven, Eight, Nine and Ten or did those areas collapse because he *did* fail on them?

Well, never mind any of that because Hubbard then goes on to implant a new idea which will reinforce the us-vs-them mentality by saying they are in fact free and independent thinkers, not submitting to mob mentality or what he calls "collective thought agreement" only when they do exactly and only what Hubbard says. This bit is actually quite some brilliant writing. He says:

"The common denominator of a group is the reactive bank. Thetans without banks have different responses. They only have their banks in common. They agree then only on bank principles."

Now that last sentence is a kicker. We agree only on bank principles? So is 2 + 2 = 4 a bank principle? Is it somehow a destructive principle to think senseless killing should be stopped? Are following the law or raising your children in a safe environment now bad things simply because most people agree they're good ideas? Well, here's more on that:

"Person to person the bank is identical. So constructive ideas are individual and seldom get broad agreement in a human group. An individual must rise above an avid craving for agreement from a humanoid group to get anything decent done."

Constructive ideas are individual and seldom get broad agreement. Ideas like freedom of thought? Freedom of speech? Civil rights? Those are all principles which get pretty broad agreement. Are those the kinds of ideas we should be looking down on with contempt simply because people agree on them?

He's just talking nonsense here. Now notice the subtleties, though. He says "in a human group" and in the next sentence, he morphs that into a "humanoid group." It's quite something what he's doing here, leading a person down a line of logic using these subtle words to get a person into a frame of mind where they believe groups of people only agree on things because they are operating on a primitive, even sub-human level.

He reinforces this by then saying

"The bank-agreement has been what has made Earth a Hell – and if you were looking for Hell and found Earth, it would certainly serve. War, famine, agony and disease has been the lot of Man. Right now the great governments of Earth have developed the means of frying every Man, Woman and Child on the planet. That is Bank. That is the result of Collective Thought Agreement. The decent, pleasant things on this planet come from individual actions and ideas that have somehow gotten by the Group Idea."

146

By emphasizing only the negative aspects of our lives as a species, he is laying the blame on an invented "Group Idea" and contrasting this with individuality being the only solution. But then, he brings Scientology into the picture and check out how he does this:

"For that matter, look how we ourselves are attacked by 'public opinion' media. Yet there is no more ethical group on this planet than ourselves.

"Thus each one of us can rise above the domination of the bank and then, as a group of freed beings, achieve freedom and reason. It is only the aberrated group, the mob, that is destructive."

Hubbard uses the word "aberrated" to mean faulty thinking or not thinking in a straight line. So groups are bad. Group agreement is bad. But we, the Scientologists, are a group of "freed beings" and therefore we are good and everything I just said about groups doesn't apply to us. Only the aberrated group is destructive. Scientology is not aberrated, so therefore Scientology is good.

He has just laid so many logical landmines into his followers; it's really quite something to break it all down, especially when he then summarizes everything he's said so far from the beginning by saying this:

"When you don't do Seven, Eight, Nine and Ten actively, you are working for the Bank dominated mob. For it will surely, surely (a) introduce incorrect technology and swear by it, (b) apply technology as incorrectly as possible, (c) open the door to any destructive idea, and (d) encourage incorrect application. It's the Bank that says the group is all and the individual nothing. It's the Bank that says we must fail. So just don't play that game. Do Seven, Eight, Nine and Ten and you will knock out of your road all the future thorns."

Hubbard spends the next couple of pages giving general, anonymous examples from Scientology history of how not ruthlessly applying his instructions resulted in people being worse off, basically instilling phobias in his followers, convincing them to not think for themselves but only to do what he says. One of the examples he gives even ends up with a woman dying of cancer because the people around her didn't follow Hubbard's direction.

This, again, has to be part of any cult indoctrination in order for it to work. Followers have to believe there will be dire consequences if they stray from the path or don't follow their cult leader's instructions to the letter, which leads to the last section.

Section 5: The Entire Universe is Counting on You

Now the last section is where Hubbard really pours on the idea of Scientology as the only hope in the entire universe for the salvation of Mankind. This idea is also a very crucial part of the cult mentality. He's taken pages to paint a picture of Mankind doing itself in at a mad rate, being totally unable to turn itself around or save itself on its own and now he must offer the one and only solution to all evil everywhere.

In Scientology, people all have these reactive minds. These are the insidious monsters in our heads making us do ourselves in. According to Hubbard, only Scientology can eradicate this reactive mind and therefore only Scientology can save Mankind.

In order to get people into a frame of mind where they are willing to forsake everything in their life for a cause, you have to put them into a fanatical state. Getting them to believe they are each ultimately responsible for the safety and security of the entire world gives people a fanatical sense of purpose and direction which is a very powerful motivating force. Here's what Hubbard says:

"When somebody enrolls, consider he or she has joined up for the duration of the universe – never permit an 'open-minded' approach. If they're going to quit let them quit fast. If they enrolled, they're aboard, and if they're aboard, they're here on the same terms as the rest of us – win or die in the attempt. Never let them be half-minded about being Scientologists. The finest organizations in history have been tough, dedicated organizations. Not one namby pamby bunch of panty-waist dilettantes have ever made anything. It's a tough universe. The social veneer makes it seem mild. But only the tigers survive – and even they have a hard time. We'll survive because we are tough and are dedicated. When we do instruct somebody properly he becomes more and more tiger. When we instruct half-mindedly and are afraid to offend, scared to enforce, we don't

make students into good Scientologists and that lets everybody down. When Mrs. Pattycake comes to us to be taught, turn that wandering doubt in her eye into a fixed, dedicated glare and she'll win and we'll all win. Humour her and we all die a little. The proper instruction attitude is, 'You're here so you're a Scientologist. Now we're going to make you into an expert auditor no matter what happens. We'd rather have you dead than incapable.'

Fit that into the economics of the situation and lack of adequate time and you see the cross we have to bear."

These are powerful words. They cast Hubbard's followers as the underdogs fighting the good fight, the toughest elite of planet Earth who are there to see to it everyone else makes it out alive. It's a cross they have to bear, a duty they have to perform in order to succeed. It sets them apart from everyone else and makes them feel superior and advanced and, at the same time, reinforces the us-vs-them mentality.

And lest anyone think I'm exaggerating, he ends it with this:

"We're not playing some minor game in Scientology. It isn't cute or something to do for lack of something better.

"The whole agonized future of this planet, every Man, Woman and Child on it, and your own destiny for the next endless trillions of years depend on what you do here and now with and in Scientology.

"This is a deadly serious activity. And if we miss getting out of the trap now, we may never again have another chance.

"Remember, this is our first chance to do so in all the endless trillions of years of the past. Don't muff it now because it seems unpleasant or unsocial to do Seven, Eight, Nine and Ten.

"Do them and we'll win."

It wouldn't be so sad if they weren't so delusional, because of course Scientology does not deliver what it promises in any sense of the word. There may well be a personal spiritual existence and immortality for us after we die, but achieving that state cannot depend on how closely someone adheres to Hubbard's delusions.

The states of being Hubbard describes in Scientology have not been proven to exist. In fact, anyone can see there is real and tangible evidence the promises of Clear and Operating Thetan are just pipe dreams with no more reality than wishes upon a star or pennies in a well. No Scientologist, including Hubbard himself, was ever able to demonstrate telepathic or mystical powers or even the ability to avoid diseases or death. It's all style and no substance.

Now more than ever, those who have followed L. Ron Hubbard's powerful words are seeing through the delusory picture he paints and extricating themselves from Scientology's destructive influence, but there is still work to do before they will all be free of it.

10. Pseudoscience and the Purification Rundown

One of the most practical uses of critical thinking in everyday life is to ferret out fraudulent or nonsensical claims made by advertisers, media pundits, political figures and religious leaders. You might be surprised to hear this, but a great many of the claims you hear coming from these people about health, beauty, diet and even the environment are total nonsense with no proof or evidence to back up what they say.

In other words, you are being lied to. A lot.

It's totally gross this goes on, right? But you want to know what is more gross? We let ourselves fall for it simply because we aren't paying attention or don't know what to look for. If we learn to recognize the clues, they will tell us when we are looking at pseudoscience.

Pseudoscience? What's that?

Pseudoscience literally means fake or phony science. People who didn't learn much about science in school, and just think it's what they see on *CSI* or in the movies, get some very weird ideas about what scientists actually do all day.

They're likely to believe charlatans like Deepak Chopra actually understand something about quantum theory simply because they throw around scientific words like *cosmic, evolution, transformation* or *synchronicity.*

They might fall for buying that new diet pill Dr. Oz is pushing because he has the letters M.D. after his name and therefore anything he says must be sound and rational. As a doctor, he is a man of science, right? Surely he would never use flowery language in order to do anything as crass as make money.

This stuff is all around us every day and far too many people fall for it. The good news is you don't need a PhD in order to know when you are looking at real science and real facts.

I thought it might be fun to demonstrate a very easy and specific way to recognize pseudoscientific claims. There are lots of ways to do this, actually, and once you start spotting them, you're going to find it easier and easier to see.

How bad a problem is this? Well, the truth is, buying into some of the pseudoscience being peddled today can actually kill you. So it's a really good idea to find out more about this phenomenon and learn to spot it when you see it.

Scientology's Purification Program

Scientology is a destructive cult which uses many thought-stopping and mind-numbing techniques to get people to spend hundreds of thousands of dollars to buy their "Bridge to Total Freedom". They offer spiritual salvation in exchange for complete loyalty and routinely give no return whatsoever in exchange for exorbitant amounts of money.

However, there is another aspect of Scientology we haven't really examined as much: the pseudoscientific claims L. Ron Hubbard made in many of his books and lectures.

The Purification Rundown is sold as a detoxification program. Within the church, they claim it's not for the direct benefit of a person's body, but for spiritual growth, impeded by toxic materials in the body. This of course excuses them from having to provide anything like evidence it works. It's Hubbard's "religion angle" all over again.

The Purification Rundown is also used in Scientology's secular drug rehabilitation program Narconon. Supposedly this will get drugs and other toxins out of a person's body so they will be free from their debilitating effects and no longer want to take drugs. That sounds exactly like "handling a person's body" to me.

Now as a person not trained in science, you could look at the materials which describe how to do the Purification Rundown and you'd be faced with literally chapters and chapters of information: a whole book describing all the ins and outs of sweating out drug toxins. There are doctor's recommendations and reviews and the material sounds impressive enough, but here's the thing: look at the words and phrases being used to describe the claims.

There are words in any language used to express uncertainty or possibility. Examples of these in English are: *can, may, might, could, should, possibly, maybe, likely, reportedly* and *pretty sure.*

If I say LSD *could* remain in the cells of a body after a person has taken it, I'm not really making a definite claim this is true. It's the same if I say LSD *can* lodge itself in the fat tissues of a person's body.

Then again, it might not, and that's the point. It's ambiguous and if you really break it down, it doesn't say anything, especially in a legally-binding context.

Language is very important when you examine claims made by anyone. The words I listed earlier are not used to state definite facts but a person could read these statements as facts and think LSD crystals are definitely lodged in their fatty tissues and they need to do something to get them out. The words chosen are used on purpose so the people who make these claims can't be held liable.

So am I cherry-picking one or two vague claims from the Purification Rundown, or is the whole book full of these non-statements? Let's take a look and see.

I actually went through Hubbard's Purification Rundown book and found every example of these words being used to express vague possibility rather than exact fact, where the meaning is ambiguous in order to create an impression different than the words actually mean. Here are three examples from just the first seven pages of the text. I've set them in bold type to help them stand out.

[in reference to food additives] *From research on these "enhancers"* *and "preservers,"* it appears *that a number of them are quite toxic, and the* *whole subject of food additives and preservatives has become a matter of* *concern to many people.*[1]

[in reference to perfume] *Findings* seem *to bear out that these* *chemicals, floating about in the local supermarket as "fragrances" are* *actually toxic and* can *end up in the food products sold there.*[2]

[in reference to toxins being stored in fatty tissue] *The* most likely *place for a toxic substance to lock up is in the fatty tissue. It* has been said *that in middle age and past middle age, a body's ability to break down fat* *lessens. So here we have,* apparently, *a situation of toxic substances locked* *up in fatty tissue and the fatty tissue is not actually getting broken down,* *and so such toxic substances* could *accumulate.*[3]

These are not definitive statements. In fact, these statements could be removed entirely because they don't say anything of substance, though they pretend to make assertions as factual as scientific axioms. They have as much validity as a cartoon or fable.

Hubbard uses flowery language about detoxification and removing poisons and harmful materials from your body so you can live a longer, healthier life, think more clearly and have more energy, but is that what he's really saying? You need to read it carefully to be sure.

One also should beware of just plain false information in the material. This is a lot harder to spot and requires you do some fact checking. For example, Hubbard says this about LSD:

"...because it is basically wheat rust which simply cuts off circulation, my *original thinking on this was that LSD must remain in the body."*[4]

To the uninformed, this may sound like an interesting and educated statement but the truth is LSD is a synthetically created chemical which has nothing to do with wheat rust and it has no direct effect on the heart or circulatory system.[5] No one knows exactly why it creates the effects it creates because serious scientific studies haven't been done on how LSD affects the brain, but they do know it's not because it cuts off circulation. One educated guess is LSD works similarly to serotonin, a neurotransmitter in the brain which regulates mood, appetite, muscle control and sensory perception, but <u>no one</u> is claiming this is a scientific fact.[6]

The cause of LSD flashbacks isn't known either, but you don't have to know what causes something in order to rule out what is NOT causing it. We know LSD is not stored in the fat cells of the body and it doesn't therefore get re-released into the body months or years after it's taken.[7] That *is* an established fact. So that shoots Hubbard's theories about this portion of the Purification Rundown right down the drain.

As far as pseudoscience goes, there is another kind of statement you should also be watching for. By law, they have to include what's called a disclaimer. In the Purification Program, here is what they say:

"There are no medical recommendations or claims made for the program. The only claim is future spiritual improvement.

"The data contained herein is a record of researches and results noted; it cannot be construed as a recommendation for medical treatment or medication, and is undertaken or delivered by any individual on his own responsibility."[8]

What does future spiritual improvement even mean? It means the only thing you are going to get out of this potentially life-threatening program is that at some point in the future your soul is going to be happier for you having done it.

What I've said about flowery and ambiguous language applies to any kind of pseudoscientific nonsense you may see peddled on TV, the internet or other media. Watch for these and you will have a good heads-up so you don't get cheated or conned.

The Dangers of the Purification Program

The Purification Program is not just about taking some harmless vitamins or being bilked out of a couple of thousand dollars. The blunt truth is it is not founded in any kind of evidence-based science and it could cause major medical problems to anyone who goes through it.

The two key elements of the Purification Program are taking mega-doses of niacin and sweating five hours a day in a sauna. It may surprise you, but neither of these activities actually do anything to rid your body of substances such as LSD or alcohol.

The reason I can say this is because it's been well established LSD and alcohol are water-soluble substances which your body completely expels within a few hours of ingestion. This has been known for decades and if Hubbard did any real research, he would have known it too. Instead, he claims he had a conversation with a Portuguese doctor about fat deposits found in cadavers and somehow intuited that drugs and chemicals are permanently stored in fat cells. There is no evidence in his materials of Hubbard doing any further experimentation or gathered any other evidence to backup his claims.

Is that good science? Of course not.

Just to point out an obvious example of why this is ridiculous, when a person does the Purification Program they take doses of vitamins every day far exceeding the doses of LSD or marijuana a person usually takes to get high. So why don't those vitamins get lodged in the fatty tissues of the body and stay there forever?

According to Hubbard's theory, wouldn't it make sense if a chemical like LSD were being stored in your body forever, then other chemicals like ascorbic acid (vitamin C), cholecalciferol (vitamin D3) or retinol (vitamin A) would also be stored forever too? Why would it only be recreational drugs and harmful toxic substances the body holds on to?

The truth is there has never been any evidence drugs stay in your body forever. Drugs are simply chemicals and the human body is extremely good at breaking down chemicals and ejecting them when it's done using them. That is what digestion and metabolism are all about. Millions of years of evolution have made our bodies quite good at it. Sure, there are some people who have abnormalities and problems with their metabolism, but those are exceptions, not the rule.

It's a commonly believed myth that all cells in the body are replaced every seven years, but that's not true. What *is* true is cells die off and get replaced and different kinds of cells deteriorate at different rates. According to a 2008 study done in Sweden, every year 10% of your fat cells die, no matter how fat or thin you are or how much weight you are gaining or losing.[9] Every year, those cells which die are replaced with new fat cells. So even if the old fat cells did contain LSD or other drug toxins - they don't, but if they did - they'd be naturally replaced.

On the Purification Program, niacin is taken at doses of up to 5,000 milligrams a day. Hubbard observed niacin can create a red flush and deduced, incorrectly, this meant radiation was being discharged from the body. Again, if he had done any real research to find evidence for his pet theory, he would have discovered the flush niacin produces is due simply to dilation of blood vessels. That flush is just a side effect. Niacin is used in much smaller doses to actually treat high cholesterol. He also would have found out you can overdose on niacin and if you do, the following can occur: severe skin flushing combined with dizziness, rapid heartbeat, itching, nausea and vomiting, abdominal pain and diarrhea.[10]

In addition, a person on the Purification Program is put into a sauna where the temperature can be as high as 180 degrees and encouraged to stay in as long as they can stand it. What can that do? Well, here are the symptoms of heat exhaustion: heavy sweating; pallor (paleness); muscle cramps and muscle pain; fatigue; weakness; dizziness and lightheadedness; headache; and nausea.[11]

If not treated, a person could then experience heat stroke, which includes the following new symptoms: rapid heart rate; difficulty breathing; loss of coordination; confusion and restlessness; seizures; and unconsciousness.[12]

Now if someone were indoctrinated to believe they were going to experience drug trips or flashbacks in the sauna, could they mistake some of these dangerous and even life-threatening symptoms of heat exhaustion and heat stroke for a drug trip? Of course they could, and the result could be disastrous for their immediate and long-term health. If these are not handled properly, they could even result in death.

Even if nothing bad happened and they recovered from these symptoms, they could still mistakenly think they just ran out some kind of drug from their body when in fact, they simply overheated themselves.

The people who deliver the Purification Rundown in Churches of Scientology are not required to have any medical training of any kind. The only materials they are required to study are those written by L. Ron Hubbard. Should heat exhaustion or heat stroke symptoms appear, they too could mistake those symptoms for drug trips or flashbacks, which is what they expect to see, and they could even send someone experiencing these symptoms back into the sauna to "run out the drugs".

How do I know this? Because one of the jobs I used to do when I worked for the Church was delivering Purification Rundowns. I realize now I had no idea what I was doing and I sincerely hope I did no lasting damage to anyone I supervised on this program.

Is Pseudoscience Really Worth the Risk?

It's amazing it requires 8-12 solid years of education for someone to become a medical professional, yet somehow all that learning and discipline is discounted by the general public in an instant when some quack utters magic words like "ancient wisdom" or "alternative medicine."

An unintended and very disturbing consequence of having the world's knowledge at your fingertips with Google is everyone now thinks they are expert at everything, when in fact the exact opposite is true. I've never seen a better example of the old adage "a little learning is a dangerous thing".

No one ever claimed medicine is an exact science which works 100% of the time. At least in the world of science and reality, we have evidence, testing and thousands of hours of research before any theory is unleashed on an unsuspecting public. Not so with pseudoscience. In the world of pseudoscience, anyone can claim anything with no need to back up those claims with evidence or proof, then rake in hundreds of thousands, if not millions, of dollars from unsuspecting dupes who believe anything they are told.

There are very sound evidence-based medical principles behind detoxifying a human body. None of these principles are evident in

Hubbard's untested pseudo scientific approach. It takes but a minute to make any claim you want. It takes years to back up those claims with real research and study.

Before you put your health or your very life into someone else's hands, make sure they know what they are talking about and have done the hard work necessary to back up their claims.

11. Why Scientologists Believe They are Saving the World (or Here's the Part about Xenu)

Scientologists do what they do for a reason. It's not a cult of morons who mindlessly repeat lyrical mantras, dance around in a circle and praise their leader. That's not what Scientology is about.

To its adherents, Scientology is about saving not only themselves as individual spiritual beings, but saving the whole world. They truly believe in what they are doing and they are very serious about it because they are convinced they have the solution to all the problems of the world.

All the abuses, human rights violations and whatnot occur in Scientology because the people committing them do so with the certain belief such sacrifices and destructive acts are necessary to pull off "the Big Win". You can't make an omelette without breaking a few eggs, as the old saying goes, and so it is in the world of Scientology.

I will talk about Xenu in this chapter but actually there is a whole lot more to this than a simple fable about an intergalactic warlord detailed years ago on the TV show *South Park*. Despite all the parodies and jokes made on YouTube and late night talk shows about this "core belief" of Scientologists, the fact is they are all getting it wrong.

Yes, Hubbard did say there is a guy named Xenu and he did horrible things so many millions of years ago, and this involved volcanoes. What most people who are relating this story get wrong is the significance of the story in Scientology. The Xenu fable is but one small part of a much larger cosmology and belief system and the specifics of the DC-8s and the volcanos are not even the most important or significant part of it. This whole story is not even the strangest thing Hubbard ever said, so why it gets such traction is actually kind of odd to me when I look at the bigger picture of Scientology and all the completely bizarre things Hubbard claimed occurred to us in the past.

It's probably because a specific price tag can be connected with the Xenu story; this is enough to create incredulous disbelief in people and that's as far as they think about it. We live in a meme-oriented, sound-byte society now and people want one-liners they can toss off and not have to think about things too deeply. With something like Scientology, that's probably for the best, but if you want a real understanding of where Scientologists' heads are at, it's inadequate to throw out a meme and think you know everything.

I'm not an apologist. I understand there's a certain degree of humor to be gotten from the ridiculous claims made by almost any religion in terms of their cosmic or supernatural beliefs. My point in this chapter is not to hold up Hubbard's claims to ridicule, though, nor to make fun of them. I will talk here about the illogical reasoning and contradictions riddled throughout Hubbard's confidential, upper level materials, but only to show how there is no way they are possible within the bounds of science and reason, not to laugh at them.

This chapter gets into the nitty-gritty of the deepest beliefs of Scientologists. The reason I'm going over all this at all is to show how and why Scientologists think they are doing the most important work in the universe and why they would forsake family, friends and everything else in their effort to save us all.

We'll start at the beginning and walk through the years of development which eventually led to Xenu and a whole lot more.

Theta/MEST Theory

In *Dianetics: The Modern Science of Mental Health*, Hubbard alludes to a life force but states it is not an individual thing but something larger and more than any one individual. He makes it out to be a sort of force of nature:

"Life forms change and die as new life forms develop just as surely as one life organism, lacking immortality in itself, creates other life organisms, then dies as itself. An excellent method, should one wish to cause life to survive over a very long period, would be to establish means by which it could assume many forms. And death itself would be necessary in order to facilitate the survival of the life force itself, since only death and decay could clear away older forms when new changes in the environment necessitated new forms. Life, as a force existing over a nearly infinite period, would need a cyclic aspect in its unit organisms and forms."[1]

Dianetics is the first place where Hubbard uses the Greek letter θ (theta) to describe the life force quantity. Here he begins a chapter on emotion with this:

"Emotion is a θ (theta) quantity, which is to say that it is so involved with life forces that Dianetics at this stage handles it with invariable success, but does not attempt to give forth more than a descriptive theory. Much research must be done on emotion; but so long as the therapy embraces it and releases it with success, further data can be dispensed with up to a point."[2]

It is this paragraph Hubbard expanded on a year later in the second book of Dianetics, called *Science of Survival*. And he didn't just expand on it; it was this germ of an idea which he used to created a whole new religion.

In early 1951, Hubbard wrote *Science of Survival,* and he started lecturing on its principles months before it was officially published in August 1951. The first of these lectures was on May 21,1951 in Wichita, Kansas, where Hubbard presented the "Theta/MEST theory"..

"Theta stands for thought. Once upon a time man talked about his soul; philosophers have talked about 'life energy' and 'cosmic consciousness.' All of these things could be called Theta. In other words, Theta is just the Greek word which comes the closest to saying 'thought.' So let's take thought as a separate energy, as something we don't know a great deal about, and we will just compartment it out of the physical universe.

"We know the physical universe. The physical universe is this desk and that chair and that light and the electricity running through that light; it is very simple. We have all had our tiffs and bumps from the physical universe. We know about the physical universe. We call that MEST. It is called MEST because it is made up of matter, energy, space and time; we take the first letter of each one of those words and put them all together and we have MEST."

He explains the interaction of theta and MEST as follows:

"We find out our first axiom is simply in the line of 'Theta has as its mission, or one of its missions, the changing of MEST.' That is not very complicated. Theta changes MEST.

"Electricity as it runs through the wires lights a light. Similarly, life energy changes MEST. A little bit of Theta gets into the physical universe and somehow organizes it to turn the laws of the physical universe into a conquest of the physical universe. Theta keeps on doing this and it builds up a greater and greater control of MEST.

"The first goal is an organism; Theta makes an organism and then this organism eventually has mobility. Then through its mobility the organism itself begins to handle MEST and change it."

He further explains:

"Now, Theta forms with MEST a union out of turbulence. Evidently, the first step in any Theta-MEST combination is a heavy impact of Theta against MEST with a resulting enturbulence. They don't go together smoothly the first time. The Theta comes back out of this, or disenturbulates to some degree, and then, and only then, begins a harmonious conquest of this MEST which it has contacted. The Theta gets into the MEST, learns something about the laws of the MEST and, pulling back, is then able to change more MEST. Then there is another enturbulence and so forth, Theta learns some more and pulls back and then comes in and changes more MEST."

"Whether this is in a single lifetime or in the sequences of lifetimes which go to make up a racial generation of many lifetimes—either way—it is the same cycle that is going on. Each time this is the same thing."

This explanation, and everything about it, one must take on faith because there is no proof or evidence of any kind to substantiate it.

Hubbard presents it as a "theory" without presenting the evidence, tests or formula which prove this theory out. Of course, this was Hubbard's modus operandi anyway, simply offering anecdotes and examples off the top of his head to prove what he claimed were invariable scientific phenomena.

The most basic part of this which does not make sense is that theta is supposed to be able to manipulate the physical universe, yet it is not part of the physical universe. It is clearly described as a separate thing, distinct from matter, energy, space and time yet able to influence and even create matter, energy, space and time. How theta manages to pull that off would be something Hubbard would work on explaining for many years to come. Clearly people kept asking him about this and wanted something substantial to hang their belief on but in the end, the answer comes down simply to "because it thinks it can."

If you accept this "theory" and cross this line of faith, everything else in Scientology's cosmology can make sense. Hubbard built an entire philosophy and religion on the premise that a nothingness called theta was life itself and this nothingness was all-powerful and all-knowing in its "native state" before it became "enturbulated" by its interaction with the physical universe.

It's humorous to realize Hubbard made a fortune basically making nothing out of everybody.

The State of Operating Thetan

Having introduced this idea of theta and convincing his small number of followers it was real, Hubbard ran with it and developed the idea into individual spiritual beings, which he called "thetans". The entire thrust of his "research" throughout 1951 and 1952 became involved in discovering the full potentials and abilities of thetans and how people could be rehabilitated to their "native state".

He offered no explanation whatsoever for where thetans came from, but merely referenced in vague terms a "separation from the main body of theta" at some point in the far distant past, initially given as 70 trillion years ago.[3] Later that timespan would become much longer and details would change over and over again as to the exact origins of theta's entry into the physical universe.

What did not change was the basic idea of a thetan and the promise of rehabilitating everyone to a state of personal godhood.

The genus of this was the idea of becoming "cause". Hubbard admitted he took a page from old Vedic lore when he related the idea of a cycle of action, meaning the stages anything goes through during its existence in the physical universe: create - survive - destroy. Hubbard invented variations on this theme and described it in different ways over the years to make it sound a lot more arcane and fancy than it is, but the bottom line was: something is created, it persists or survives until it is no more and it is destroyed.

To be at "cause" was to be the originator of cycles of action. This is always positioned in Scientology as the best position to be in. One desires to be at "cause" since the opposite is "effect". If you are not causing something to happen, you are instead being effected by someone else's causative actions. Since this opens you up to being hurt or having something happen to you which you don't want to have happen, it is always better to be cause than effect.

The term "Operating Thetan" or "OT" was introduced in Philadelphia during an intensive series of lectures given in December 1952, later referred to as the "Philadelphia Doctorate Course". The material in these lectures has always been considered by Scientologists to be very deep and hard to understand, since Hubbard goes into electronic phenomena (waves and energy flows and such) as well as pretty esoteric sounding terms as the "Qs" (the highest form of knowledge possible), Theta Clear and Cleared Theta Clear and other states he describes in a very roundabout way using lots of hand-drawn charts and scales.

Throughout the course of these lectures, Hubbard described how thetans control bodies and MEST using energy flows and beams (as in tractor beams which pull and pressor beams which push) and these beams emanate from the thetan onto the body and make it do things. This sort of thing makes no sense given a thetan is not supposed to have any location, mass or wavelength in the physical universe, so how

166

can a nothingness be emitting energy beams? But again, this is a matter of faith and not hard science. One simply accepts what Hubbard says because he's saying it and everything follows from that. Hubbard's followers do not think too deeply or critically about this material, otherwise they would no longer be Hubbard's followers.

In a lecture given on December 13, 1952 titled "Development of Scientology - Characteristics of Living Science" he described an OT as a being at the top of every scale.

"What's an Operating Thetan? An Operating Thetan's a guy who can handle MEST without beams and travel without energy. And uh... that's not too hard to achieve. We have those techniques. We've talked about this sort of thing."

Throughout these lectures, Hubbard also described an earlier threshold just below an Operating Thetan called a Theta Clear who would be "a person who operates exterior to a body without need of a body."

This Theta Clear was touted as the first condition to work on reaching. OT was thrown out as a sort of not-yet-achievable goal but something to be attained eventually. Hubbard says in the quote above they had techniques to attain OT but that was just a tease because almost all the Philadelphia Course techniques emphasized achieving Theta Clear and no one was making it even to that level yet. Partially, this is because Hubbard was extremely vague in his definitions of what a Theta Clear even was or how to attain it exactly.

The only definite thing he said about it was Theta Clear meant someone could operate outside their body and stay there - a kind of permanent out-of-body experience. OT was where they could influence or move matter and energy and go anywhere in the universe at will. This put the state of OT as a sort of unattainable theoretical which Hubbard could keep selling for many years to come.In fact, they still sell it to this day.

The basic premise of what an OT is and what it is capable of have not changed much since 1952. What has been worked on and talked about *ad absurdum* is how to go about attaining this state. Hubbard's "research trail" throughout the 1950s and into the 1960s and 1970s

167

was actually just a way of continually moving the goal post farther and farther out while promising each time he moved it *this time* he had found the way to ensure everyone made it all the way to the top, to the state of full OT. To this day, this state is still completely unattainable but Scientologists believe it can be achieved by doing all the as-yet-unreleased upper OT levels. So they stick with it and keep going.

There were some key milestones along the way which Hubbard spent quite a bit of time developing and which became part of the bigger picture of saving the world, starting with implants.

Implants and the Whole Track

Hubbard coined the term *time track* in *Dianetics* to describe the film-like stream of mental pictures which made up a person's memories going back to the beginning of their life. In Dianetics counselling, preclears were directed to go "down their time track" to earlier moments in time and recall what they saw, heard, felt, etc.

Once past lives came into play and people went down the track hundreds or even thousands of years, a new term was created to describe the pictures prior to a person's present lifetime: the whole track. This was the sum total of *all* the mental image pictures from every lifetime the person ever lived.

How far back does the whole track go? According to Hubbard, thetans have been around for so long it's almost impossible for the human mind to conceive of the periods of time used. A trillion, for example, is not a number anyone can easily think with. The American definition of a trillion is one thousand billions. A billion is one thousand millions. And a million is one thousand thousands.

When I was a Scientology course supervisor and I had to get students to really understand these numbers, the only way I could get them across was to use an analogy of counting. If you were going to count to a million, one number at a time spoken every second without taking any breaks or even going to sleep, it would take you a little over 11½ days.

To reach a billion, it would take you 31.7 years.

To reach a trillion, counting 24/7 all day everyday, it would take you 31,688 years.

That sort of communicates how big these numbers are and gives you perspective on Hubbard's claim thetans have been around for 70 trillion years. He later expanded on this and said thetans had been around for a trillion trillion trillion years - numbers so large they required pages of zeros to write down. It just became ridiculous and at that point as a course supervisor I simply said to my students that thetans had basically been around for a "near infinite amount of time." That seemed to settle the issue for most people.

Hubbard claimed the physical universe and all the galaxies and planets in it were far older than modern science thought. It was easy for him to come up with pseudoscientific explanations for why or not even bother with explanations at all but just say "Nope, these physicists and astronomers don't know what they're talking about." In one lecture, for example, he explained they had carbon dating all wrong and this threw off all their calculations of life on this planet, because they grossly misestimated how much carbon exists in the universe. To people who can barely remember their high school science education and are prone to put their faith in cult leaders, explanations like this made total sense, especially when this reasoning is leading to them achieving godlike states with supernatural powers.

All this is important only because of the tales Hubbard told about what thetans were up to all this time.

Thetans did not always attach themselves to bodies. There was a period of time, vaguely spoken of in various lectures, where bodies and this physical universe did not exist at all. Thetans were just thetans who created things in their own spaces or what Hubbard referred to as their own universes, and sometimes they would share universes with one another and mutually create things. There is also mention made at least once of a "magic" universe where wizards flew on the backs of great creatures and anything you could imagine existed including sorcery.

It was, Hubbard hypothesized, the merging of these various individual universes which brought about the existence of the physical universe, a new common universe of agreement which punished any individual who disagreed or tried to do his own thing instead of what the physical universe mandated. I'll save you the trouble of looking for further details or explanations of that statement because there weren't any. The exact nature and precise origin of the physical universe and the life in it is given this gloss-over explanation and that is all you get.

However, through the 1950s and especially in the early 1960s, Hubbard talked extensively about implants. An implant in Scientology is an incident of brainwashing on a scale never before imagined or even possible here on Earth. Hubbard defines an implant as *"an unwilling and unknowing receipt of a thought. An intentional installation of fixed ideas, constrasurvival to the thetan."*[4]

Hubbard's research "uncovered" hundreds, even thousands, of different kinds of implants which took place at various times and places in the universe. Most of them are variations on a theme: use beautiful or interesting imagery or art to attract a thetan to a specific location, pin him down or trap him using electronic beams and then hurt the thetan while showing him pictures or imagery which gives him very specific ideas. Then make him forget the whole thing and send him on his way, or sometimes eject him to a specific place.

Implants come in all shapes and sizes with all sorts of specific purposes and goals, all of which boil down to the control of spiritual beings and getting them into loyal or more pliable states of mind so they will follow orders or think along certain specific lines.

If you can imagine the most heinous and hideous torture session possible, involving the most excessive use of force and with the sole intention of ripping a person's mind apart so new ideas could be installed in their place; that is an implant. Here on Earth, implanting is done by governments, destructive cults and other military or religious groups by physically torturing a person. On the whole track implants are done directly to a spiritual being and involve levels of force using electronics so great, that kind of technology doesn't even exist here yet.

They are gruesome, horrible traumatic episodes carried out by uncaring, evil beings who knowingly and with malice aforethought are not just ruining a person's life but are corrupting their soul to ruin all future lives as well.

Hubbard claimed almost everything we see, hear or experience in the various civilizations which have existed throughout history, all the way up to modern times, are a result of implants which make people say and act out pattern responses. There have been earlier civilizations and whole galactic empires which looked very much like Earth does because we are merely copying those civilizations from our implants and our whole track, subconscious memories.

Almost all the important and heavy duty implants were carried out millions or even hundreds of trillions of years ago. He describes implants which contain a lot of nonsensical animal and mechanical paraphernalia. For example, there is one called the "Aircraft Door Goals" where a thetan is given false life goals or purposes by being held in front of aircraft doors and being subjected to explosions. Another was called the "Gorilla Goals" where a thetan was taken to an amusement park with a single tunnel, a roller coaster and a Ferris wheel; gorillas were always present in some form and implant goals were laid into a thetan "to end", "to be dead", "to be asleep" and the like using blasts of raw electricity, explosions and fantastic motions. As you can see, Hubbard had a lot of imagination to dream up these very bizarre incidents which he said occurred to most of the people of Earth. Of course, Hubbard claimed it is their very bizarreness which makes them so unbelievable and keeps them hidden from view.

Hubbard also described Heaven in exact detail and said the entire concept of Heaven (and most of organized religion including the very existence of Jesus Christ) was the result of whole track implants. This one about Heaven specifically happened 43,891,832,611,177 years, 344 days, 10 hours, 20 minutes and 40 seconds before 10:02:30pm on May 9, 1963.

There are so many logical fallacies, inconsistencies and outright nonsense throughout all these implants, including the very idea of how a being who has no physical existence could even be affected by electronic waves or how such beings could be tossed around or made to go from the "universe of theta" to the physical universe by force in the first place. None of this really makes a whole lot of sense but implants are a vital part of the cosmology of Scientology because they are

Hubbard's explanation for why the world around us is so screwed up and why spiritual beings on this planet, and everywhere in the universe, have forgotten their true nature and lost their abilities.

The way Hubbard describes it, thetans in their native state, before the existence of this physical universe, were ignorant of the terrors of implants and unaware that by agreeing to play with physical bodies or objects, they were insidiously fooled into eventually agreeing they themselves *were* these physical objects they were playing with. It's analogous to a child playing with dolls and then somehow agreeing to the idea he was the doll and reacting to anything done to the doll as though it were being done to him. A kind of spiritual voodoo, if you will.

The whole subject of implants go back to the 1950s in Scientology. None of the information I've covered so far is confidential. You can open up a book called *Scientology: A History of Man* from 1952 and read all about many of the first implants Hubbard "discovered" back then. He built up a catalog of these things over the years which went back further and further in time and had a larger and larger impact on the spiritual beings they were done to.

Most Scientologists have heard of them or read about them and many, after reading about them in Hubbard's books, have promptly claimed to recall them in their own auditing.

The Cyclic Aspect of Existence

One other important aspect to this (and to all auditing, really) is not only are preclears looking for times in the past where they were implanted but also times when they implanted others. Something like the Aircraft Door Goals or the Gorilla Goals may have been done to a thetan but it's also something he then turned around and did to others, and that also messed him up and caused him to be affected by the implant even harder.

The idea is that over the course of time, thetans have taken on different roles and jobs and those include being both the cop and the criminal, both the saint and the sinner. A near infinity of time has given thetans lots and lots of opportunities to do just about everything you can imagine, over and over and over again. This includes not only being implanted but also taking on the role of the implanter.

Implants control not just ideas a person may have or goals they may want to attain, but also cause forgetfulness about past lives. Thetans were implanted many times to forget their last lifetime automatically and then, upon dying, go to a hospital and assume control of a newborn or as-yet-unborn fetus shortly before it is born. Since being on Earth at least, this is how thetans are caught up in an endless cycle of life after life. Since earlier galactic civilizations operated pretty much the same way life on Earth goes, one can assume life for a thetan in those places was pretty much the same.

Scientologists believe it was implants which were used to fool and entrap them all those millennia ago so they would agree to have bodies. However, learning this basic truth is not enough to free these beings now and let them escape from their physical bonds.

For one thing, the implants are extremely powerful and kick in hard on a thetan whether he wants them to or not, in the same way a fear of heights might keep a person from going near a cliff. They may intellectually know the fear is ridiculous or unfounded, but they still are emotionally affected by it.

It was research and development on implants which led Hubbard to eventually formulate the upper levels of Scientology and make them all confidential.

The Grade Chart

In September of 1965, Hubbard took a very important step in the development of Scientology by creating a chart which he called the Classification, Gradation and Awareness Chart of Levels and Certificates. No one calls it that in Scientology though.They refer to it as the Grade Chart or the Bridge to Total Freedom. In short, it's a big chart which lays out a step-by-step guide to progress from the bottom (a beginning Scientologist) through all the various services of Scientology to the top (a full OT).

This chart was needed because Hubbard developed thousands of different auditing processes or procedures (or ripped them off from others, but that's another subject entirely). There was not a lot of rhyme or reason to the order in which someone would be audited or what procedures should be run first, second, third, etc. There had been some stabs at organizing things in the early 1960s but it was still pretty haphazard and up to the whim of whichever auditor a preclear saw as to what he was going to receive.

With the Grade Chart, a Scientologist has an exact route he can look at and see what he needs to do next. All the various processes were categorized into subject matter and type. For example, communication difficulties are a big subject and lots of different auditing processes were invented to tackle this. All these were put together under Grade Zero, the first of the Scientology Grades a person does on the way to going Clear (Hubbard had a thing for starting lists at zero instead of one). Grade One addresses problems, Grade Two addresses moral transgressions, Grade Three addresses traumatic or abrupt changes in a person's life and upsets they've had with themselves and others, etc.

Each step on the Grade Chart would tackle a particular subject or area and the end result of each step would be freedom from trouble with that area of life. About half-way up the Chart is the State of Clear. Above it are some preparatory steps to ready a person for OT, and then the vaunted OT Levels themselves, each one totally confidential. The OT Levels are where the real meat and potatoes of Scientology are. Everything a person does in Scientology is directly or indirectly meant to get them onto and through the OT Levels.

The OT Levels

Hubbard made the OT Levels confidential because he said the material covered on them is so powerful, anyone not ready to know about them or audit them yet could be spiritually damaged or even killed. This is taken very seriously in Scientology. They are the best kept secret and no one who has seen or done the OT Levels ever talks about them casually, even with other OTs when they are alone. There are a lot of written forms and security bonds people have to sign before they are allowed to see these materials, but more importantly they know if they were ever to reveal anything about them, they would be immediately and mercilessly kicked out of Scientology and never allowed back in. They would be declared a Suppressive Person and would also lose any Scientology friends, family or connections. Nothing is taken more seriously than the security of these confidential scriptures.

However, despite all the security measures, this material has leaked out over the years by disaffected ex-Scientologists who realized Hubbard's promises were so much dust in the wind and none of the promised supernatural abilities and godlike powers were a reality. The story of how these materials got out into the public domain is a whole interesting and amusing tale itself, but not the point of this chapter.

The first three OT Levels are done Solo, meaning the person puts himself on an E-meter and does the instructions for each level by himself in a quiet, locked room. Hubbard said an auditor was not needed because the speed with which the person is handling mental phenomena is too fast to be able to talk about it or describe what is happening. Part of the setup for the OT Levels is doing a whole course to learn how to be a Solo Auditor.

The first OT Level, called OT I (Roman numerals don't have a zero), is sort of an "orientation" which is pretty mundane actually. There are no secrets revealed nor new information imparted. Instead, the person simply Solo audits some common lower-level procedures to get the hang of Solo auditing. This is supposed to give a person a "fresh, causative perspective as an OT" but personally I think it's a rather huge and obvious waste of time.

However, the second OT Level jumps right back into implants, specifically implanted goals and purposes from ages past which have created dichotomies (opposing ideas) in a person's head which cause them to bounce back and forth from one goal to another, all not of their own choosing. Over the millennia, this had the effect of making thetans into slaves and robots where each life is sort of a cookie-cutter pattern: grow up, get a job, get married, have a dog, have a cat, have

175

kids, drive a car, go to work, grow old, die. Rinse, repeat. Thetans were implanted thousands of times so they wouldn't want anything else than this humdrum, boring existence and would stay out of trouble.

This keeps thetans busy and occupied in a sort of eternal Hell on Earth, which is how Hubbard describes life on this planet. The population is carefully and systematically controlled, both by having been implanted in ages past and also by being re-implanted when their bodies die and they need a "refresher" before being sent back down to assume control of another newborn body.

There are implant stations in various hidden places on Earth, such as in the Pyrenees Mountains in Europe, as well as on Mars. There are also electronic screens and force fields which keep thetans trapped on Earth when they die so they can't escape to other parts of the galaxy and stir up trouble. Of course, all these implant stations are heavily screened off so as to avoid detection by Man's current primitive state of technology.

Hubbard spent a lot of time in the early and mid-1960s working out these dichotomies so they could be addressed in auditing. There are hundreds of them with a lot of very odd wording and the procedures for addressing them are very complex. It's not necessary for me to go into any of that here.

The point of OT II is that thetans are leading lives not of their own choosing and are stuck in an endless rut they not only can't get out of but don't even know exists. Their once carefree and spiritual existence has been reduced to that of an automaton with pre-programmed thought patterns and responses which have removed any sense of self-determination or free will. Only when a person gets up to this level do they realize the extent and nature of the trap they are caught in and can start doing something about it.

Once these dichotomies are addressed with OT II, a person is supposed to now be able to deal with the whole track and what has been done to them for real, versus all the imaginary memories and desires they thought were their own thoughts. Another aspect of this is supposedly to separate the person himself as a spiritual being from what are known as his body thetans so they are ready to tackle OT III.

176

Incident 1 and Body Thetans

There are two parts to OT III, which Hubbard dubbed "The Wall of Fire" in his first briefing about it in late 1967. Hubbard was in Las Palmas and recorded this lecture sitting alone and outside, claiming he just made the most fantastic and dangerous spiritual journey of all time and it almost killed him in the process. This lecture, known as *Ron's Journal 67*, is legend in Scientology. It is used to entice and intrigue Scientologists with a vague allusion to a "catastrophe which happened 75 million years ago" but no further specifics about OT III are given.

Only when a person has gone up The Bridge through OT II are they allowed to sit in a confidential, locked course room and read the actual materials of OT III.

Hubbard first describes one common implant which happened at the exact moment all of us, every single being in the whole universe, entered the physical universe for the first time. He calls this "Incident 1."

This happened four quadrillion years ago. The thetan was simply flying around or doing whatever it was thetans did before the physical universe existed when he was suddenly subjected to a loud snapping noise, followed by a flood of luminescence, then saw a chariot followed by a trumpeting cherub. After a loud set of snaps, the thetan was overwhelmed by darkness. Apparently upon waking up from this or emerging from out of the darkness, the thetan was trapped in the physical universe.

It's unclear who would have put together and executed Incident 1 for the first time. That's one of the many things about it which makes no sense considering someone had to "come through" into the physical universe to begin with and then figure out the cherubs and chariots and clapping noises in order to start trapping everyone else in it. Who or what executed this plot is never made known. However, Hubbard did say implants of all shapes and sizes were eventually used by almost every galactic civilization in order to control their populations and the practice got pretty out of hand. One imagines a sort of *1984* Big Brother kind of universe out there where whole populations are subjugated in the same way Communist Russians or North Koreans were and are held in thrall by their leaders but using much more heavy-handed methods. In his universe, it all started with Incident 1.

Hubbard does make reference elsewhere to the concept there were earlier universes before this one, many of them in fact, so it's entirely possible all this has been a cyclic activity from one universe to the next and everything in Scientology so far has just been the tip of the iceberg. In Scientology one never quite knows where the train stops and you've reached the end of the line.

More importantly, as far as the OT materials are concerned, there is more going on than just this one-spirit-to-one-body relationship. If that was all, it would be an easy matter of going back and "running out" Incident 1 using Scientology auditing techniques and it would be game over and everyone could be OT again.

There is one more wrinkle in this whole thing which makes it a lot more complicated. Before tackling Incident 1, Scientologists first have to deal with the other part of OT III. This is the story of Xemu and the tragedy of how most life in this sector of the universe was reduced to an unconscious, almost dead, state of existence about 75 million years ago. No one here has recovered since and the reason Earth and the other occupied planets in this region are in such a sorry state is because of what Xemu did.

I am using the spelling of Xemu with an "m" and not Xenu as popularized on *South Park* and other places, because "Xemu" is what Hubbard calls him in the actual OT materials. Hubbard very clearly writes the name with an "m" but because a cursive "n" can look to some like an "m", some people get confused. Hubbard not only wrote this name but also spelled it and said it aloud in confidential OT lectures. The Xenu variation seems to have come from a later work Hubbard wrote based on this material but not exactly this same material.

Spelling issues aside, the Xemu story has gained a lot of notoriety for its bizarre and grandiose narrative of an intergalactic ruler who decided to solve overpopulation issues by instituting a Final Solution of mass genocide. However, what people don't really understand is to

Scientologists, the details and specifics of the story are actually the least important part of what OT III is all about.

On OT III, the story is told in Hubbard's own handwriting. While much of the lower level material and other OT materials were transcribed or typed out, when a person gets on to OT III, they read it exactly as Hubbard wrote it. Unfortunately, they are not really given the whole story. Hubbard gives a lot of additional data about the incident in confidential lectures for advanced auditor trainees in 1968 which those who do OT III are not privy to. However, all this information is out there on the internet; putting it all together, you come up with the following narrative:

This sector of the galaxy was ruled 75 million years ago by a Galactic Confederation consisting of 76 planets circling the 21 adjacent stars to Earth (which he also describes as "the larger stars visible from Earth"). The head of this Galactic Confederation (or Confederacy, as Hubbard also described it) was named Xemu and he was a tyrant in the same vein as Stalin or Pol Pot.

One of the planets in the Confederacy was named Coltus and orbits Polaris, the North Star. Their technology allowed for faster than light travel and it apparently was a nine-day journey from Coltus to Earth. I would take this apart in terms of faster-than-light travel not being possible but I don't have to, because there is a much more fundamental problem with Hubbard's claim about Polaris which doesn't rely on Einstein's time-space relativity theory.[5]

Earth was part of this confederacy and was known back then as Teegeack. The Confederacy's government consisted of Loyal Officers, who represented the citizenry, perhaps similarly to our present-day Congress, except these Loyal Officers were the ones who elected the supreme ruler and they had the power to impeach him as well.

Despite the Loyal Officers being a safeguard against this, Xemu carefully replaced administrators and heads of planets in various places with people who were loyal to him began a campaign of feeding false information to the military so they were suborned to his rule.

Overpopulation was a very serious issue. Hubbard's math is creative on this point, but apparently the average population of each planet was

179

178 billion people. He says in the same sentence there were upwards of 250 billion per planet, so the numbers are little unclear. He clarified in a later lecture the 250 billion figure was the number of people on *this* planet (Earth). Regardless, there were a lot of people, dwarfing Earth's current population problem of only 8 billion people.

Probably because of Xemu's despotism, there were major social issues and unrest throughout the Confederacy. Xemu was about to be recalled by the Loyal Officers and he knew he had to act fast. So what did he do? Xemu's solution was, in short, genocide on a scale unimaginable here on Earth

How do you round up something on the order of 13.5 trillion people and do away with them? What's more, how do you do this if you know they are not just bodies but are going to come back? Xemu and the Galactic Confederation had implant technology at their disposal and knew how to capture a thetan and keep it prisoner.

What is even more interesting is Hubbard said death itself did not really exist for these populations. Their bodies just went on and on and on and in fact, the process of us now growing old and dying was one of the results of this whole OT III incident. A person back then could die a violent death or be killed accidentally, of course, but dying by old age was something which didn't happen very often.

You would think these two factors alone would have changed things quite a bit with the way the Confederation was run and how people lived their lives, but apparently that was not the case in Hubbard's fantasy. Consider this: if you didn't die in the first place (at least not of natural causes) and you knew you were coming back around in a different body if you did die, just think about how you would go about doing things. What would be different in the world? Quite a bit I would imagine. Our culture's values, morality and concepts about the purpose of life and whatnot would be radically different from how we understand things from our current perspective.

Instead, Hubbard describes this world as being remarkably similar in dress, culture and appearance as 1950s and 1960s Earth. This part of the narrative really makes absolutely no sense at all considering a confederation population of trillions of people who lived for many millennia, experienced no natural death and had implant technology.

Regardless, Xemu had his body of loyal troops gather up these trillions of people. One of the ways this was done was by having them called in for tax audits. Apparently there were other methods used as well but Hubbard never elaborated on what those were. It took months to carry out this Confederacy-wide roundup and apparently no one noticed it was happening while it was going on, at least not soon enough to fight back or put a stop to it.

The citizens were knocked unconscious as they came in using a mixture of alcohol and glycol (injected straight into the lungs with a needle) and then frozen, perhaps in some kind of cryogenic storage or just literally frozen into ice cubes. The alcohol and glycol mixture would, according to Hubbard, knock thetans out. These frozen bodies - trillions of them - were then loaded into spaceships Hubbard described as looking like DC8 airplanes without "fans" (jet engines). Perhaps these spacecraft were also a hundred times the size of a DC8 and there must have been thousands of them to transport this many bodies, otherwise the idea of transporting trillions of people in DC8s is so ridiculous as to not even be conceivable.

Not all the population, of course, was captured this way. Apparently one of the maneuvers Xemu pulled was to have certain bodies of troops go in and collect up or exterminate mobs of citizens. Then a different body of troops would go in and eliminate the first body of military troops. In some fashion which is not made entirely clear, as these troops were killed off, they would be implanted and Hubbard says they "implanted each other" and laid waste to a lot of real estate in the process.

Hubbard describes those who were doing the capturing, flying the spacecraft and carrying out the implants as "renegades" but the explanation sort of stops there as to what their fate was. He simply says "they are gone." Details like that were apparently not really important to his narrative.

These thousands of DC8 space vessels flew the "billions and billions" of captured and unconscious Confederation citizenry to Teegeack. They dumped them in boxes all over the world.

The 250 billion people who were already here on Earth weren't dealt with the same way exactly. Hubbard said "nobody bothered to pick them up." The planet's administrators, government centers and other control points were just taken out, meaning only the Loyal Officers were gathered up specifically to keep them from getting in the way. Then the genocide was enacted and it engulfed all Teegeack's inhabitants in the process.

Over the course of thirty six days, all these trillions of people were killed and run through an extremely vicious series of implants. This was done using hydrogen bombs which were blown up specifically on the primary volcanoes in the world. I assume they did this because Hubbard thought it would have a greater destructive impact on the planet itself to blow up volcanoes and thus be more efficient in killing everyone off. He never does make it clear why they set the bombs off on volcanoes exactly.

These bombs vaporized everyone in an instant but before any of the trillions of now freed thetans could fly off or escape, electronic ribbons of standing waves (a type of force field) were erected and the winds sweeping over the planet from the explosions trapped them all. Over the next three days, they were transported back down to the surface, packed up and put in front of 3D projectors which implanted them with many of the OT II dichotomies (described above) and lots of other implants as well. These contained a lot of religious symbolism about God, the devil, crucifixion, space opera, etc. Additional imagery contained trains, cars, helicopters, crashes and other things which serve to make it even more confusing. Hubbard said the entirety of Catholicism was implanted during this time. At the same time, there were also implants given forcing us to only live for a short period of time, to get colds and illnesses as well as to suppress sexual urges.

Lastly, they were implanted with four or five different explanations for what just happened to them and who did it. The reason for all these implants was not only to confuse the thetans and distort their reality about who and what they are, but also get them to not be so keen to create things and thus, knockout any desire to procreate in the future.

The whole thing was an obvious solution for overpopulation. There might be a slight degree of sarcasm in that statement.

This went on for weeks until everyone was then brought to one of two places depending on where they landed geographically after the explosions. Everyone ended up in either Las Palmas or Hawaii. A sort of factory assembly line was setup and boxed everyone up again but this time these thetans were ejected out into space. Remember, this whole time, all this implanting was being done on thetans who did not have bodies. The bodies were destroyed by the atomic explosions.

Xemu remained back on the capitol planet but he was not as secure as he thought he was. There were surviving Loyal Officers who evaded or were missed by the pickup crews and renegade forces who rounded everyone else up. Xemu's administrators and renegade troops were caught off-guard when these Loyal Officers organized themselves and fought back. It took a year of fighting and what was left of the Galactic Confederation was in ruins, but the Loyal Officers did succeed in capturing Xemu. Within six years, they captured or killed the remainder of Xemu's followers.

Xemu and those followers who still lived were sentenced by the Loyal Officers to an eternity of prison. They were locked up in a mountain on one of the planets of the Confederation (Hubbard doesn't say which one), using a wire cage charged by an eternal battery. So Xemu is still alive out there somewhere but is not likely to ever get out.

Having no civilization left to rebuild and too few people to really build a new one, the Galactic Confederacy's few remaining inhabitants died out (despite their incredibly long life spans) and that was the end of that. This sector of the universe has been a desert ever since. It apparently didn't occur to any of the surviving Loyal Officers to come back to Teegeack and do anything about all the trillions of souls who were left to wander aimlessly for millions and millions of years with no clue as to their true nature or even identity.

Because of the implanting, no one involved has been able to remember any of what actually happened. Anyone who did manage to shake it off or start to recall bits or pieces of this have literally died (often by pneumonia, extreme insomnia or by having accidents, etc.). The nature of this incident is such that you cannot safely remember it without going through the procedures Hubbard laid out first (achieving Clear and the prior OT Levels), which is why this and all the OT Levels are kept confidential. Hubbard stated there is little chance of anyone just suddenly remembering any of this anyway, because thetans in an uncleared state (not having any Scientology) have too little awareness to be able to deal with anything like this.

Had that been all there was to this whole thing, it would have been horrifying enough. It would explain why people are so screwed up in this sector of the universe, at least, and give quite a beefy incident to run out using Scientology procedures. However, the most important part of this whole OT III incident is not the narrative, but the consequences of that narrative: *"One's body is a mass of individual thetans stuck to oneself or to the body."*

An apparent phenomenon in thetans who are killed together or experience traumatic episodes at the same time is they will sometimes cluster together as a group. They will be confused and act as a unit entity rather than a bunch of individuals. Thetans in such a condition are in a near unconscious state and lose their sense of individuality and personality. *Clustering* like this is a natural phenomenon due to the way thetans operate and make mental image pictures, which apparently attract other thetans. Knowing this, Xemu used this phenomenon. As thetans were gathered up after the explosions and packaged up in Las Palmas and Hawaii, they were purposefully clustered.

It is the clustering and mental confusion accompanying it which screw up these thetans so much, because they cannot differentiate between their thoughts, goals and intentions and those of the other thetans they are clustered with. It is a sort of ultimate in schizophrenia because while the individual thetans are often asleep or unconscious, from time to time they do come awake and start looking around or responding to what is going on. These reactions are confused by the main thetan occupying a body with his own thoughts, feelings and reactions.

Imagine a group of people stuck in a dark closet all talking at the same time. After weeks or months of this, the individuals in this closet would probably start having a hard time being able to tell the difference between what each of them were saying versus what other people were saying. They would start thinking other people's statements were actually something they themselves thought or said. I'm sure psychological studies of some kind have been done about this, but you don't need a study to imagine what kind of mental state these people would be in if they were in that closet for centuries or millennia. They would go quite insane. According to L. Ron Hubbard, this is the current spiritual state of every person on Earth.

Through the Solo auditing procedure of OT III, one sits silently in a room by oneself with an E-meter setup, and telepathically contacts each of these body thetans (BTs) and one-by-one releases them from this immobilized state so they can go off and have their own independent lives again. This is done by running each body thetan one contacts through the entirety of Incident 2 and then Incident 1. This releases them. This is all done silently with no verbal commands necessary.

The number of BTs varies from person to person, for obvious reasons. Clusters are random and stray thetans could also just come along and adhere to the body itself without being part of any of its existing clusters. A person could have many clusters attached to him at one time. Clusters are created by a common bad experience which they all share and which holds them together. There are many thousands of BTs adhered to each person on Earth.

When Xemu's genocide took place 75 million years ago, these clusters of thetans were so immobilized and stupefied by the whole catastrophe, most of them were unable to go anywhere else. They stayed here until mankind started to develop again about 20 million years ago on Earth. It's not clear how or why this new "body line" developed but once it did, these clusters started inhabiting these bodies and adhering to them.

These body thetans don't actually make up a body. They are simply attached to a body, either individually or in these clusters. Once they are contacted telepathically by a Scientologist using the OT III procedure and rehabilitated, they fly off and can get a body of their own or, as Hubbard puts it, they can just as easily go off and admire daisies. They are free of the clustering, though and will not be as susceptible to falling into such a trap again.

There is a lot of ancillary material in the OT materials to handle various complications and problems people have in handling BTs, but the above information is the mainline account of what it is all about and what Scientologists believe they are handling on the Wall of Fire. They are freeing trapped thetans who have been stuck for millions of years and giving them a chance at life again. In the process, they are also "emptying their closet" of all the ghost voices and random thoughts which they mistakenly believed were their own ideas and thoughts. This is supposed to have the effect of removing any and all feelings of life being overwhelming or confusing.

Scientologists who get to the level of OT III believe they have been given a window on the world which no one else has or even could have. This is *the* explanation for the horrendous state of existence all Mankind finds itself in, and the ultimate answer to bring about a world free of insanity, criminality and war, since it is Xemu's genocidal act which created what Hubbard called the Fourth Dynamic Engram. This is his term for the implant which literally creates urges to act insane or criminal and to make war.

The story is outlandish and more than a few ex-Scientologists who got to OT III said they had a hard time accepting it as literal truth. However it needs to be understood, in order for the OT Levels to "work" on someone, they have to accept this as literal truth a not as a parable or fable. I said the Xemu story is the least important part of OT III but that doesn't mean it's not supposed to be taken seriously. In fact, a person can't really move forward as an OT if they don't take all this as literal truth. They do believe Xemu really lived and all the rest of it really happened right here on Earth.

The original goal of OT III was to get rid of all the body thetans. However, Hubbard found that to be a much harder task than he originally thought, and so more OT levels were developed.

Becoming Cause Over Life

The next two OT Levels, IV and V, are delivered by an auditor and are not Solo auditing like OTs I-III.

As I described in the chapter on the Purification Rundown, in the late 1970s Hubbard came up with a scientifically unsound (and later invalidated) theory stating when a person takes drugs, residuals of those drugs stay in the body forever and can randomly go into "restimulation," meaning the drugs affect the person again. He believed this could even happen years after the drugs were taken. The fact Hubbard believed this indicates he never cracked a book on biochemistry, toxicology or actual biology but was just making up facts, like everything else he was a supposed expert on. Toxicologists know drugs and toxins do not stay in the body for any significant period of time, especially water-soluble drugs such as LSD or alcohol, which pass completely through the body within just hours of intake.

After coming up with these crank theories about drug toxins, Hubbard developed a whole new set of ideas about how drugs and drug residuals would affect clusters and BTs, and therefore a whole new OT Level had to be designed to deal with the "drug restimulation" these BTs experience. This is OT IV, the OT Drug Rundown.

The mental side of this picture is because thetans create mental image pictures of events and store them in a mind, these pictures can later come back and impinge on a person, making him act or think things similar to the contents of the pictures. This theory goes all the way back to *Dianetics: The Modern Science of Mental Health* and is a fundamental idea to Scientology. Taking drugs reactivates earlier pictures of taking drugs and can make a person experience the sensations, feelings, emotions and attitudes of earlier drug trips, in addition to what the current drugs are doing to the person's body in the here and now. Plus, once those earlier drug pictures are reactivated or restimulated that way, they can tend to stay stuck in place for a very long time (like years) and leave a person unable to think clearly or easily.

When clusters and BTs are added to the mix, they have their own sets of pictures from their own earlier experiences and many of those pictures will include incidents of taking drugs. Hubbard said earlier cultures on the whole track were much more heavily involved in drugs than our current one, and drugs were also used in implants as well.

To make matters worse, Hubbard claims the BTs and clusters who are stuck in whole track drug incidents not only continue to create (mock up) those earlier incidents but they also mock up the drug as well. He claimed the BTs were literally capable of creating drug tissues in a person's body in the here and now based on their memories of taking drugs in the past..

None of this really makes any sense because it's founded on unsubstantiated junk science which Hubbard literally invented out of thin air, but it makes for interesting reading. He claims by doing the Purification Rundown, getting rid of drug toxins in the body in the here and now actually "destimulates" the drug incidents of the person's BTs and can cause some of them to rehabilitate enough to leave the person's body. So this is a whole new additional benefit to the Purification Rundown which was heretofore unknown.

Conversely, OT IV was invented because some of the BTs and clusters are so stuck in earlier drug incidents they can't be run through Incident 1 and Incident 2 until the drug incidents are handled first. So OT IV is the procedure for handling them.

Once the BTs who have been stuck because of drugs have been dealt with, the next phase of BT/cluster handling is started with OT V.

The Living Lightning

Hubbard refers to OT V, VI and VII as the NOTs Band (the abbreviations and neologisms truly never end in Scientology). NOTs is New Era Dianetics for OTs. Without getting too detailed or involved in a bunch of technical details, there was a period of time after the initial release of OT III where Dianetics techniques were still being used on OTs to handle Incident 1 and Incident 2 but this was difficult for some OTs to do.

A Clear in Scientology is someone who no longer has his own reactive mind and is not supposed to think using mental image pictures. When a person runs Dianetics, they are supposed to be going back in time by looking at their mental image pictures and relating to the auditor what they see, feel, hear, etc. So in explaining why OTs were having difficulty running Dianetics, he said the reason for this had to do with the BTs and clusters furnishing pictures from their own past; this would confuse the hell out of the person trying to run the Dianetics recall procedures and it would just end up in a big ball of mess. They weren't running their own pictures, they were running a BT's pictures.

NOTs was originally developed to handle this situation and get these OTs straightened out. It seems odd because after OT III and OT IV, a person should not really have any more BTs to have to deal with, but Hubbard said the end result of OT III only gives one the *apparency* of having run out all the BTs and clusters. OT IV uncovers more BTs who were hidden by drug incidents but this is only the beginning.

As mentioned earlier, the phenomenon of clustering and thetans adhering to bodies didn't start with the Xemu incident. Degraded and/or near-unconscious thetans have been wandering the universe for millennia and can come along and light on a body at any time. Hubbard said "...you're living in a universe which is crawling with this type of stuff."[6]

When a person completes OT III, they have only reached those BTs and clusters which were *easily* communicated with. NOTs was developed to reach the rest of them, what Hubbard refers to as Dormant BTs. And what's more, he says there are lots of them.

The first part of NOTs is OT V, done with an auditor. Various procedures and methods are run which address different aspects of why a person would have difficulty spotting and handling BTs and clusters. There are many such steps. These are done with the auditor until the person reaches a point of stability and gain and can then move on to handle the rest of the BTs himself as a Solo auditor.

At this point, the person does a long course (OT VI) which teaches them how to be a Solo NOTs auditor. It is strictly a training step done in a course room (only delivered at the Flag Service Org in Clearwater, Florida) until the final steps when they practice Solo auditing under supervision.

Once ready to carry on by themselves, the Scientologist is allowed to go home and do Solo auditing sessions multiple times per day, every single day, until they telepathically get rid of all their BTs. This is OT VII. They are not allowed to skip even one day, rain or shine, and are expected to do up to five or even seven Solo sessions a day. Usually sessions last anywhere from 5-30 minutes.

In the NOTs materials, Hubbard makes many claims about the problems of life caused by BTs. Chronic illnesses and physical conditions are all explained in terms of the BTs causing them, even deafness or blindness. By addressing these BTs, chronic physical conditions are supposed to be relieved or healed fully. Scientologists truly believe NOTs will deal with these things despite the easily demonstrated reality of many Scientologists who have done NOTs auditing still wearing glasses, developing the same problems in old age everyone else does and dying of such usual conditions as heart disease and cancer.

Another interesting but very odd thing Hubbard says on this level is the massive collection of body thetans and clusters form an image of the person's body and this is what a thetan perceives when he looks at the body he is running. The solidity of the body is this mass of BTs and clusters and not the body itself, because once all the clusters are gone, the *"basic biological structure of the body is transparent to a thetan."* This doesn't really make any sense but it has to do with the end result of the NOTs band, so it has to be mentioned.

Hubbard specifically states the goal of NOTs is *"a transparent body which does not interfere with the sight of the thetan and is free from unwanted sensations, pains or pressures."*[8]

As more and more BTs are blown off, the person's "mass" becomes less and his attention goes more and more out to the environment around him. Soon he's directly perceiving the physical universe rather than using the body as a conduit, e.g. the thetan is able to directly perceive the feeling of walls without having to have the body walk over and touch it with its fingers.

Also, the person doing NOTs can also start to perceive and blow BTs off *other* people's bodies in their environment. This happens once he has gotten rid of so many of his own BTs he begins casting around in the environment looking for more and may find other people's instead. OTs sometimes claim they have handled situations or problems with people who are remote from them, even on the other side of the country. This story explains why they think they can.

The end result of NOTs is the person has a transparent body and a clear area around it to some distance. There are no more BTs stuck to them in the here and now. As a result, the person is supposed to realize he is alive and very much himself (as opposed to all these old personalities he was confusing himself with). This is interpreted in Scientology as being "cause over life."

All Roads Lead to Auditing

Ever since Scientology first started, all roads have led to auditing. The key to improving individuals in Scientology, the most important thing it can do, is to eradicate the reactive mind and, having done that, release all the BTs and clusters trapped on and around a pre-OT. Once those things are done, and only with those done, can a person have any chance of regaining supernatural powers and realizing their true potential.

All the training, study and social betterment activities Scientologists perform mean nothing if the above is not being achieved. This is why there is so much emphasis in the Scientology world on "getting up The Bridge" and getting into auditing sessions at all. In the end, nothing else matters.

This is also why if Scientologists pay attention to social betterment activities at all, such as passing out *The Way to Happiness* books, getting people off drugs through their Narconon program or going out to provide relief at disaster sites, such help is given grudgingly if at all. Most Scientologists would rather write a check than actually go do something themselves or get their hands dirty. This isn't pure laziness on their part nor are they mean-spirited or don't want to see things get better.

It's that they truly don't think those activities are going to do much of anything compared to what they can do as OTs when they can sit down in a room by themselves and telepathically command their personal demons to go away.

They believe by erasing their reactive minds and releasing their BTs, they convert entheta into theta. Every BT they release is one more live, causative being restored to life and who will go get a body and hopefully, eventually turn up in a Scientology organization to do the rest of The Bridge. The higher they go up the OT Levels, the more theta they believe they are releasing.

Scientologists have credited their auditing with producing miracles in the real world such as healing chronic life-threatening illnesses, changing dangerous weather conditions and even bringing down the Berlin Wall.

South Park got it right: upper level Scientologists really do believe in Xemu and the whole story with the volcanoes and the DC8s. As I've laid out here, they also believe a whole lot more.

This is how Scientologists believe they are saving the world. It sounds ridiculous because when you get down to it, it is ridiculous. And that is Scientology.

12. Scientology's PR Problem
(Let's talk about OSA)

To anyone who pays attention to the Church of Scientology on a fairly regular basis, it has become obvious over the past couple of years its public image has taken repeated (well-deserved) beatings. It's so bad at this point I believe it has passed the point of no return. There is no road for Scientology to regain a favorable public image and it's only going down from here.

What's not so obvious is why this has happened.

We critics of the Church can only stand with our mouths open in shock when we see some of the more insane displays of hate and fear high-level Scientologists demonstrate when the cameras are rolling. I can only imagine the horror Church members themselves must feel when they see how their organization represents itself to the world at large. Believe me, despite the Church's internal demands on its members to not watch or read anything bad about Scientology, the widespread accessibility of mass media in this day and age makes it impossible to censor the truth anymore.

There are reasons the Church of Scientology acts so blatantly against its own best interests and I'm going to break down some of those reasons for you. With more exposés and full-blown documentaries about Scientology on the horizon, I want to also lay out what we can expect to see from the Church in response to these and why their responses are only going to make matters worse for them.

The Office of Special Affairs (OSA)

I think most people who have any awareness of Scientology know about the Office of Special Affairs, the Church's legal division. In fact, much of the Church's bad PR is due to the hard work of OSA's Investigation and Legal departments, including the non-Scientologist lawyers and private investigators they hire to actually carry out most of their dirty work. When you see Scientology stalking and harassing its ex-members, for example, you are seeing these investigators and lawyers doing their daily work.

What many may not realize is OSA also has a Public Relations department fully responsible for the Church's external public image and media representation.

Public Relations is an important subject for any group, company or organization. Technically, it's the practice of managing the spread of information between the individual or group and the rest of the world, the public. Billions of dollars are spent every year on PR. Some do it better than others, but it's safe to say almost anything you see in any mass media outlet has been directly affected by professional PR work.

By any yardstick you care to use, OSA has done an absolutely horrendous job for many years. It's degenerated so badly there hasn't even been a public media representative or international spokesman for Scientology since Tommy Davis disappeared in 2011. It took two years just for the public to find out Mr. Davis left the employment of the Church along with his wife and does his absolute best to stay out of the limelight now. No one is stepping up to take his place.

When you look at the press releases, promotional materials and commercials put out by Scientology, it's difficult to understand just what public image they are trying to create or maintain. All they ever seem to talk about is fundraising for bigger buildings, giving money to their International Association of Scientologists membership fund or making their members re-do services over and over again because supposedly they weren't doing them right the last time. Of course, their members have to pay for the privilege of these re-dos each time, making this hamster wheel an endless source of incoming cash for Scientology's coffers.

It seems as if this organization does nothing except raise money for itself.

Hubbard's PR Series

L. Ron Hubbard wrote a series of policies in the early 1970s called the "Public Relations Series". These gave the operational directions for anyone in the Church who was going to engage in public relations. It's interesting to look at a few of these and see how Hubbard set the stage early on for the cataclysmic failures they are now experiencing.

Like every other subject he wrote about, Hubbard claimed he was the only person able to figure out the real laws and workable procedures to execute successful public relations. Instead, what he actually offered was a contradictory set of rules which look like they might make sense on the surface, but when you try to use them you end up in a total mess.

One example is when Hubbard talks about the use of truth in PR in a policy letter from August 13, 1970, PR Series 2, THE MISSING INGREDIENT:

"The more lies you use in PR the more likely it is that the PR will recoil.

"Thus the law:

"NEVER USE LIES IN PR."

Scientologists read this and they think it's Church policy to never tell lies and therefore everything OSA ever says must be true. Right? Not so fast. Because just a little later in this same policy Hubbard then says:

"Handling truth is a touchy business also. You don't have to tell everything you know.... Tell an acceptable truth.

...

"SO PR becomes the technique of communicating an acceptable truth - and which will attain the desirable result.

"If there's no chance of obtaining the desirable result and the truth would injure, then talk about something else."

In PR Series 16, PR TEXTS, Hubbard even faults a PR textbook because *"It continually advises frankness with the press to a point where a PR, using that, could easily create situations of out-PR."*

The problem here is in Scientology an 'acceptable truth' is defined as anything they want it to mean, so long as it is used to attain what they consider to be a desirable result.

Orwellian Redefinition of Terms

George Orwell was the pen name of author Eric Arthur Blair, famous for such works as *Animal Farm* and *1984*. He was a brilliant essayist and a lifelong opponent of totalitarianism. Amongst many other things, Orwell wrote about the clever use of language in politics and media, and how language can be altered for PR purposes to fool the masses into agreeing with losing their own rights and freedoms. To demonstrate what he was talking about, Orwell is the one who invented terms like *cold war, Big Brother, thought police* and *doublethink*. If you have never read any of Orwell's essays or books, I cannot recommend them enough.

Hubbard knew of Orwell's work. He wrote a whole issue about the redefinition of words for propaganda purposes on October 5, 1971 in the PR Series.

But instead of agreeing with what Orwell had to say about this dangerous practice in thought control, Hubbard actually encouraged its use in Scientology PR. In what has to be considered a truly Orwellian twist, Hubbard wrote:

"Many instances of this [re-definition of terms] *exist. They are not 'natural' changes in language. They are propaganda changes, carefully planned and campaigned in order to obtain a public-opinion advantage for the group doing the propaganda.*

"The technique is good or bad depending on the ultimate objective of the propagandist.

"'Psychiatry' and 'psychiatrist' are easily redefined to mean 'an antisocial enemy of the people.' This takes the kill-crazy psychiatrist off the preferred

list of professions. This is a good use of the technique as for a century the psychiatrist has been setting an all-time record for inhumanity to man.

"The redefinition of words is done by associating different emotions and symbols with the word than were intended."

"A consistent, repeated effort is the key to any success with this technique of propaganda.

"One must know how to do it."[1]

Hubbard literally advised Scientologists to do the very thing Orwell spent his entire life fighting against, trying to prevent totalitarian dictatorships from destroying the rights of Man. These are the kinds of curves Hubbard threw into almost every subject he wrote about.

So how does this get done in Scientology? Well, here's one recent example.

Scientology was founded on the precept its counseling procedures, called auditing, would free a person of past trauma and stress and eventually they will reach a state of personal spiritual immortality. Hubbard was crystal clear such a state was only achieved through lots and lots of auditing. The full amount of spiritual trauma any person carries around is called their "case" in Scientology, so personal improvement is called "case gain".

If you look at recent promotional mailers and flyers from building fundraisers and the IAS, they are promising case gain can be had by just the act of donating money.

There is certainly nothing wrong with feeling good by giving money to what someone thinks is a worthy cause. People do that every day with thousands of different charities. Scientology is not a charity and giving money to the IAS is the equivalent of burning it in a fireplace, but that's not my point.

The real point here is case gain has now been re-defined by the IAS to mean the feeling you get when you give money to them. This is a purposeful, calculated promotional action to redefine the very basics of what Scientology is all about.

By the way, L. Ron Hubbard never authorized or approved of the IAS. Despite his numerous shortcomings (and they were legion), he was very clear in his policies: people were supposed to get materials and services for their money. There was supposed to be an exchange. The IAS is the brainchild of David Miscavige, who used it to rake in millions of dollars to pay for his own legal defense so he could avoid prosecution by the IRS and other government agencies. There is no evidence Miscavige even let Hubbard know the IAS existed.

If you wanted to turn Scientology into a purely money-making enterprise, it would be necessary to first redefine the terms used to describe the gains you get from Scientology. It would be necessary to make it seem like giving money for nothing was just as good, if not better, as giving money for something. They have succeeded in this and Scientologists are now so deluded they think giving money to criminals gives them personal spiritual immortality.

Creepy People doing Creepy Things

When the chips are down and things aren't going their way, many people can get desperate and start to do desperate things. When you cannot compete in the arena of ideas and tell the truth about what you are actually doing, all that's left is to attack and resort to violence. So we come to where Scientology is now and their responses to critics.

Since Anonymous started exposing the Church of Scientology's criminal activities on an international scale in 2008 using the power of the internet, Scientology has been reeling from blow after blow. The truth is a powerful weapon and the internet is a platform Scientology cannot control.

Despite claiming to have recall of advanced galactic civilizations dating back trillions of years, somehow Hubbard never conceived of the internet, nor was he able to write any operating policies for the Church to deal with mass media dissemination of anti-Scientology information. Up until he died, Hubbard's policies all concerned censorship and intimidating his enemies into silence through threats and force. These kinds of strong arm tactics only work on individuals, similar to how grade school bullies intimidate children into never tattling on them. That's not possible with the internet, so the truth about the Church remains out there despite its best efforts to stop it.

Realizing they were not going to have much success using their old tactics, Scientology attempted a series of attacks using disinformation, trying to paint Anonymous as a terrorist organization. The Church literally made up a story Anonymous threatened to blow up bombs on church property. This was later disproven and recoiled back on the Church badly.

In addition, on February 4, 2008 a video was posted by Ruthie Heyerdahl. This was in response to a specific video Anonymous posted with a Call to Action to publicly demonstrate outside Scientology churches against the human rights abuses Scientology perpetrates on its members.

Ruthie appears to be spontaneously speaking out as a non-Scientologist against Anonymous. However, as with everything associated with Scientology, looks can be deceiving.

She was, in fact, a Scientologist actress or at least someone who had Scientology services as far back as 2002. How far she got or whether she is still doing services is not clear. She removed her entire YouTube channel and almost all online traces of herself after the massively negative responses she received to her pro-Scientology stance back in 2008.

The negative feedback was well deserved, but why am I even talking about a video from 2008 now? Because this video was, in fact, a carefully scripted and orchestrated work by the Office of Special Affairs to counter not only that Anonymous protest, but every attack brought against the Church since.

This video represents the best OSA has to offer in terms of a seemingly reasoned response against people critical of the Church. The lines used in this video are still in use by the Church today and are the same ones they are going to continue to use to try to shut down critics.

You can find the Ruthie video online easily enough and since this is a book, I can't reproduce it here but I am going to quote from it and analyze the important statements she makes. These lines are used by OSA in print as well as video media to counter critics and anti-Scientology media to this day, which is why this analysis is applicable to more than just the 2008 Ruthie video.

They begin the video with these two lines:

"I just saw something that totally creeps me out. Wow."

"I just think it's really weird."

These purposefully set the tone for what's coming, using these exact phrases to describe the Call to Action video from Anonymous. Using words this way is a technique called "guilt by association". The listener is supposed to get the idea Anonymous is now creepy and weird. Later in the video she also describes Scientology protesters themselves as "strange" "fake" and even uses the word "evil".

"I don't know what exactly they plan on protesting. Religious freedom? Constitutional rights? C'mon guys, really?"

Now this part is crucial. In fact, most of the video hangs on this statement. This is called a straw man argument, and all it means is she is inventing completely different reasons for why Anonymous is protesting Scientology, and she will then use these invented reasons to ridicule Anonymous throughout the rest of her rant.

This is a very common technique in PR and is used all the time by people who can't argue the facts and instead want to distract from the real issues by putting words in their opponents' mouths.

She is specifically avoiding the real issue, which is Scientology brutalizing its members, especially those in the Sea Org, and engaging in outright criminal activity on an almost daily basis. Those are the issues OSA PRs cannot and will not address directly. Instead, they throw out misdirectors every single time these issues are brought to light.

This also conforms with the Hubbard PR policy I mentioned earlier of avoiding the truth by simply not talking about it.

Right after this misdirection, Ruthie reveals her actual loyalties by showering unwarranted praise on the "ton" of Scientologist friends she has. She describes all of them as *involved, ethical, friendly, so happy* and says they *have such a purpose in life.* They *try to make a difference.* She implies they vote without saying they do, but then says they are *the most involved people* she's ever met, they *care* and are *great.* She even reiterates they *make a difference.*

I have no doubt all these qualities came from surveys Scientology did of the general public to find out what would be desirable qualities in friends or relations. These words have nothing to do with how Scientologists actually act, as proven over and over again by the horror stories literally thousands of ex-Scientologists have told over the past three decades.

Now just stop and think about this for a second. When was the last time you saw a Scientologist making a difference in any community anywhere? Beyond maybe a few random acts of kindness from individual Scientologists, have you ever seen the Church of Scientology do much of anything for anyone which didn't serve its own interests?

Even non-critical journalists and students who have gone into Churches of Scientology have come out writing articles about how the staff were uncaring, robotic, pushy and only wanted to sell them something.

Keep in mind Scientology is not supposed to be a business. It calls itself a religion. When was the last time you went into a Catholic church, a Jewish synagogue or even a Mormon temple and someone tried to sell you something?

Ruthie goes on to say:

"To protestors, all I can say is I don't really understand what you expect to accomplish, like the US government is going to be like 'Oh right, Scientology, no it's not actually a religion. We were just kidding.' I don't think that's going to happen."

She now addresses the protesters directly in an attempt to discourage them by setting up another straw man. She purposefully exaggerates and alters the goal of the protests to be taking away the Church's religious recognition when that's not the issue at all.

"I mean, I'm not a Scientologist but I'm not the type of person that's just going to sit there and let a religious group be bashed. What time do we live in where it's normal to bash someone's religion? Are you joking me?"

This is interesting because she's positioning herself as a non-Scientologist, something we know OSA has done many times when they comment on websites or blogs or news articles to try to make it look like the general public is in agreement with the Church when the exact opposite is the truth. This is more than a PR action and actually goes over into a kind of covert operation; something which Hubbard said was sloppy and desperate in his PR policies.

As for the religion-bashing, this is just another misdirection because no one was protesting their religiosity.

She then plays the "think for yourself" card by challenging anyone watching to actually go into a Scientology organization and ask questions. She even goes so far as to accuse the viewer of being afraid to find out directly from Scientology what they are all about.

There's absolutely nothing wrong with thinking for yourself. In fact, I highly encourage it in every aspect of your life. I've talked at length in my videos and articles about how Scientology refuses to let its own members think for themselves, so I won't belabor their hypocrisy again here. If you have never been in a Church of Scientology and you want to go into one, go for it.

However, realize going in and talking to one person at the lowest levels of an organization is not going to provide you with any real information about its true operations because you're talking to people who themselves don't know. The corruption in Scientology is at its highest levels, not its lowest.

Beyond all that, let's talk about the underlying assumption behind this "think for yourself" challenge. Scientologists assume if you don't like Scientology, it's simply because you don't understand it or know anything about it. Because they think it's the greatest thing since sliced bread, they are absolutely certain you would too if you only give it a chance.

This is an unwarranted assumption but it is a fundamental thread which runs through all their promotion and marketing materials and every Scientologist's view toward the rest of the world. They believe this because L. Ron Hubbard tells them to in his books and lectures. Like any other destructive cult, they are absolutely sure they have all the answers to every single issue to plague anyone.

The facts they are failing miserably in their own conquest of the world and Scientologists continue to die of cancer and other diseases, file for bankruptcy and have the same life problems as the rest of us, do not seem to shake their faith in the slightest.

No amount of talking to Scientologists or reading L. Ron Hubbard's works is going to change the fact Scientology just isn't universally workable nor does it have universal appeal.

The Joker in the Deck

Everything I've gone over here is how Scientology PR operates according to Hubbard's directions. However, there is another joker in the deck and this person has actually radically altered the entire face and character of Scientology. That person, of course, is David Miscavige.

None of Scientology's PR activities make any sense if you look at them against the gauge of what an organization should be doing to expand itself.

Unlike Hubbard, Miscavige does not care at all about Scientology expanding or growing or conquering the world. He really doesn't.

You can listen to the words someone says, even if they continue to mouth them year after year, and think that's what they're doing, but any executive or leader is going to reveal his true intentions through the actions his organization takes under his leadership and what it actually produces versus what it says its producing.

For example, if someone leading a religious crusade in this day and age was serious about it, they would be promoting their crusade on every conceivable media channel, repeatedly and continually, using as many of their resources and as much of their money as they could possibly round up.

Yet where are these campaigns? Where is Scientology in the mass media? The last time there was any international media campaign of any note was in the 1980s when *Dianetics: The Modern Science of Mental Health* was being marketed with TV commercials as well as radio and print ads. Dianetics household name recognition rose from 30% to 90% over the course of a year and *Dianetics* hit the New York Times Bestseller List again in 1988, thirty-eight years after it was first written.[2] Jefferson Hawkins was the mastermind behind that campaign and he was ousted by David Miscavige personally for treasonous conduct. What treasonous activity was Jeff carrying out? Trying to promote Scientology!

David Miscavige's actions show he does not care one bit about the dissemination of Scientology. He only cares about himself. And when you look at Scientology's more recent media activities in that light, everything starts to make sense.

A few years ago, Scientology purchased the old KCET television studios a couple miles away from their Los Angeles headquarters. Miscavige has been promising they are going to renovate these studios at great expense and open up a 24/7 broadcasting station emitting L. Ron Hubbard's works on all media channels.

Now why would they do this when they've already invested millions of dollars in facilities to do the same thing more than twenty years ago? They're called Golden Era Productions and not one Scientologist could argue with me about this because they've seen the pictures and videos of their beautiful multi-million dollar, state-of-the-art audio and video production facility in Hemet, California.

If Miscavige wanted Hubbard on the airwaves 24/7, he could have had it 20 years ago.

This broadcasting station is just the latest gimmick, a pack of lies designed to keep Scientologists pumped up and giving more and more of their money. As I write this, these new KCET facilities were supposed to have been opened up 6 months ago and each new opening date is pushed further and further back, yet the fundraising for this facility never stops. Like the Super Power building in Clearwater, Florida, which did not open for 25 years, this KCET studio is a money pit which will not be opened until millions upon millions of dollars are fundraised for it out of Scientologists' pockets. Not because this money is needed to open the facility, but simply because Scientologists are so gullible they think that is the case and they so desperately want to see Scientology thought well of by their non-Scientology family and friends.

I think it's clear I am no fan of L. Ron Hubbard but after studying the man's works for decades, I have a pretty good sense of what he was about. He was a narcissist and megalomaniac. Yet despite that, Church expansion was important to him. He wanted Scientology to succeed. He cared about dissemination and marketing, so much so he worked hands-on to make films and promotion himself to ensure it was done the way he wanted it done. It might not have been very good promotional material, but under Hubbard's watch, Scientology grew. That is undeniable, historical fact.

Since Miscavige has taken over in the 1980s, it has been one disaster after another and Scientology is now the world's fastest shrinking religion. The Church has always refused to give any hard numbers when it comes to their membership, but all evidence points to the fact there are less than 30,000 members worldwide, including their own staff.

Scientology now is just a parade of flashy gimmicks and vacuous statements made by a dancing clown on a stage to keep the money coming in. Every single thing David Miscavige does is done for only one reason: to keep himself in a position of power which he can lord over others. Whether Scientology grows or shrinks is inconsequential next to his selfish purpose.

It's pretty sad when you think about all those thousands of people through the years who have been conned. They can't seem to throw their money at Miscavige fast enough.

On second thought, maybe Hubbard's PR policies aren't so ineffective after all.

Chapter 13. The Insanity Which is Scientology's Organizational Structure

All Scientologists wonder why Scientology isn't as successful as they think it should be. The Ideal Orgs are not filling up with new people and the church takes a beating in the media and courtrooms almost every day. Working in a Scientology organization can be a maddening experience but it's not immediately obvious to most people why this is so.

Everyone in the organization believes it should make sense and should work because it was designed by L. Ron Hubbard, and as far as they are concerned, he is infallible. But the proof it doesn't work is right before their eyes: empty buildings and a shrinking membership.

The structure Hubbard designed actually violates his own rules for how life operates, yet somehow he thought it would work anyway.

But there's more to the story than this. A lot more. Because while most Scientologists believe Hubbard's system is how things are run, there are all sorts of things which don't make any sense even after you understand the management system. The reason for that is the entire structure was actually subverted almost from its very inception in the early 1980s. I'm going to show you exactly how this happened.

By the end of this chapter, you will understand more about how the Church of Scientology operates than most people who are in it. If you are a member of Scientology right now, or were a member in the past, I think this is going to explain a lot about why you might have found your experience with the church has been so....unsatisfying.

We'll start at the bottom and work our way up. There is a chart in Appendix 3 which shows the entire org structure from top to bottom.

Class V Organizations

A Class V organization - called an "org" for short - delivers beginning and intermediate Scientology services. They are called Class V orgs because the highest level of training they provide is called the Class V Course on the Scientology Bridge to Total Freedom. An org is also supposed to be able to take its parishioners all the way up to the state of Clear, but most of them lack the trained personnel to do this. Orgs are usually located in major or capital cities.

Sea Org Organizations

Above Class V orgs, there are Sea Org orgs, meaning larger service organizations staffed only by Sea Organization members and which deliver higher level Scientology services such as the confidential OT Levels. These are located on Sea Org bases around the world such as in Los Angeles, California; Clearwater, Florida; East Grinstead, England; and Copenhagen, Denmark.

The Sea Organization

The Sea Organization was formed in 1967 and is a group of Scientologists who are bound together around the common purpose to forward, uphold and carry out Command Intention, meaning they swear an oath to follow the orders of whomever is in charge of the Church of Scientology. Originally their leader was L. Ron Hubbard. When he died in 1986, David Miscavige publicly took over running all Scientology operations and has been the leading officer of the Sea Org ever since.

Anything Miscavige orders is considered Command Intention.

Hubbard told Scientologists Sea Org members are the "aristocracy of Scientology". They are run with military-style discipline and traditions, such as wearing uniforms, holding naval ranks like Petty Officer and Lieutenant and calling seniors "Sir".

Brevet ranks exist in the SO, meaning ranks one gets temporarily because of a job or position they hold. For example, someone could be a Commander temporarily because they are holding a senior executive position at the highest levels of the Church, even though the rank they have earned as a Sea Org member could be quite lower. When Hubbard was alive, he designated himself as Commodore, but he was the only one who ever held that rank; now the highest position is a Captain. According to documents the Church filed with the IRS in 1992, Captain David Miscavige is the only Captain in the Sea Org who holds the rank on a permanent basis. In other words, he is the highest ranking officer in the Sea Org and has been for decades. However, besides personnel at Int Management level, rank has very little importance in the Sea Org beyond conferring a little bit of status.

Only Sea Org members may hold management positions in the Church's hierarchy and only Sea Org members are given the rights to deliver the confidential upper level services. Sea Organization members also hold positions of authority in every lower-echelon Scientology service organization. They keep an eye on things and act as representatives of senior management authority.

Sea Org members move between different posts and different organizations at the whim of Sea Org executives, who decide how to meet whatever personnel demands are the order of the day. A Sea Org member can be a senior Scientology executive at the highest levels one day and re-posted as a janitor in a lower organization the next day. I've actually seen such demotions happen right in front of me by verbal order. There is very little stability in the life of a Sea Org member.

In fact, no matter what their rank, position or standing, Sea Org members can be removed from their positions at any time and sent to the Rehabilitation Project Force if it is deemed they have somehow betrayed the Sea Org or not followed Command Intention.

What's so interesting about the Sea Org is it has no legal existence; it's not a corporation or even a membership trust like the IAS. Yet it *is* the group which unquestionably runs Scientology internationally, which is why it is impossible to talk about Scientology's management structure without understanding it.

Continents

For administrative purposes, Scientology divided the world into nine arbitrary "continents". They are Canada, Western United States, Eastern United States, Latin America, United Kingdom, Europe, Italy, Africa and Australia/New Zealand. There is a satellite office for Russia which is under the domain of Europe, while East Asia falls under Australia. Each of these continental areas has a Continental Liaison Office or CLO which manages all the Scientology activities in its area. The CLOs are like umbrella organizations which house all the various Scientology management activities for their zone.

International Liaison Office and Int Base

In Hollywood, California is the International Liaison Office or ILO, which runs all the CLOs. ILO also houses various management units, all run by the Sea Org and similar in structure to the CLOs. ILO is run by International Management, which is located on the Gold Base in Hemet, California. This location is kept secret from Scientologists but it's a well-known fact on the internet.

ED Int and Int Management Executive Committee

At the Gold Base, you have the Executive Director International (ED Int) and his staff, collectively known as the International Management Executive Committee. This is the highest managing body in the Church of Scientology. ED Int and his staff develop international strategies to expand all parts of Scientology.

For example, one of ED Int's staff is responsible for all audio-visual aspects of Scientology like the films and videos used in orgs. Technical Training Films are a key part of auditor training and show Scientologists who are training to be auditors what auditing is supposed to look and sound like. So the Audio-Visual Executive International

(A/V Exec Int) might work out a strategy to get all the films popularized so more people want to see them (and therefore get more people wanting to train). He would write programs for orgs to popularize the films.

However, he and the other Executive Committee staff do *not* directly tell the orgs to do those programs. Instead, the A/V Exec Int sends the program to ILO and it sends the program down to the CLOs and on down to the orgs. There are people in ILO and CLO who then follow through step-by-step and get the orgs to perform each step of the program. ILO and CLO don't write programs; they get programs done. This is how Scientology management is supposed to work at its most basic level.

What I've explained so far is roughly as much as the average Scientologist understands about the management structure. It seems like it makes sense and should be easy to run. Most Scientologists probably think David Miscavige is the Chairman of the Board of this international management council and that's where he sits in the big picture.

But, no...that's not how it works.

Watchdog Committee

Let's take a look at another body which fits on top of this whole thing, called the Watchdog Committee. Now why have a committee of watchdogs over this management structure?

After the Guardian's Office was caught in the mid-1970s infiltrating the US Government, something had to be done to make sure no one was going to get carried away with violating the law so flagrantly. It's not that the GO operated independently of Hubbard's wishes or he didn't know what they were up to. It's the fact they got caught and from Scientology's point of view, that was totally not okay.

In order to keep it from happening again, Hubbard came up with the idea of the Watchdog Committee. They oversee all the various sectors of Scientology - the locals orgs, the missions, the upper level Sea

Org organizations like Flag and the Freewinds, and even internal bodies like Golden Era Productions and the Office of Special Affairs.

There's an individual in the Watchdog Committee for each of these sectors and then an overall chairman for the Committee known as the WDC Chairman. Their job is not to personally run their sectors. They aren't "management" per se. They are supposed to make sure management actually manages, each sector is receiving correct direction and guidance, the policies governing their sectors make sense and everything within each sector is smooth as glass.

To be crystal clear, the WDC Chairman is *not* David Miscavige. He has no position with WDC.

In order to do their jobs, WDC members need to get information, issue orders and confirm compliance to those orders. How do they do that? WDC was given a police organization called the Commodore's Messenger Org or CMO.

Commodore's Messenger Org (CMO)

When Hubbard was running things on ships back in the 1960s and 1970s, he had children and teenagers working for him as message carriers and basically servants. They would run around the ship being his eyes and ears. When Scientology management operations moved from sea back to land in the mid-to-late 1970s, Hubbard retained his messengers and made them into their own little sub-organization. Some of them carried on as his personal servants while others were put in higher positions of trust. Being directly under L. Ron Hubbard, they carried a great deal of authority. When one addressed a Messenger, one acted as though he were addressing Hubbard personally.

When Scientology management was reorganized in the late 1970s and the Watchdog Committee was created, it was only natural for these Messengers to be placed under command of the Watchdog Committee as its eyes and ears. That way they could continue to ensure Hubbard's directives and orders were followed. In fact, the WDC Chairman is the Commanding Officer of the CMO.

You see, from the late 1970s up until Hubbard died in 1986, he wasn't supposed to be managing Scientology directly. To avoid criminal prosecution for the whole Guardian's Office fiasco as well as tax evasion and other legal situations, Hubbard supposedly removed himself from management lines entirely. So the CMO were the people who openly took over handling all Scientology management. Of course, Hubbard was still giving orders but these were called "advices". If you've ever heard of LRH Advices and wondered why they were called that, it's because they couldn't legally be called "orders" even though that's exactly what they were.

So here were WDC and CMO overseeing Int Management and all the other levels down to the orgs. And this is where we start getting to the crux of the problem; this is where the structure of this whole thing actually violates basic Scientology principles.

Conditions of Existence

In Scientology, there are Conditions of Existence. Simply put, a *condition* is the operating state or situation any individual, group, body or nation is in at any time. There is a table of conditions in Scientology, from top to bottom:

Power
Affluence
Normal
Emergency
Danger
Non-Existence

There are conditions below Non-Existence but we won't go into those here because they aren't important to the point of this chapter.

It should be obvious in looking at this chart one would strive to maintain at least Normal and would want to be in Affluence or Power most of the time. One would certainly not want to be stuck in Danger, because that's just one step up from Non-Existence. And Non-Existence means exactly what it says - you don't exist.

So a fundamental law about these conditions, according to L. Ron Hubbard, is if someone is on a command line and they are bypassed by anyone for any reason, the bypassed person is immediately in a condition of Danger. For example, let's say Joe is the head of a division. One day Joe's boss comes in and directly orders one of Joe's juniors to do something. His boss has bypassed him - meaning he ignored Joe and skipped the chain of command.

This puts Joe in a bad spot because what if he didn't even know what happened? He is working with his division to get Project X done on a tight schedule and now Joe finds one of his juniors is randomly hard at work on Project Y because his boss told them to. That is exactly why Hubbard called it a Danger condition. Just by the fact a senior person to Joe issued orders to one of Joe's juniors and then Joe's junior accepted and acted on those orders - that alone puts Joe in the condition of Danger.

There is a *lot* more to know about these conditions in terms of how they are used in Scientology, but for this purpose of this chapter, the above is all we need cover for now. Scientologists use these conditions to govern their lives and actions and decide how well they are doing personally, in relationships, their jobs, etc.

Let's now look at how WDC and CMO are supposed to do their jobs.

How WDC Works

Golden Era Production makes films. So let's say WDC Gold wonders why the Films Unit at Gold is not getting out enough new films on schedule. He sends a Messenger in to investigate. The Messenger does so and determines it's because the Films Unit is undermanned and it's just physically impossible for them to meet their production quotas no matter how many hours of sleep they lose or how many of them are threatened with the RPF.

WDC Gold then writes a program, meaning he issues a series of orders which should result in more personnel in the Films Unit. The executives of Golden Era Productions get the program and decide to send out some recruiters to get more people for the Films Unit. Now, that's not the end of the story, it's just the beginning.

WDC Gold wants to make sure those personnel are recruited, so he has Messengers continue to go to staff in Gold and direct them on the program he wrote and make sure they get it done. The Messengers are not going to follow the command channels inside Gold. They don't care about any of that. Their job is to get that program done.

Messengers have the authority to go to anyone in the organization at any time and tell them what to do. If anyone were to disobey a Messenger's directions, they would be in serious trouble. So here you have an immediate danger condition on every single person the Messengers bypass when they issue orders to people like the Personnel Director, the Finance Secretary or the Staff Training Officer.

At any one time, there could be any number of WDC programs being run into Gold. *This same pattern also applies to every other echelon of management.*

There is a CMO Unit physically adjacent to each management body. For example, CMO Clearwater is at the Flag Land Base in Florida. There is a CMO unit at Saint Hill in England. There is another in Los Angeles.

Messengers from every one of these CMO Units are physically running around in those management units every single day issuing tons of written orders and verbal directions, totally bypassing the standard command lines, putting every single manager up and down the line in a permanent danger condition.

Down In the Class V and SO service orgs, there isn't a CMO unit, but that doesn't mean the service org staff aren't subjected to this same kind of insanity. They have what are called *networks*.

Networks are independent command personnel in these service orgs who are supposed to act as "management's eyes and ears." These network personnel have specific activities and jobs they are supposed to get done and in order to do them, they issue orders to anyone in the org they want to, similar to how the Messengers operate. There are supposed to be five or six network staff in each org. Most of them are Sea Org members, such as the Flag Representative or the Flag Banking Officer. Each network has its own special zone of operation, but the net effect is the same: constant bypass of the org's command lines.

Supposedly all this bypass is handled with the use of what LRH termed "coordination committees". These are another bureaucratic band-aid which are supposed to coordinate the orders and activities coming in to an org at each level. I watched these committees go on for years and to just tell it to you straight, they don't work.

Permanent Bypass is Built In

Everything described above is what Scientologists and Sea Org members believe is the *totality* of their management structure. If you read through all L. Ron Hubbard's policies and issues inside the Church of Scientology about its management system, this is what you come up with. Everyone inside the organization is trying to do their jobs according to this system, but they can't do their jobs because of all the crazy bypass going on. Everyone has at least four seniors who come in and give orders at any time of the day or night. This creates stress, tension and frustration beyond belief because they are living in a bureaucratic nightmare and they can't make sense of it.

As crazy as this is, it actually gets worse. This entire system was completely subverted decades ago.

There is a hidden management system added to this structure which is so obvious everyone knows about it but no one in Scientology realizes what they are actually looking at.

Now we are finally getting to David Miscavige and the Religious Technology Center. Let's look at where this fits into the whole picture.

The Religious Technology Center

RTC is an organization sitting above and apart from the rest of Scientology. According to the RTC website, "Its purpose is to protect the public from misapplication of the technology and to see that the religious technologies of Dianetics and Scientology remain in proper hands and are properly ministered.

"Mr. Hubbard personally oversaw the orthodox practice of Scientology. As an integral part of that endeavor, he also registered as legally protectable trademarks many of the religion's identifying words and symbols, such as 'Dianetics' and 'Scientology.'

"It is RTC that grants Church of Scientology International (CSI), the mother church of the Scientology religion, the right to use the trademarks and to license their use to all other Scientology churches. Without CSI's written authority and RTC's ultimate approval, no entity can legally use the marks or call itself a Church of Scientology."

However, RTC's purpose never said anything about managing or directing Scientology affairs, nor is it supposed to have any power over individual Scientologists. RTC is supposed to enforce proper use of the trademarks. As an organization, that should be the entirety of its power.

David Miscavige took control of RTC in March of 1987 and made himself the Chairman of the Board of RTC, a job he has held ever since. In 1994, Miscavige declared in a court of law "RTC is not part of Church management, nor is it involved in the daily affairs of various Church of Scientology organizations or missions...In fact, a major reason for its formation was to have such a Church organization that performed these functions in a capacity entirely separate from the actual management of the various Churches and Missions of Scientology. Not only is RTC not involved in the management of the international hierarchy of Scientology churches, but its very existence and performance of its true functions depend on the fact that it is not part of Church management."[1]

I want you to keep this testimony in mind as I break down what Miscavige and RTC have been up to for the last 30 years.

The History of Scientology Management

Let's talk about some Scientology history. Odds are, anyone still practicing Scientology these days does not know what I'm about to tell you, yet this information is key to understanding how the church operates. In fact, the reason this is kept covered up, the reason the history of the church has been so carefully revised, is because to know about this is to know how the sausage really gets made behind the flashy facade Miscavige presents to his followers.

There's a lot to know about the period from the late 1970s to early 1980s and I'm not going to pretend to cover every significant event or important detail. This was a time of tremendous change for Scientology and I can only give you a brief summary of what was going on.

From its inception in 1953 up until the mid-1970s, L. Ron Hubbard directly managed the Church of Scientology. He set up a bureaucracy in the 1960s to take over this job called Worldwide Management Control Center. Yet by 1971, Hubbard disbanded Worldwide because he said they weren't doing the job. Then he formed a new management system which operated from the Sea Organization's flagship, called the *Apollo*. Since then, the Sea Organization has been directly managing all Scientology churches around the world.

Many different management structures and organizations existed throughout the 1970s, far too many variations to describe here. None of them are really important anyway. What is important is by the 1970s, Hubbard was in a lot of legal trouble.

For example, in 1967 the Church lost its tax-exempt status in the United States because the IRS found out Hubbard was personally profiting from Scientology. This was a real problem because taxes were suddenly owed but Hubbard still refused to pay them.

He was also in legal trouble in other countries like France, where in 1978 he was convicted for illegal business practices and sentenced to four years in jail. Of course, he never went to France for the trial, nor to serve his sentence.[2]

Instead, Hubbard put together a program called Operation Snow White to try to get his name cleared legally and try to clean up the files of the various governments so Scientology could operate in the clear. However, they didn't do this legally or openly. Instead, they resorted to illegal means and stirred up a lot of trouble.

The Church's legal bureau at the time, called the Guardian's Office, infiltrated the US government in the mid-1970s and got caught. Eleven Scientologists ended up going to jail over this, including the person who ran the Guardian's Office: Mary Sue Hubbard, L. Ron Hubbard's wife. This fiasco prompted a great deal of cover-up and reorganization to protect Hubbard and the Church from full scale elimination.

Earlier I said because of all the legal trouble, Hubbard was not supposed to be seen managing Scientology directly. In fact, by 1980, Hubbard was in hiding, in a location known to literally only a couple of CMO Messengers who were physically with him and cared for his personal needs. These were Pat and Anne Broeker and Steve "Sarge" Pfauth. No one else knew where Hubbard was located, nor would they until his death in 1986.

It was Hubbard's hermitage which enabled a young CMO Messenger named David Miscavige to establish his own power and authority.

With all the fallout from the Guardian's Office indictments, there were two top priorities for the Church: (1) get Hubbard's name cleared legally so he could come out of hiding and start running things openly again; and (2) get Scientology's corporate status sorted out so it would be legally defensible and continue making money for Hubbard.

Two Sea Organization units were initiated to get these done: Mission Corporate Category Sort-Out began in February 1980 and the All Clear Unit was established in 1981 to clear Hubbard's name legally. Included in the All Clear Unit was the Special Unit (or Unit X) which took over all the old GO/legal functions and even brought in some of the old Guardian's Office staff.

You see, from the time it first started in the late 1960s, the GO was not manned by Sea Org members; it had been an independent group operating side-by-side with the Sea Org, sort of in competition with it. Once the FBI moved in and uncovered the extent of the Snow White Program, the GO's days were numbered. Once it was eviscerated and its executives taken out by Miscavige and the CMO, the functions of the Guardian's Office were fully taken over by the Sea Organization.

David Miscavige ran both of these units. At this point in time, it was the CMO who ran everything while the whole WDC/Int Management structure I described earlier was being formed up and established. While Miscavige was not yet at the top of the Church hierarchy nor in command of all the organizations, his position in running these projects gave him almost full autonomy. Those in charge of the CMO had their hands full handling the GO fallout and a myriad of other operations Hubbard directed from his secret location.

So while Miscavige was not "in command" so to speak, he did one other thing which ensured his future success. While running the Special Unit and overseeing the Corporate Sort-Out, he managed to get himself into the position where he was the filter point between L. Ron Hubbard and everyone else in Scientology. He was the one who would rendezvous with Pat Broeker at predetermined locations to deliver mounds of written communications for Hubbard. Anything going up to Hubbard or coming back down from him first went through David Miscavige's hands. He did this to "take the load off" the other CMO executives and at first, they were happy to have the burden of this job off their plate with everything else they had to handle.

It was easy for Miscavige to orchestrate getting rid of anyone he felt threatened by or just wanted gone. He simply reported to Hubbard the individual he was targeting was "out-ethics" (up to no good), not loyal to Hubbard, up to criminal activities or working against Scientology. Hubbard would respond by banishing that person or ordering them sent to the RPF or whatever. It quickly became clear Miscavige was not someone to be trifled with.

The goal was to get Ron back into a position of running things openly. However, things were too hot legally for him to ever be able to show his face. Until he was back, those in charge wanted to be as close to Ron as they could and "flow him power". When Author Services Inc (or ASI) was formed in 1982, David Miscavige took charge of it and made himself the Chairman of the Board of ASI.

Chairman of the Board is a unique post because it doesn't officially do anything and yet holds all the authority and power over the entire organization. There has never been anyone else in all Scientology's history who has held the sole job of "Chairman of the Board" at any level. It's something Miscavige dreamed up just for himself.

In the early 1980s, ASI was important because it was Hubbard's literary agent. In other words, it was the organization in charge of collecting all the royalties owed to Hubbard for his writings and getting said money sent up to him. It was a clearinghouse for all the money Hubbard was secretly collecting from the Church and putting into his own accounts. While Hubbard was alive, this organization was the power hub of Scientology.

Miscavige stayed COB ASI until 1987 and continued to run the All Clear Unit from this position. In fact, he ran everything from this position, with the heads of RTC and the Church of Scientology International reporting directly to him almost daily. Hardly anyone in the Church outside of the senior management echelon knew Miscavige had this much control over Church affairs. Everything was still done in Hubbard's name. However, anyone who crossed Miscavige, tried to bypass him or stop him was either declared suppressive, sent to the RPF or otherwise put in their place so they were no longer a threat to him.

As part of the corporate reorganization, RTC was formed up in 1982 along with ASI. As covered earlier, one of its roles was to safeguard the trademarks over Scientology. Vicki Aznaran was its President. She answered only to David Miscavige and, through him, to L. Ron Hubbard.

The first actions RTC took as an organization involved getting its name known, registering trademarks in other countries and starting legal action against people who left the Church and started their own auditing groups. RTC was important, but ASI was where the real power was.

Fast forward to the next major turning point in this story in early 1986. Despite a lot of work, Hubbard's name still wasn't cleared. But the WDC/Int Management command structure was in place and Scientology had weathered the storm of the Guardian's Office disaster. The International Association of Scientologists had also been formed in 1984 and began aggressively collecting funds into what was known as the "war chest" which were supposed to be used to fight the lawsuits and legal battles OSA was embroiled in. Dianetics had started to be nationally marketed and was on its way to getting widespread name recognition across the US. Golden Era Productions studios had been constructed and was creating new promotional items and producing new technical films for Scientology. The Int Base was established and operating. Things were actually starting to look up. Then in January 1986, L. Ron Hubbard died.

What followed was a year-long power struggle between David Miscavige and Pat Broeker for ultimate control of Scientology. Because Broeker was so close to Hubbard and supposedly held the rest of the OT Levels from OT VIII all the way up, Broeker was in a power position himself and was the only person Miscavige felt could challenge his authority. Details of the intrigues between them are beyond the scope of this book, but suffice it to say when the dust settled, Miscavige was the one still standing. Pat Broeker and anyone loyal to him were either kicked out of the Church entirely or sent to the Rehabilitation Project Force and had to earn their way back through hard physical labor and promising loyalty to Miscavige.

With Hubbard dead, it became clear to Miscavige the situation with ASI had changed. As Hubbard's literary agent, ASI was directly connected to Hubbard and his works and all the money flowed to him. With Hubbard out of the picture, the Church of Scientology was going to continue to produce income and have a base of followers to be led. Miscavige wanted to be on top of that.

So it was in March, 1987, David Miscavige and his hand-picked crew marched into the offices of RTC and kicked its President and Inspector General, Vicki Aznaran, and the Deputy Inspector General, Jesse Prince, out of the picture. It was a classic coup. Miscavige assumed the position of Chairman of the Board RTC. Greg Wilhere was the new Inspector General, with three assistants: Marty Rathbun was the Inspector General for Ethics, Ray Mithoff was the Inspector General for Tech and Marc Yeager was the Inspector General for Admin. The Church of Scientology had a new seat of power.

Since that day, many people have gone in and out of a lot of positions in management, but David Miscavige has been steady as the

222

head of the Sea Org, running Scientology from his position as Chairman of the Board RTC.

Until 1993, Miscavige's primary focus was tax exemption. It was imperative the Church re-gain the tax exemption it lost in 1967 for a number of reasons, not least of which was Hubbard specified in his will only a tax-exempt organization could actually take possession of the Dianetics and Scientology trademarks. However, that didn't stop Miscavige from putting himself on the approval line for every key issue and program Scientology management wrote before they could be released. This was in direct contravention of the entire purpose of RTC but Miscavige didn't care. He was a dictator and his word was law. He was going to run things exactly the way he wanted and to hell with what anyone else thought about it. If anyone did try to speak up or buck his authority, they soon found themselves the subject of intense investigation and relegated to the RPF or booted out of the Sea Org. There are numerous eyewitness accounts by ex-Scientologists of Miscavige also using physical violence to get his way, literally beating people into submission.

New releases of previously uncompiled materials started to be put together. For example, there was the release of OT VIII in 1988, all Scientology basic books in 1991 and the big release of the Key to Life Course and Life Orientation Courses also in 1991. All this and a lot more needed Miscavige's personal approval before any of it could be released.

While Miscavige held no management position, there was no question in anyone's mind who was actually in charge. In fact, his first major public appearance in 1992 on Nightline with Ted Koppel confirmed it to the entire world.

Once tax exemption was secured in 1993, Miscavige was truly an unstoppable force and he then started remaking Scientology into his own image. Behind the scenes, he began intruding more and more directly into the day-to-day affairs of the Church and its management, even issuing his own bulletins and corrective actions on org staff under the heading of Inspector General Network Bulletins.

In 1996, Miscavige began to re-position himself as the actual source of Scientology with the release of what he called the Golden Age of Tech. This was basically a total rewrite of the entire subject of Scientology training. Like so many things Miscavige took on, he managed to utterly ruin training, making it impossible for Scientology auditors to ever graduate. Thus began Scientology's steep decline as a service-oriented organization, as more and more of the staff's attention was forced onto straight fundraising activities instead of service delivery.

As part of this Golden Age of Tech, Miscavige gained micromanagement control of every Scientology continental zone. He did this by sending RTC Representatives directly loyal to only him to every Sea Org base, where they usurped control of the local CMO units. He even announced he was doing this at the 1996 Golden Age of Tech event. There was nothing hidden about this takeover and Scientologists fully supported anything Miscavige said because he was the new leader of Scientology and the hero who won the "war" with the IRS.

Since that time, Miscavige slowly but relentlessly dismantled the international management structure I described earlier. He doesn't just approve programs and issues for the orgs to execute. Since 1996, Miscavige is the one who writes them.

It's hard to believe, but Miscavige has personally removed almost every person of any significance at Int Management. There are no Watchdog Committee personnel, there is no Executive Director International or Int Management Executive Committee. All these people are ordered about at Miscavige's whim to do whatever he tells them to, including clean out trash bins, scrub floors and sit in crowded, dirty quarters writing down all their moral transgressions and bad thoughts against him personally.

He has no interest in reestablishing or maintaining a management structure, because anyone who is allowed too much power or authority could become a threat to him. He simply won't allow that to occur. Since he is the head of the Sea Organization, whatever he says is

Command Intention, meaning all Sea Org members are required to obey him.

A Recipe for Disaster

The structure of Scientology's management is a recipe for disaster and that is exactly what they have on their hands.

Perhaps this might explain now why things seem so insane in the world of Scientology and why they can't manage to expand any of their organizations no matter what orders they issue or how many people they yell and scream at.

In fact, it might just be all the yelling and screaming is going on because these people are caught up in a bureaucratic nightmare preventing anyone from getting anything constructive done.

The only things holding this whole thing together are the belief of the parishioners in the system and the almost slavish amount of overwork by those who still work for the church. Their faith in this system and Hubbard's organizational genius is touching but it is completely misplaced.

In the future, David Miscavige will announce all Hubbard's policies have been reviewed. He will detail how a bunch of suppressive persons twisted Hubbard's words and how Miscavige stepped in and saved the day. He will tell the Scientologists they *now* have the most perfect organizational structure in the universe. The only reason he will say these things is so the parishioners will continue to believe and will continue to give over their hard-earned money because none of what he is saying will have any truth to it.

The good news is, given Scientology's shrinking membership, it looks like more and more Scientologists are catching on to the fact this group is not capable of delivering on its promises, and in fact is just ripping them off for all the money it can get before it collapses.

How much longer this can go on is anyone's guess. It really depends on how much longer Miscavige can continue to fool Scientologists and the courts. And it's my hope he won't be getting away with this for much longer.

14. Scientology's Most Powerful Lie

"It's hard for me to understand how it is that you and I effectively subsidize the Church of Scientology by allowing them to take tax-deductible donations in order to be able to go hire private detectives to harass and intimidate people, to coerce children to sign billion-year contracts which effectively consign them to permanent servitude, to threaten people with the loss of their homes, to practice this policy of disconnection that destroys families. Why is that considered a charitable activity? I don't get that." Alex Gibney, writer and director of *Going Clear: Scientology and the Prison of Belief*

It's not overstating the case to say Scientology is a house of lies, built on one careful deception after another after another. Through this ongoing practice of duplicity, L. Ron Hubbard and his successor, David Miscavige, have been able to keep Scientology going all this time. The organization indoctrinates its members into an "end justifies the means" philosophy where anything is acceptable so long as it forwards Scientology's existence. What none of those members realize is by buying into this, they are actually contributing to what amounts to an international criminal organization.

In recent years, many of the lies the Church is built on have been exposed, each time lessening its influence and power. However, it is still able to maintain its facade as a religious charitable organization because it has one last weapon in its arsenal. It is a weapon used over and over again to beat down opposition, stop court cases in their tracks and justify its cult behavior.

What weapon is this?

It's not its faith, what Scientologists refer to as their technology. There is nothing special or unique about Scientology in this regard. While they claim to be able to create what Hubbard termed *Homo novis* (New Man), there is no scientifically validated evidence for anyone who has practiced Scientology achieving any higher state of mental or spiritual existence. These states are totally subjective and any Scientologist would have to acknowledge this as true because they cannot point to any tests or physical evidence to indicate they have the abilities or powers Scientology promises. In fact, rather than being more able and extroverted, Scientologists actually become more insular and elitist, refraining from close ties with non-Scientologists and even shunning family and friends who refuse to go along with what Hubbard or Miscavige demand.

It's not its money. Although Scientology has billions of dollars at its disposal, almost all those assets and reserves could be made to disappear in a surprisingly fast period of time, given the right circumstances. Just ask any tin-pot dictator or 1990's dot.com company president whether their untold millions could save them when push came to shove.

This weapon is much more powerful than either of these. What I'm referring to is the means by which the Church of Scientology ensures it has the full protection of the United States justice system to harshly discipline its members with grueling physical labor, violate their basic human rights in the process and and inflict emotional blackmail upon even its most devoted members.

Quite simply, this weapon is Scientology's tax-exempt status in the United States, granted by the Internal Revenue Service, which opened the door to Scientology being legally recognized as a legitimate religion.

On the surface, this may not sound very impressive, but as I will show you here, Scientology can only continue to exist as long as it can convince the IRS it is a religious institution which should enjoy the full protection of the First Amendment of the US Constitution and the gigantic tax breaks which come with that status.

Scientology deserves no such recognition, because in order to get it and keep it, they lied about practically every single aspect of their entire operation. I will show you the exact ways they have done this, and what needs to be done now to take this apart. That way Scientology not only loses this tax-exempt status, but also receives the justice it deserves for its long list of crimes against its members and the general public.

What is Tax Exemption?

Why is tax exemption so important to Scientology? Why was Scientology willing to "go to war" (as David Miscavige put it) with one of the most powerful institutions in the world and why was it so important for them to win?

Taxes have been with man almost as long as civilized society. Which is not to say taxes are civilized, merely that governing bodies have to pay for common properties and goods which all citizens benefit from such as roads, education, transportation etc. Taxes are the means by which governing bodies do this.

Tax exemption is when a government grants exemptions from taxes for certain types of organizations or individuals because they do something *which benefits the public good.*

Rarely does this mean a full pardon from all taxes. More often, it is a kind of partial exception made for specific circumstances. Charitable organizations like the Red Cross, for example, are granted freedom from certain taxes because, in theory, the vast majority of their resources go to providing that benefit. Not only that, but because the Red Cross exists, the governments of the countries it operates in do not have to pay to make those same services available.

Soldiers who have fought in wars give not only their time and energy to fighting for the common good, but sometimes are permanently disabled in the line of duty. Because they gave their all to their country for the benefit of everyone, their country in turn exempts them from having to pay the same amount in taxes as other citizens.

There are many different kinds of taxes: property, income, employment, sales etc. Different countries deal with exemptions from these taxes in different ways depending on the country's history, culture and political attitudes.

Churches and Tax Exemption

Charitable and religious organizations have a long history of relief from taxation going all the way back to ancient times. This is, first, because they are supposed to be serving the public good and second, serves as a protection for the free practice of the religion. The idea is if a religion is open to taxation, an oppressive government who disagreed with it could tax it out of existence.

One important point about this in the US is the government is not supposed to favor any one religion over any other. In fact, it's supposed to keep its fingers out of the religious pie altogether. So in deciding if an organization is religious and should be granted tax-exempt status, *it does not do this by evaluating the religion's belief system.* This is important because the reason Scientology should lose its tax-exempt status has nothing to do with its belief in aliens or OT powers or anything like that.

Strictly speaking, the US government does not grant approval or recognition to any religion. According to our the First Amendment, Congress cannot pass any law to officially regulate religious affairs or conduct. Instead, it reviews the organization applying for tax exemption against a series of requirements laid out in section 501(c)(3) of the US tax code.

These requirements are not complicated:

- the organization must be organized and operated exclusively for religious, educational, scientific, or other charitable purposes,
- net earnings may not inure to the benefit of any private individual or shareholder,
- no substantial part of its activity may be attempting to influence legislation,
- the organization may not intervene to win political campaigns, and

230

- the organization's purposes and activities may not be illegal or violate fundamental public policy.

If the organization can pass these requirements, the IRS isn't supposed to care what its beliefs are. It grants tax exemption, not religious recognition. This might seem like a fine point, but it's commonly misunderstood and answers the question of why other controversial churches with unusual beliefs or religious practices can be tax-exempt. The government is not putting its stamp of approval on the group's practices. It is merely verifying the points listed above are valid.

Conversely, it also means if the Church of Scientology loses its tax exemption, it will not lose its religious recognition. The courts have given the Church the ability to hide behind the First Amendment separately from the IRS granting tax exemption. Scientology uses this as justification for human rights abuses, human trafficking, fraud and all the rest of a long list of very un-church-like behavior, much of which violates the last point of tax exemption against illegal purposes and activities.

I mentioned the two go hand-in-hand earlier to make the point the IRS opened the door to the courts recognizing Scientology as a religion and made it easier for Scientology to sell it to them. If the IRS revokes tax exemption, Scientology does not automatically lose religious recognition. However, losing tax exemption would still be a gigantic blow to Scientology, a blow they would not be able to recover from.

How Much Does Religious Tax Exemption Cost?

According to estimates from The Washington Post, the bottom-line figure for religious subsidy and tax exemptions in the United States is $82.5 billion per year.[1] Yes, billion.

For example, states don't require churches to pay property tax, which saves these organizations an estimated $26.2 billion per year.

Because ministers don't pay income tax, there is another $1.2 billion in tax exemptions annually via the parsonage allowance.

So this is a big business with a lot of money at stake. Taxpayers end up footing the bill for everything churches don't pay for.

In many cases, these exemptions are sensible and of real benefit to the public good, so I'm not making any case here to revoke all tax exemption for all churches. Quite to the contrary. Many charitable institutions and churches should definitely maintain their tax-exempt status, or society will suffer. All organizations which truly operate for the public benefit should be supported to the fullest extent possible.

How is Tax Exemption Abused?

Given how much money is involved, there is a lot of controversy over whether churches should have tax exemption at all. One of the reasons for this is the abuse over the years where corrupt individuals within church and charity organizations take advantage of their positions to line their own pockets.

This is called inurement and it is illegal. *Inurement* is an unusual word which just means "benefit." The inurement prohibition forbids the use of the income or assets of a tax-exempt organization to directly or indirectly benefit an individual or other person who has a close relationship with the organization or is able to exercise significant control over the organization.

If this happens even once and can be proven, then the organization could theoretically lose its tax-exempt status almost immediately. More often, the individual who benefited is made to give the money back and is assessed a stiff fine for what was taken.

Scientology is not the only group to abuse this privilege. There are many "charities" and "religious institutions" which are no such thing and operate almost exclusively to benefit one or a few individuals with palatial estates, jet planes and a Kardashian lifestyle on the backs of senior citizens, disabled/handicapped people and religious followers who are too ignorant and trusting to see they are being conned out of their hard-earned savings. In the United States in particular this is so common, and tax exemption is so abused, the IRS has a lot to answer for in allowing this kind of criminality to go unchecked for as long as it has.

For example, Jim and Tami Bakker were famous televangelists in the 1980s who created Heritage USA and the *Praise the Lord* show. They were making an estimate of $1 million a week in donations. Investigation found Jim Bakker siphoned off $3.4 million of this for himself as a bonus and kept two sets of books to conceal the accounting irregularities. In 1989, he was found guilty on 24 separate counts of fraud and conspiracy, and sentenced to 45 years in federal prison and a $500,000 fine. Jim was out of prison by 1994 but he and his now ex-wife Tami still owe the IRS millions in unpaid back taxes.

The comedian John Oliver recently did a series of episodes on his HBO show highlighting just how easy it is for these vampires to suck the life out of their followers with empty promises and blatant hypocrisy. To these leeches on society, the televangelists and swindlers, I say no mercy should be given. I would gladly applaud any effort to see them put behind bars for their crimes against humanity and just plain common decency.

Scientology's Religious Status

I've detailed in earlier chapters how Hubbard created an overnight sensation with Dianetics, built up a nationwide organization, led it into bankruptcy (twice) and eventually resolved the issue by abandoning the whole thing and starting anew with Scientology after he came up with the "religion angle."

Since this new subject of Scientology dealt with non-physical realities and Man's spiritual state, it leant itself to a religious angle. He defined it as dealing with man's relationship to himself, other spirits and the universe itself.

This is a very important point because it gave him the legal right to make the most outrageous claims he wanted and no one could touch him in a court of law. A big part of the success of early Dianetics was the promise it could cure physical problems and Hubbard didn't want to stop making those claims. Once he had religious protection, he could make such claims and not be sued for practicing medicine without a license.

In November, 1953, Hubbard got the rights to Dianetics back after wearing out his former business partner, Don Purcell, with litigation. However, he didn't want to repeat the same mistakes of the last three years, so he moved forward with the Scientology religious plan. He would later re-incorporate the word Dianetics in to Scientology practices and integrate its use into the church.

On December 18, 1953, Hubbard personally incorporated the Church of Scientology, the Church of American Science and the Church of Spiritual Engineering in Camden, New Jersey. These three church entities were controlled by the Hubbard Association of Scientologists International (HASI) which was *a religious fellowship and association for research into the spirit and the human soul and the use and dissemination* [of Scientology materials]."[2] The HASI, interestingly, was incorporated in London, not the US. It required membership dues from all Scientologists, similar to its current incarnation, the International Association of Scientologists (IAS).

A few months later, on February 18, 1954, Burton Farber established the Church of Scientology of California (CSC), which eventually became the mother church for all of Scientology and remained so until the corporate restructure in the 1980s. This wouldn't take place, though, for quite a few years. At the time it started, CSC was contracted to the Church of American Science and paid a 20% tithe.

Having learned some lessons from the disaster of Dianetics, Hubbard kept a much tighter grip over the organizational structure and the copyrights he created by setting up a franchise system. He licensed new Scientology organizations and they paid 10% of their income to the HASI each week. With the help of his third wife, Mary Sue, and a small but intensely loyal group of followers, Hubbard grew the organization and it became very profitable again as new followers were attracted to what was now presented as a church.

According to Jon Atack in his landmark book *A Piece of Blue Sky*, one very important control point was put in place at that time and

234

which continues to this day. The board members of each Scientology church signed undated letters of resignation and gave those letters to Hubbard before they were officially appointed. Hubbard didn't have to hold a formal position on those boards himself, he merely had letters which gave him the power to do away with anyone should they end up giving him trouble. He also had direct access to and control of all church bank accounts.[3]

It was a church in name only, though. Members understood the church status was there for mere legal and tax reasons and no one took it too seriously. Hubbard inculcated a basic distrust of all things bureaucratic and governmental in his followers and it was easy for them to go along with the con because, after all, they were engaged in spiritual cleansing and creating higher states of being. Not only did it sound kind of religious, but it was also another way to stick it to "The Man". No one really took the religion angle seriously and they would have chafed at any formal religious doctrine or methodology being pushed on them.

To this day, the same spirit and attitude prevails throughout Scientology. When faced with adversity or legal challenges, Scientology trots out its religious status and members make grandiose claims about their freedom of religion being attacked. Yet in their day-to-day practice, no Scientologist thinks of Scientology as a religion in the same way people of other faiths think of theirs. They know and acknowledge to each other the whole "religion angle" simply exists for the purposes of "wog law."

The Beginning of the War

Scientology does not actually meet the IRS' definition of a church, but it fits in the tax code under a "religious organization." This means they could not automatically claim tax-exempt status as many other churches, synagogues or mosques do. They had to apply for it.

According to all information to hand, this was not a difficult process. Each individual Scientology Church which sprung up in the US was incorporated and shortly thereafter gained tax-exempt status.

For example, the "Founding Church of Scientology" in Washington DC was incorporated in July 1955 and gained tax-exempt status in 1956.

Hubbard pushed religious cloaking right from the start. For example, on March 20, 1957 he wrote an issue called "Ministerial Ordination" for the DC church, stating *All ministerial ordinations of the Church must be in full force for the current year before income tax provisions can be claimed.*

However, it was this same church which just a few years later started the chain of events which led to Scientology's tax-exempt status being revoked, challenged in court and ultimately beginning a war with IRS which lasted until 1993.

Money rolled in hand over fist and Hubbard made not only a salary of $125 a week (about $1,063 now) but was also paid speaking fees for lectures and regular congresses held 2-3 times or more a year. All the materials of Scientology (books and E-meters) were sold exclusively through the HASI and Hubbard made royalties and commissions from these sales. He came down hard on any off-brand or "squirrel" E-meters being put together in the field because those cut into his own profits.

None of Hubbard's income went to living expenses because the HASI also provided him and his family a house and a car. He finally didn't need a regular salary once he started getting a direct percentage of the profits instead. Between 1955 -1959, he made $108,000 (equivalent to $885,000 now), a hefty amount of income. And he wasn't shy about drawing money from any individual church account if he needed it and calling those withdraws "loans".[4]

What Hubbard was doing was the very definition of inurement and it didn't take the IRS long to catch on to the scheme.

In 1958, the IRS revoked the Founding Church's tax-exempt status. They stated in part *the tenets set forth in the books of L. Ron Hubbard, and related instruments of instruction relative to 'Scientology' in training courses, clinical courses and otherwise* did not constitute an exclusively religious or educational activity.[5]

According to a later court filing, the reason for the revocation was Hubbard, as the founder of Scientology:

"...was not only paid, in addition to his salary, commissions and royalties but he and his family received unexplained payments in nature of loans and reimbursements, church was not entitled to exemption from federal income taxation under statute, which includes among those organizations exempt from taxation a corporation organized and operated exclusively for religious or educational purposes, no part of net earnings of which inures to benefit of any private shareholder or individual."[6]

In response, Hubbard attempted to institute a campaign of public protest against the entire concept of income tax. It was a topic he railed against for years in his lectures, saying it was a Marxist concept straight out of *Das Kapital* and an unfair punishment of those who were holding society up on their shoulders through their hard work. Without mentioning or broadcasting he was doing this because of the income tax revocation, he issued a policy to every Scientologist in the United States on July 18, 1959 called "Income Tax Reform" where he asked them to write a letter to their local newspaper and to their local congressional representative which said, in part:

"While fighting a cold front with communism, the US is violently cooperating with communist aims by destroying her individual confidence and initiative with a Marxist tax reform. The basic principles of US income tax were taken from Das Kapital *and are aimed at destroying capitalism. Unless the US ceases to cooperate with this Red push, communism could win in America.*

"The reform of all income tax laws is needed for other reasons. (1) To increase government revenues in order to support defense. (2) To prevent spiraling inflation and another stock market collapse and (3) to return the US to the basic principles of democracy as opposed to economic tyranny."

As can be seen, Hubbard was not at all above playing to public fears about Communism and appealing to Cold War sentiments.

At the same time, Scientology wasted no time in appealing this IRS decision in the courts. This battle went on for years but was a losing one for Scientology. In fact, because this was fought so hard, the Justice

Department requested the IRS review *all* Scientology church tax exemptions.

"Sometime in the fall of 1966 the Department of Justice asked respondent to review the tax status of several Scientology churches including petitioner. The request was made as the Department of Justice prepared to defend a case against the Founding Church of Scientology (Founding Church) in the United States Court of Claims. In that case, the Founding Church sued for refund of its Federal income taxes which it had paid after its tax-exempt status had been denied. The *405 exemption was denied on the grounds that the Founding Church was organized and operated as a commercial venture benefiting private interests and that Scientology did not serve a religious purpose. Believing that respondent's recognition of the tax-exempt status of other Churches of Scientology was inconsistent with the defense of the Founding Church case, the Department of Justice asked respondent to investigate the matter and rescind recognition of all similar Churches of Scientology prior to the trial of the Founding Church case."[7]

Hubbard fled the United States and set up shop in England at Saint Hill Manor in 1959. He tried unsuccessfully to get tax-exempt status there too. He failed because Scientology was unable to pass the much more stringent public benefits test the Commonwealth countries (UK, Australia and South Africa) have for religious tax exemption. He incorporated "limited companies" in the UK in an effort to gain freedom from taxation but the UK would never grant non-profit status.

In a policy dated October 29, 1962 called "Religion" he talked about the religious nature of all Scientology organizations worldwide and also of the E-Meter as a diagnostic tool used in Scientology confessionals. It was quite important to Scientology practice the E-Meter be accepted as a religious artifact and therefore not be subject to FDA regulations.

There was an additional bit which has been edited out of modern versions of this policy letter where Hubbard also stated his intentions to have all US and international Scientology organizations come under one tax-exempt umbrella group. He wrote:

"For information of the London and Commonwealth offices, they will soon be transferred to Church status when the Founding Church of

238

Washington DC is given full tax exemption, and HASI Ltd. and HCO Ltd. shares will be converted to equally valuable Church certificates. Scientology 1970 is being planned on a religious organization basis throughout the world. This will not upset in any way the usual activities of any organization. It is entirely a matter for accountants and solicitors. I have evidently failed in designating HASI Ltd. as a non-profit organization and cannot transfer HASI Inc. assets to any but a non-profit corporation. Therefore other arrangements must be made, but these in no way shatter any organization or change its personnel or actions in the slightest.[8]

There were a lot of corporate shell games and behind-the-scenes shenanigans going on so Hubbard could keep all the money coming in for himself. He hated taxes and he hated the idea of anyone cutting into his profits. The whole religion angle was set up to prevent this, yet here the US and UK governments were not cooperating and continued to probe deeper and deeper into the various bank accounts and shell corporations.

With US Scientology churches no longer protected from taxes, it seemed there was no safe haven for the massive amounts of funds to go where they would be free of some government's meddling and greedy fingers. Then Hubbard realized there was one corporation which successfully evaded the IRS's scrutiny: the Church of Scientology of California.

In an Executive Letter dated March 12, 1966, Hubbard told his followers a tall tale of how the various corporate structures of Scientology had struggled over the past 13 years to support themselves despite the best efforts of the UK and US governments to tax them out of existence and how Hubbard had to support the whole thing with his own monies in order to keep everything afloat. The long and short of it, though, was every international and US holding was transferred to the CSC including all HASI monies. CSC was chosen to take over as the "mother church" for Scientology because it still had tax-exempt status in the US.

Even this was only a temporary respite though because in 1967, the IRS caught on to this tactical move and revoked the CSC's tax-exempt status. It was checkmate for Hubbard and Scientology. They no longer had a tax-free haven anywhere in the world.

However, instead of throwing in the towel and conceding Scientology was, in fact, exactly what the governments of the US and Commonwealth could easily see it was, Hubbard instructed no taxes be paid by any organization, period. And so the checkmate turned into a stalemate.

The FCDC continued to fight but lost again in 1969 when the court ruled:

"...that plaintiff [FCDC] has failed to prove that no part of the corporation's net earnings inured to the benefit of private individuals, and plaintiff is not entitled to recover. The court finds it unnecessary to decide whether plaintiff is a religious or educational organization as alleged, since, regardless of its character, plaintiff has not met the statutory conditions for exemption from income taxation. In any event, the Government has not raised this issue....we need not and do not determine whether plaintiff's operations were exclusively for religious or educational purposes."

It didn't matter whether Scientology was or was not a religion, it was not abiding by the IRS's 501(c)(3) tax code because Hubbard was profiting personally and the Church could not make a case otherwise. Even the US Supreme Court agreed.

It was during this period Hubbard disappeared from England and set off on the high seas, forming the Sea Organization in 1967 and removing himself from the easy reach of any government or tax collector. He formed more shell corporations and Swiss bank accounts to hide his money, hoping a deeper labyrinth and harder-to-follow paper trails would keep his growing millions secure.

Officially, Hubbard never did come out of hiding until his death in 1986. He was determined to not give any government any part of Scientology's (or his) profits. It was all his money and he didn't see any reason to share it.

Over the next three decades until Hubbard's death in 1986, no US Church of Scientology paid taxes to the government. Instead, they simply refused and fought tooth and claw in the courts, stating because they were a religion, they should not be taxed. They went to extreme measures to hinder or block IRS investigations. As one example:

"During [1970-72], petitioner [Scientology] advocated and practiced the use of obstructionist tactics to thwart IRS investigations of petitioner and affiliated churches. In 1970 petitioner's tax returns for the taxable years 1964 through 1967 were under audit. In June or July of that year Martin Greenberg, the Church's accountant, told an assembled group of Scientologists that he purposely made the audit difficult. He said he gave the examiner boxes of original records, disbursement vouchers and invoices in no semblance of order with the intent of so hopelessly overwhelming and confusing the examiner that he would be forced to give up the examination and accept petitioner's version of the facts. In April 1972 Mr. Greenberg instructed a member of the financial staff at an affiliated Church of Scientology to use similar tactics if IRS agents ever came to her church to examine records. She was told to give the IRS agent a bunch of records in a box in no semblance or order, to place the agent in a dark, small, out-or-the-way room, to refuse to give practical assistance like locating records, and to notify petitioner's Guardian Office immediately of the agent's presence. Henning Heldt, petitioner's vice president and the Deputy Guardian Finance in petitioner's Guardian Office, gave this staff member similar instructions."

While it may seem like fun and games to thwart an IRS investigation and run them around in circles, the Church of Scientology cost taxpayers millions in legal and administrative fees over the years without once contributing anything of benefit or gain to society, and won a tax-exempt free ride in the process.

Doubts and Reserves

While in hiding and running things from his secret locations, Hubbard gave serious thought to losing the religion angle. It was certainly costing the organization a lot of money in legal fees all on its own. Scientology was also spending money hand over fist on other matters in the 1970s too, namely the Snow White Program and other illegal Fair Game activities against people like journalist Paulette

Cooper for daring to expose Scientology's deceitful and criminal nature to the world at large.

Nancy Many, an international executive in the late 70s, recalled Hubbard talking about this in her book *My Billion Year Contract*:

"Hubbard expressed to me the thought that going with the whole church angle for Scientology might have been a mistake in the first place. He felt that the trouble we were currently having with the IRS would not exist if he had not listened to those around him at the time and just stayed as a for-profit corporation and just made more money to pay the taxes. This conversation with him was not upsetting to me or out of the ordinary. I myself had often wondered why we were pursuing the church status. Self-help was big business in the late '70s, and I felt that if anyone had the best self-help around, it was Scientology."

Richard Behar seconds this in a 1987 article he wrote for Forbes magazine where he quoted a "former high church official, *"Hubbard told me at one time the biggest mistake we made was going religious and that we should have kept it straight as a business. That would have avoided all the trouble with the IRS."*[10]

Given the fact if he converted it to the actual business model it was, Hubbard would have to start paying not only taxes but minimum wage to Church employees, health benefits and all the rest, it ran too much against his greedy character to allow this to happen.

Bill Franks, a former senior executive in Scientology, said in the Forbes article by the time he was on the scene in the late 1970s and early 1980s:

"The question was always how to get more money into Hubbard's pocket and how to hide that from the IRS. There was literally cash all over the place. There would be people leaving from Florida for Europe with bags of cash on a weekly basis. There were hundreds of bank accounts."[11]

According to Behar's article, here was how just one of many schemes operated over the years:

"In 1981 Franks started taking Hubbard's name off these accounts as signatory - 15 years after Hubbard was said to have retired from the church - to hide the connection to church funds they represented.

"Instead, much of the organization's cash reportedly wound up in the Religious Research Foundation (RRF), which former church members say was a Liberian shell corporation with bank accounts in Luxembourg and Liechtenstein. RRF was set up by three otherwise unimportant board members who had submitted their resignations in advance. The RRF was used as a way station for money from the church to the unseen Hubbard's own accounts in Switzerland and Liechtenstein. Franks claims that RRF accounts alone totaled well over $100 million by 1981.

As all this was going on, the Snow White Program had been running since the early 1970s to try to clear Hubbard's name legally and make it so he could come out of hiding. Scientologists were secretly installed in government positions of employment and also were infiltrating government organizations and stealing documents having to do with Hubbard and Scientology. If they weren't able to gain legitimacy through legal means in the courts, they would do it illegally through subterfuge and illicit intelligence operations. As far as Scientologists were concerned, any means necessary were acceptable to protect their leader.

This ended up blowing up in their face in 1977 when the FBI got wind of what was happening and raided Church headquarters. They found mounds of incriminating evidence against Scientology, sending 11 of its members to prison including Hubbard's wife, Mary Sue. She took the fall for Hubbard since there was not enough evidence to indict him directly.

As Hubbard's personal secretary, Ken Urquhart, later stated:

"[Hubbard] was privy to almost all of it, he was as guilty of conspiracy as Mary Sue. There were a number of reports that could be interpreted that way. He didn't mind the fuss, flaps or errors he made. One thing I find hard to forgive was that he allowed his wife to go to jail for crimes he was equally guilty of. He publicly abandoned her. He made it perfectly clear within the org that she was abandoned."[12]

This whole operation did little to help Scientology's status in the courts and the IRS continued to press for back taxes owed and by 1984 was putting together a criminal case against Hubbard for tax evasion.

243

It was at this time, in the late 1970s and early 1980s, a new character entered the scene who was to change everything. That character was David Miscavige.

Scientology's Corporate Shake-Up

There was so much happening in Scientology in the early 1980s it's impossible to easily detail or summarize it all. A great deal of shaking up was going on internally as a younger, new breed of executives were taking over from the old guard on the heels of the Operation Snow White disaster. David Miscavige was leading the shake-up, in tight communication with L. Ron Hubbard, who coordinated everything from his hidden locations and gave Miscavige detailed instructions on how to handle "enemies" of the Church. Included in that list of enemies were Scientologists who had worked slavishly for Hubbard and Scientology for years. Paranoia was the order of the day, with anyone and everyone a potential suspect of working for the FBI, CIA, IRS or worst of all, "the psychs."

Gaining protection for Hubbard and tax exemption were at the forefront of the list of priorities, though, and Miscavige was working with other Church officials hard to make this a reality. A Sea Org mission was begun in 1980 to reorganize the entire Church structure. It had the unenviable task of legitimizing several decades of criminality by setting up a corporate structure to which the IRS would be able to give its stamp of approval. This whole corporate reorganization effort was detailed in the last chapter so I won't go into the specifics of it again except to say while its stated purpose may have been to give Scientology legal legitimacy, what it was really doing was setting up a structure where Hubbard and Miscavige would be able to continue to bilk millions and millions of dollars for witless parishioners and not let the IRS or any other government agencies find out what was actually going on.

Internally, Scientology wasn't particularly being circumspect in what they were doing. For example, in October of 1982 there was a large gathering of Scientology franchise (mission) holders in San Francisco.

The newly appointed Corporate Affairs Director, Lymon Spurlock, gave a briefing about the reorganization. Parts of his briefing were deleted from the official transcript (underlined here) but in the recording he said:

"Prior to the end of 1981, a few of us from the CMO got together and took a look at the corporate structure of the Church with the view in mind of making it more defensible and more regular <u>and particularly not understandable by the traditional enemies of the Church such as the IRS,</u> and to make an overall improvement"[13]

Once the corporate reorganization was done, Scientology had a new air of legitimacy and a bullet-proof labyrinthine structure which would be unassailable by any government or tax organization. The best minds had been put onto this and no expense was spared in its organization and setup. Larry Brennan was the Sea Org member who was the chief architect of this scheme; he would later leave Scientology and become one of its most damning critics. Here is part of what he said about it:

"...it would be a whole new evolution in Scientology's corporate status and management. It would be honest and straightforward and that's what the corporate sort out was designed to do. But the problem is - it didn't do it, it just made it look like that was the case. And, for example, and I don't want to bore anybody on this but as an example - prior to the corporate sort out, in the years prior there were several million dollars funneled to Hubbard through a phony corporation called Religious Research Foundation.

"Now the Mission Corporate Category Sort Out, those guys were trying to figure out how to make that legally defensible, retroactively, like oh my God! What a mistake. What a horrible, thing, that this money, cause Hubbard was putting out issues to all Scientologists that he never benefited from Scientology, he never took any money. But the fact is, he was taking several million dollars while staffs were starving."[14]

Even when it was figured out and made to actually be a legitimate and legal operation, the leaders of Scientology (Hubbard and then Miscavige) continued to run it in a criminal fashion because, as I've made the case in other chapters in this book, Scientology at its heart is nothing but a money-making scam meant to enrich one man. Even the people who worked for Hubbard at the highest levels actually believed in the lies Hubbard put forward about Scientology being an applied religious philosophy which was supposed to save the world and all the people in it. Yet when it came down to brass tacks, Hubbard and Miscavige operated like criminals and continue to do so to this very day.

For example, in setting up the numerous new corporations which would make up the new structure of Scientology, new boards of directors were instated around the world. According to Brennan, here is how this was done:

"Well, it was us, the missionaires under Miscavige who decided who was going into which corporation. And, even they're quote, unquote 'board members' the people we picked to be that, they didn't even know who was going on. We would just say - this one's going to be in this corporation, this one would take the orders from that one. And we were setting up all the window dressing. In fact, we pulled a bunch of students off courses at Flag and sent them all around the world to get the churches to sign the new agreements with the new mother Church of Scientology International.

"The local churches for the most part didn't even know who their board members were, they never met. And they weren't allowed to read the agreements. I myself was sent my Miscavige to 'Pubs,' the New Era Publications in Copenhagen, Denmark, to get them to sign the new royalty contracts with Hubbard. They didn't even get to read them. So, it's not just that, maybe there's a little bit of an out corporate integrity, it's a one hundred percent controlled by Hubbard and then Miscavige with just a whole bunch of camouflage put around it to make it look like it's not."[15]

On September 24, 1984, Scientology lost an appeal over tax assessments made on the Church of Scientology of California (remember this had been the umbrella corporation for Scientology since 1966). The Los Angeles IRS office also began a criminal investigation into Hubbard, leading with accusations from former members alleging he skimmed money from Scientology.[16]

Scientology not only appealed the legal decision with further legal machinations, but within months began to exert external pressure on the IRS in an attempt to back them off.

Attack, Never Defend

The National Coalition of IRS Whistleblowers was a Scientology front group started by Freedom Magazine, an outlet of Scientology's legal division, the Office of Special Affairs. Stacy Young, then editor of Freedom Magazine and an OSA staffer, said:

"The I.R.S. was not giving Scientology its tax exemption, so they were considered to be a pretty major enemy. What you do with an enemy is you go after them and harass them and intimidate them and try to expose their crimes until they decide to play ball with you. The whole idea was to create a coalition that was at arm's length from Scientology so that it had more credibility."[17]

To give the coalition an air of legitimacy and make it appear to be something it was not, i.e. a Scientology-financed attack on the IRS, Stacy hired Paul J. DeFosses, an ex-IRS agent turned advocate, to run the coalition. They quickly put together a white paper called "The Internal Revenue Service: An Agency Out of Control" and started sending this around to anyone who would read it.

Hubbard died in January 1986. In 1987, Miscavige was running Scientology as the Chairman of the Board of Religious Technology Center, the corporation which was supposed to control all the copyrights of Dianetics and Scientology.

Hubbard had doubts about whether Scientology should remain a religion, but he worked through those before he died. He insisted the Church of Scientology become a tax-exempt organization officially recognized by the US government and wrote into his will for this to be done before the Scientology trademarks could be transferred under Church control. Even after he was dead, he did not want anyone outside the Church getting their grubby hands on the money.

So if Scientology were going to continue, tax exemption had to be reclaimed. If Miscavige was going to be able to run this operation for any real length of time, tax exemption had to be reclaimed. Faced not only with these facts but also with the very serious problem he could be facing his own legal problems if the IRS continued to push forward in their investigation of his own wrongdoings with Church monies, Miscavige had to deal with the IRS once and for all.

There were two basic tacks Miscavige decided to take with the IRS to get them to reconsider the Church's position and grant tax exemption. The first was to liberally apply the Hubbard policy to "attack, never defend" so as to overwhelm the IRS and force them to make mistakes. The second was to tell the IRS whatever it wanted to hear about how Scientology had reformed and changed their evil ways, painting a facade of corporate integrity which would pass IRS scrutiny.

What is so amazing is this strategy actually worked. However, it did not happen overnight.

The Heat is On

The IRS was playing hardball. They wanted to make a definite and emphatic statement to Scientology even though Hubbard was no longer in the picture, they were still intent on getting their money and not letting Scientology get away with its decades of abuse of the tax system.

The criminal probe by the IRS's LA division was dropped after two years. They continued to try to make a case against Miscavige and the Church but felt they lacked credible witnesses since Scientology successfully smeared every ex-Scientologist who dared go to bat against Scientology in court.[18]

On July 9, 1988, the IRS denied tax-exempt status to the triad of corporate entities which were supposedly now running Scientology: the Church of Scientology International, the Religious Technology Center and the not-so-public Church of Spiritual Technology. The IRS demanded for-profit income tax returns for all years back since their inception and put full-time auditors (the IRS kind) on the Church of Scientology of California for 1967 - 1984.[19]

In November of that same year, arguments were made before the US Supreme Court in Hernandez vs IRS Commissioner regarding individual Scientology parishioners deducting their donations to the Church as charitable contributions. On June 5, 1989, the US Supreme

Court decided against Scientology, stating basically charitable contributions should not be made for a promised return or quid pro quo. This had been a hotly contested point for many years and with the Supreme Court's decision final, that argument was over. This was another major blow against the Church.

Meanwhile, DeFosses' Coalition of Whistleblowers made waves in exposing very real IRS abuses and criminal activities.

"The coalition's biggest success came in 1989 when it helped spark Congressional hearings into accusations of wrongdoing by I.R.S. officials. Using public records and leaked I.R.S. documents, the coalition showed that a supervisor in Los Angeles and some colleagues had bought property from a company being audited by the agency. Soon after the purchase, the audit was dropped and the company paid no money."[20]

While Capitol Hill was listening, Scientology also moved in with its usual covert investigations against IRS principals, namely agents and executives within the organization they wanted to get dirt on for blackmail purposes. Private investigators were hired and no expense was spared to get them. They snooped and pried around IRS meetings and investigated individual agents for any kind of personal or professional wrongdoing but there is little evidence anything substantial was found which would lead to effective blackmail material.

However, that didn't stop Scientology from taking out full page ads in *USA Today* citing abuse after abuse the IRS had committed against individual taxpayers and families. Many of these stories were horrifying and fed fuel to the very large PR bonfire Scientology was fanning.

In June 2009, the Tampa Bay Times reported this about the Church's battle with the IRS:

"Armed with IRS records obtained under the Freedom of Information Act, Scientology's magazine, Freedom, featured stories on alleged IRS abuses: lavish retreats on the taxpayers' dime; setting quotas on audits of individual Scientologists; targeting small businesses for audits while politically connected corporations were overlooked. Scientologists distributed the magazine on the front steps of the IRS building in Washington."[21]

In 1990, Scientologist Steven L. Hayes started another anti-IRS group called Citizens for an Alternative Tax System. Their idea was to institute a federal sales tax which would, in effect, make income tax unnecessary and the IRS useless. They worked to rally support as a grassroots movement and get politicians to take up their cause. David Miscavige personally made a video on the steps of the IRS promoting the group and its purposes. While the system it proposed was unworkable in the extreme, the whole point of this was to merely to bring more pressure to bear on the IRS.[22]

In addition to public relations pressure, Scientology also brought the heat on legal channels:

"The church filed about 200 lawsuits against the IRS, seeking documents to prove IRS harassment and challenging the agency's refusal to grant tax exemptions to church entities.

"Some 2,300 individual Scientologists also sued the agency, demanding tax deductions for their contributions."[23]

Some of those "cookie-cutter" lawsuits grew into full blown legal cases all on their own. For any group, even something as large as the United States Internal Revenue Service, this truly was an overwhelming amount of work to deal with. According to one IRS memo, the Scientology lawsuits alone tapped the IRS's litigation budget before the year was over.[24]

Something else to keep in mind is the millions of dollars required to pursue these cases were all paid by parishioner donations. IAS fundraisers toured the world telling Scientologists that the US government was trying to destroy Scientology forever because they hated the idea of Scientology freeing beings and this was literally Scientology's last hope for survival. If the Scientologists didn't act now to give everything they possibly could and more, Scientology would be destroyed by the "psychs" and "government SPs" who colluded for decades to undo the good works of the Church and bring down Hubbard. Now he was gone, they saw blood in the water and were working overtime on their "Final Solution for Scientology." They referred to the IAS coffers as the "war chest" and demanded Scientologists make any sacrifices necessary to fill it.

Even with all this going on, it seemed the IRS' Final Solution was rolling forward despite Scientology's efforts to pressure them to back down.

The Secret Meeting

A key moment came in October 1991. In fact, this is considered the pivotal moment in the war between Scientology and the IRS, when the whole nature of the relationship between them changed forever.

Miscavige was in Washington DC with Marty Rathbun, the second most senior official in Scientology at the time. Miscavige wanted the battle to end and thought it was time he take matters into his own hands since clearly all the lawyers, money and PR pressure weren't effective. They walked into the IRS headquarters and asked to speak with Fred Goldberg, the IRS Commissioner. He agreed to meet with them a week later.

Rathbun, now an ex-Scientologist and one of its most feared critics, is the only person in that room who said anything about what happened there. His account has been called biased and even pro-Scientology, even after he left the Church behind him. Regardless, it's the only account there is, as reported in the Tampa Bay Times:

"Rathbun says that contrary to rumor, no bribes were paid, no extortion used. It was round-the-clock preparation and persistence — plus thousands of lawsuits, hard-hitting magazine articles and full-page ads in USA Today criticizing the IRS.

" 'That was enough,' Rathbun said. 'You didn't need blackmail.'

"He and Miscavige prepped incessantly for their meeting. 'I'm sitting there with three banker's boxes of documents. He (Miscavige) has this 20-page speech to deliver to these guys. And for every sentence, I've got two folders of backup.'

"Miscavige presented the argument that Scientology is a bona fide religion — then offered an olive branch.

"Rathbun recalls the gist of the leader's words to the IRS:

"Look, we can just turn this off. This isn't the purpose of the church. We're just trying to defend ourselves. And this is the way we defend. We

251

aggressively defend. If we can sit down and actually deal with the merits, get to what we feel we are actually entitled to, this all could be gone.

"The two sides took a break.

"Rathbun remembered: 'Out in the hallway, Goldberg comes up to me because he sees I'm the right-hand guy. He goes: 'Does he mean it? We can really turn it off?'

" 'And I said, turning his hand for effect, 'Like a faucet.' "[25]

Personally, I believe this account. Knowing what I know about David Miscavige and his craven nature, I do not believe for a second he walked into the office of the head of one of the most powerful organizations in the United States government and threatened him with blackmail. That is a federal offense for which Miscavige could have literally been arrested on the spot. If Goldberg were looking for a way to escape the pressure Scientology was bringing on the IRS, that would have been all he needed. Imagine what would have happened to Scientology if Miscavige were led in handcuffs out of the Commissioner's office. That truly would have been game over for Scientology. I'm positive Miscavige would never take any such risk.

Those who have a conspiracy mindset may call me naïve or blind, but I don't think anyone who is claiming conspiracy is looking at all the facts. The sheer volume of pressure Scientology exerted against the IRS and was prepared to continue exerting was unlike anything the IRS encountered before. It was a war because Scientology was making it a war and they were not ever going to surrender.

Regardless of what happened during the meeting, or whether any backroom deals were made, Goldberg could not just wave a magic wand and grant Scientology tax-exempt status on his word alone. Instead, he bypassed the agency's Exempt Organizations Division which normally handles church and charity organizations, and created a five-member working group under Howard M. Schoenfeld to resolve the Scientology matter.

Given the thousands of lawsuits and PR pressure from Scientology, it really isn't hard to fathom why Goldberg would do such a thing. He wanted this dealt with and he wanted Scientology to stop their vigorous attacks. He had the courts on his side with decision after decision against Scientology, so it was not a matter of fearing a legal loss. Goldberg knew if something didn't change, the IRS was going to eventually win. It was the sheer magnitude of the costs involved to his agency and to the taxpayers to get that win which would have concerned him, as well as all the additional Congressional oversight Scientology was creating with their exposes and advertisements.

Also, during the entire two years this special working group was collecting information to decide on Scientology's tax-exempt status, the IRS was still doing a complete audit on the CSC and moving forward on tax assessments including penalties and interest. So there was no effort made to shut down movement against Scientology on standard IRS channels.

The Pack of Lies

Between 1991 and 1993, the IRS asked the Church about every aspect of their operation. There were three different sets of lengthy questions asked and answered. They had the Church explain in detail how their command lines operated, how the finances were managed at every level of the church, what the church's myriad corporations actually did, who was on the boards of directors of each corporation, how were Hubbard's policies applied to finance, etc.

This is where Miscavige, high-level Sea Org members and the Church's tax attorneys really went to town. Their "cooperation" with the IRS and claims of being "completely open" were bald faced lies.

I don't blame the Church's non-Scientologist lawyers so much as I do the Sea Org members involved. Tax attorneys and court lawyers who work for Scientology are just shills who will say or do anything for money. They park their ethics at the door and I have nothing but contempt for them, but in the end they are just mouthpieces and don't understand how things really work behind the scenes. They are not members of a destructive cult; they are merely paid to represent them. I'm not giving them a pass, I'm saying that they are doing their jobs and as despicable as those jobs are, it isn't personal for them.

The Scientologists and Sea Org members who did this work, though, are a whole different story. There is no way they were not fully aware of the facts but altered and changed them to paint a completely different picture from reality. They lived and worked under MIscavige and knew what went on behind the scenes. They knew of the abuses, the human rights violations and all the rest, and they purposefully lied about all of it. This is where Hubbard's policy of telling an "acceptable truth" really came into play.

"Handling truth is a touchy business also. You don't have to tell everything you know....Tell an acceptable truth. ... So PR becomes the technique of communicating an acceptable truth — and which will attain the desirable result."[26]

The following are some of the most important specific lies and deceptions the Church reported to the IRS.

MISREPRESENTATION OF SCIENTOLOGY MANAGEMENT OPERATION

In the Church's second series of responses to the IRS (June 29, 1992), a great many pages are dedicated to explaining the administrative hierarchy of the Watchdog Committee, International Management and the lower echelons, describing the same system I laid out in chapter 13. However, by the time these documents were submitted to the IRS, this entire system had already been subverted by David Miscavige.

Starting from back in the early 1980s when he ran the Special Unit (or Unit X) and then assumed the role of Chairman of the Board ASI, and now as COB RTC and the highest-ranking officer of the Sea Organization, Miscavige routinely bypassed anyone and everyone in the Scientology command structure at his whim. Anyone at any level of the Scientology hierarchy (including non-Sea Org personnel) who dare to question any small part of an order he gives are immediately interrogated and disciplined for such temerity, regardless of who their actual senior personnel are or their post assignment. Nothing but unquestioning loyalty and immediate compliance are expected to any order Miscavige issues. Should such compliance not be forthcoming, RTC staff will enforce compliance directly and without mercy.

In 1992 when these answers were submitted to the IRS, ED International and his Management Committee as well as the Watchdog Committee personnel were still nominally holding these positions and reporting to post each day, provided they were not removed permanently or temporarily by order of David Miscavige or some other RTC personnel for whatever petty grievance or offense they felt warranted the removal. Personnel shifts, demotions and transfers by order of Miscavige and RTC staff were routine among WDC, ED International's Management Committee and other International Management staff.

The entire Scientology command structure operated then and continues to operate now on Miscavige's caprice, verbal orders or directions and his written programs, making this entire submission to the IRS a complete and knowing lie.

MISREPRESENTATION OF CHURCH HISTORY AND CORPORATE SORT-OUT

It has been said history is written by the victors. Nowhere is this more true than in the Church of Scientology, where the events of the corporate and management takeover in the 1980s by David Miscavige were told to the IRS in a very creative and deceitful fashion.

As part of the second series of responses, reference is made to the Guardian's Office and the necessity of RTC and its Inspector General Network. The following statements are made in this section, each of which is a bald-faced lie and pure historical revisionism to give the IRS the impression Scientology had cleaned house and was no longer a corrupt, criminal organization:

"...during the 1970s, the Guardian's Office had become an autonomous and unsupervised splinter group, portions of which engaged in questionable and often illegal activities in serious violation of Church policy and the law."

The Guardian's Office was never a splinter group. It operated directly under the authority of Mary Sue Hubbard, who met on an almost daily basis with her husband and reported on its activities and progress in carrying out Hubbard's orders and programs. At no time was the Guardian's Office autonomous, meaning operating under its own volition without answering to a higher authority.

"Sea Org management bodies had been unable to detect and handle this situation before it got out of hand."

When you consider L. Ron Hubbard and Mary Sue Hubbard were the two leading officers of the Sea Organization (Hubbard was the self-appointed Commodore while Mary Sue was a Captain) and the directors of all Scientology operations internationally, there is no interpretation of this statement which makes it true. Hubbard claimed he held no management position in the Church after "turning over his hat" in 1966, yet there are reams of orders, evaluations, programs and despatches written throughout the 1970s which show the exact opposite was the case.

"The then Commanding Officer of the CMO INT attempted to block an internal investigation into the GO and Laurel Sullivan formulated plans to revise the Church's corporate structure to place the GO in control of the religious marks."

Laurel Sullivan is simply being made a scapegoat because it's convenient for the Church to do so since she was in no position to defend herself or offer true testimony as to what her involvement was with the corporate sort-out.

According to Stewart Lamont in *Religion, Inc.*:

"[Sullivan] left the Church of Scientology in 1981 after serving fifteen years, the last eight as Hubbard's personal public relations adviser. From 1972-81 she was in charge of a secret operation to transfer money from church funds to Hubbard through a corporate shell, the Religious Research Foundation (RRF), incorporated in Liberia with accounts in banks in Lichtenstein and Luxemburg. When she left Scientology in 1981, she said that the RRF's assets were between $200 million and $300 million, and at one point in the 1970s they totalled $330 million."

Laurel Sullivan reportedly worked with Mary Sue Hubbard, who David Miscavige despised and later ousted from any power position in the Church (this was after the Snow White Program indictments but before Mary Sue was sent to jail). Sullivan knew the actual intent of the corporate restructuring was to protect Hubbard and continue funneling money to him. Whether the Guardian's Office was going to gain control of the religious marks would have been irrelevant if it suited the purposes of Hubbard and Miscavige. In re-writing history, Miscavige claims bad apples in the Church were trying to stop him and his band of "good guys" from expunging the criminal elements back in the early 1980s. This, of course, also justifies why Laurel Sullivan and her ilk were all declared Suppressive Persons and no longer in the Church. One positive consequence of declaring a person Suppressive (as far as Scientology is concerned) is they're no longer around to defend themselves from any accusations Scientologists make about them.

The Church's historical revisionism goes on to state to the IRS:

"Further, Mr. Hubbard was not actively involved in Church affairs at that time; having decided to devote his time and energies to completing his researches into the highest levels of spiritual awareness. Thus he was not in a position to monitor the use of the religious marks."

As has already been documented in the last chapter, Pat Broeker and David Miscavige had a whole private communication system in place to relay written orders and dispatches to and from Hubbard's hiding place from the time Hubbard went into hiding until his death in 1986. There was no period of time when Hubbard was out of touch with Scientology's affairs.

In fact, during this time in the early 1980s when he was supposedly not involved in Church affairs, Hubbard authored specific directions to all Scientology churches internationally, giving them directions on how to play "the Birthday Game" (a competition amongst the churches to see which can grow more in size over a year's time) as well as giving a complete review of Scientology's progress in the world in issues called "Ron's Journals". These are publicly available documents and prove by his own hand he was very much on top of what was going on with Church affairs.

I've described in detail how Scientology's corporate sort-out reorganized its internal management structure. There was a whole other aspect to this which is just as involved and was also subverted in just as deceitful a fashion. This involves a checks and balances system which was put into place with the three primary corporate entities which hold power in Scientology. These are not internal management entities, but corporate bodies which hold control over Scientology's bank accounts, trademarks and copyrights.

The system is quite involved so only a brief summary will be presented here, enough to show how Miscavige represented it to the IRS and how he then immediately subverted it for his own ends, removing any threats to his own personal power and giving him dictatorial control over the Scientology empire.

Corporately speaking, there are three entities which are the core controlling groups of Scientology: Church of Scientology International (CSI), Religious Technology Center (RTC) and Church of Spiritual Technology (CST). This triumvirate are set up with boards of directors and trustees so as to present a picture to the world of checks and balances, to prevent exactly what has already happened: one man taking over the entire operation as a dictator.

Perhaps if that one man had not been present for the formation of this whole structure and not taken steps to subvert it from the very beginning, these checks and balances would actually work. However, as I've already made the case for, Scientology was never about checks and balances or about limiting the control of its leader. It is about keeping that leader in power and given unlimited financial resources to have his way.

In the real world, corporations have boards of directors. and trustees. These individuals control things on a broad basis and have the ability to appoint or remove corporate executives if they are not doing their jobs or are doing something criminal or the like. Then there is a CEO or President or someone with a similar title who controls the day-to-day operations through an executive team. The board members and trustees do not run daily operations or even involve themselves in that level of decision making. They are there to make sure things are running smoothly over the long haul and to keep the CEO on his toes. This is how people are used to looking at corporate entities and how they think they are controlled. Normally they are right. In the case of Scientology, they are dead wrong.

The people who were put into these positions were almost all Sea Org members. As described in the last chapter, the Sea Org is the paramilitary group who have dedicated their lives to Scientology and have sworn a very binding oath to uphold, forward and carry out Command Intention, meaning anything that the leader of Scientology says to do. Every single Sea Org members reveres David Miscavige. As he is the ranking officer of the Sea Org, they also have no choice but to follow his orders. If they don't, they will face immediate consequences including being sent to the Rehabilitation Project Force for their insolence. None of these people are going to stand up to David Miscavige or invoke corporate bylaws to remove him from power.

CST is the most unique of the three key Scientology corporations, in no small part because it has Special Directors who are not Sea Org members. It was founded in 1982 by Lymon Spurlock (a Sea Org member who was also a trained CPA), Meade Emory, Leon Misterek and Sherman Lenske (none of them are SO members). It's not clear now who exactly its Special Directors are; Lymon Spurlock and Meade Emory have died. The only person I know for sure is a Special Director right now is Monique Yingling, a tax attorney who is a Church mouthpiece trotted out whenever they need some clout from Capitol Hill, which is where Yingling works.

CST's Articles of Incorporation state its purpose is to *"espouse, present, propagate, practice, ensure and maintain the purity and integrity of the religion of Scientology..."*[27]

CST does this by creating massive, insanely expensive archives of Hubbard's written and spoken works. Using the highest end archival and space age technology, they have created vast underground vaults which store titanium plates and gold-plated records upon which are inscribed Hubbard's books, bulletins and recorded lectures. There are no less than four of these underground vaults built in the western United States, all out in remote locations and heavily secured to prevent anyone from coming near the vaults themselves.

When Hubbard was still alive, the CST had another purpose: to be a depository for the bulk of his testamentary estate. CST's founders wanted to accomplish "*the creation of an organization to which Mr. Hubbard would be willing to (and did) bequeath the bulk of his estate, and most importantly his copyrights and patents (which include copyrights to scriptures of the religion and patents on the E-Meter)."*[28]

CST was founded using money from the Flag Service Organization (a "one-time startup grant" of $17.9 million dollars) in 1983 and annual unrestricted grants from RTC ranging from $623,000 to $2.8 million.[29]

Much has been made out about the significance of the non-Scientologist Special Directors by those who see conspiracies around every corner. For example, from 1975 to 1977, Meade Emory was an Assistant to the Commissioner of the IRS, one of the many jobs he held as a tax attorney and expert in the US tax system. He died in October 2010, living in Seattle and a Professor of Law Emeritus at the University of Washington School of Law.

Conspiracy theorists believe somehow the IRS is now secretly in charge of the Church of Scientology because of tenuous behind-the-scenes connections like Emory. Such a conspiratorial view requires one to accept the IRS as some kind of old boy's club where once one is part of it, one is forever part of it and continues to take orders from it for the rest of one's life. This view also requires ignoring that despite the IRS getting their "inside man" into the Church at the head of CST, they took another 12 years to get around to granting tax exemption, after spending millions more prosecuting tax cases against Scientology. This conspiracy claim is frankly ridiculous at every level.

Rather than some vast conspiracy to control Scientology, the real explanation behind these non-Scientologist Special Directors is because they ensure CST never, ever loses its tax-exempt status. CST is the final bastion, the last line of defense for Scientology if everything else falls apart. It must maintain tax exemption at all costs. That's why tax specialists are an integral part of its very structure. There is a rumor of some other shadow corporation waiting to take over should CST fall or be corrupted, but I could find no solid evidence of its name or existence.

There are lots of complications to the bylaws and articles of incorporation of all three of these corporations which create the illusion Scientology is not a dictatorship. However, in the end, the boards of directors and trustees of CST, RTC and CSI are nothing more than window dressing, a veneer placed there to satisfy inquisitive tax collectors or those in the "wog world" who try to understand who is really running Scientology. The checks and balances between these corporations exist on paper only but are never going to be exercised in the real world.

For example, if the Board of Directors or Trustees of CST see RTC or CSI have gone off the rails, they are supposed to be able to buy back the copyrights and trademarks from RTC for just $100. The last record I could find of the Board of Directors of CST is from 1993: John Allcock, David Lantz and Russell Bellin, all Sea Org members. In case anyone has any doubt about what I have said about Miscavige being able to control these boards through the Sea Org, when I was on the RPF from 2004 - 2008, John Allcock was there with me. Not much of a Board Member and certainly in no position to challenge Miscavige's authority.

Meanwhile, the Special Directors of CST, the non-Scientology tax attorneys, were all put there by David Miscavige and their positions really are sinecures (an office requiring or involving little to no responsibility, labor, or active service but for which one receives a hefty salary anyway). Miscavige is the one who has final say on their appointments and signs their checks. Their purpose is not to usurp authority from Miscavige but to ensure tax exemption is maintained so he can continue to hold authority and power. None of those Special Directors are motivated to do anything to remove Miscavige.

A House of Lies

As I have shown, the very structure and integrity of Scientology were misrepresented to the IRS in the grossest possible way, giving them an impression very different from the reality of what Scientology is and how it is run. It was on this basis tax exemption was granted, since the case was made Scientology is not a dictatorship, does not exist for the inurement of one individual and has some actual public benefit. None of these things are actually true.

There were many other lies and deceptions in the questions and answers to the IRS. For example, there is the assertion all Scientology auditors are ordained ministers, easily disproven by reviewing course completion rosters of any Scientology organization to see which auditors have or have not done the Minister's Course. There is the assertion IAS donations are not mandatory requirements in order to move up the Scientology Bridge, easily disproven by the numerous and repeated testimonies of former members who were quite clear on the fact they had to donate exorbitant amounts of money to the IAS before they would be granted "ethics clearance" to proceed to the OT Levels.

I could take up another two chapters worth of material in documenting them but I think what I've shown thus far has proven my point.

It's been said if you tell a big enough lie enough times, it will eventually be believed no matter how outrageous it is.

The church is a house of lies built for one basic reason: to shield and protect L. Ron Hubbard for having to accept the consequences of his destructive policies, mismanagement and financial inurement. David Miscavige built on that and to this day continues to get away with the same lies and mismanagement.

15. Converting the Converted

Change is Possible

There's this funny idea I've heard, usually spoken in a cynical tone, saying people can't or don't ever change.

This is patently ridiculous as people make important life changes every day. I would have sworn on a stack of Dianetics books I would never give up my Scientology beliefs and would never be argued out of them. Yet I changed, and so can anyone else.

In fact, isn't it true many of today's atheists and skeptics were at one time, believers in faith of one kind or another? There's nothing worse than an ex-smoker, right?

Making the Change

In the arena of critical thinking and skepticism, the favorite opponents seem to be religious fundamentalists or destructive cult members (same thing). When trying to "talk some sense" into these fundamentalists, some people fail to make any immediate or visible change and so feel they have failed in their efforts, and conclude people can't or don't even want to change. This is especially true of close family and friends of cult members who are trying to convince them how dangerous the cult is or why they shouldn't be involved with it.

What they fail to realize is the real reason those cult members don't change their tune is the actual reason for their beliefs has not been isolated.

Generally speaking, unless you are dealing with a truly insane person, you can find some rational reason behind anyone's belief in just about anything. You might talk to 100 different Christians and in isolating why they believe God is good and Jesus is their personal Savior, you are going to probably find 100 different reasons. Every person is unique and they each have their own experiences, viewpoints and reasons for believing what they believe.

I'm not saying all Christians are cult members, by the way. Far from it. There are plenty of good religious groups without the characteristics of a dangerous cult and if you are part of one of those groups, I have no issue with you or your beliefs. However, I think it's pretty easy to see when you look at the Westboro Baptists or Quiverfull movement, you are dealing with people who are involved in very destructive activities.

Tolerance is Key

When talking to one of these people, if you isolate what their reasons for belief are and then argue against them with rationality and intelligence and don't make the person feel like a moron in the process, you have a very good chance of changing their minds. I'm not just talking about religion either. This applies to any firmly held belief or point of view, especially when belief becomes rigid and fixed and the person is absolutely unwilling to consider changing.

The number one thing you can do wrong when you are trying to change the hearts and minds of others is to make them feel stupid, wrong or bad for believing what they believe. Human nature is such that, when faced with direct or indirect opposition like this, it will fight back by holding on to those beliefs even harder.

Maybe the reasons people have for believing things are silly, illogical or irrational. Telling them so is not going to score you any brownie points. The last time someone told you you were stupid or didn't know what you were talking about, did that contribute to a constructive conversation?

16. N is for Narcissism

After coming out of a cult experience like Scientology, I've seen a lot of former members try to make sense of the experience. It's not easy because when you are in a bubble world surrounded by like-minded people who are constantly reinforcing whatever belief system, customs and morals your group subscribes to, you get a skewed world view. You start thinking about everything in the same terms and how people are either on your side or on the "other" side. Walls get put up and it's so very easy to start thinking of yourself (or your group) as being better than everyone else.

Hubbard preached reality is agreement. There is a certain degree of truth there, in that people in any group certainly agree to see things a certain way and actively block out anything opposing "their reality."

I wish I could say Scientology or destructive cults are the only places this happens, but unfortunately that is not the case at all. I see this every single day with regular religious and political groups, social activities etc.

I try to stay away from labels or name calling, because I generally think that sort of thing is unproductive and harmful to critical thinking. At the same time, though, there are certain words we use to describe motives and behaviors which fit well enough and also serve to make a point. And in this case, the word I'm looking at is *narcissism*.

I'm not here to say all Scientologists are textbook narcissists. I'm saying Scientology heavily indoctrinates its followers in narcissistic behavior and the entire culture within the Church encourages this.

265

Perhaps the same thing happens in other mass movements or closed-belief systems too.

Narcissism has been described as a personality disorder. I don't know if I'd call it a disorder so much as a frame of mind, but that is completely open to debate. I just want to be clear I'm also not trying to saddle all Scientologists with the stigma of being "mentally ill" or bad people.

This is not an effort to summarize all Scientology or explain the whole subject. I'm writing this to try to help explain the behavior of Scientologists and perhaps offer some suggestions as to how to help those trying to get out of the Scientology mind-set, whether this means you personally or someone you know.

It's All About Me

The term *narcissism* comes from the Greek legend of Narcissus. He was a handsome young man who fell in love with his own reflection in a pond after rejecting the nymph Echo. According to the myth, he sat and stared in adoration at his reflection for so long he eventually turned into a flower, the narcissus.

Narcissism has been defined as extreme selfishness, with a grandiose view of one's own talents and a craving for admiration. There's a great article on it by Dr. Kelly Neff at The Mind Unleashed website.[1]

Here are some of the characteristics of narcissism:

1. Has a grandiose sense of self-importance (e.g., exaggerates achievements and talents, expects to be recognized as superior without commensurate achievements)

2. Is preoccupied with fantasies of unlimited success, power, brilliance, beauty, or ideal love

3. Believes he or she is "special" and unique and can only be understood by, or should associate with, other special or high-status people (or institutions)

4. Requires excessive admiration

5.   Has a very strong sense of entitlement, e.g., unreasonable expectations of especially favorable treatment or automatic compliance with his or her expectations

6.   Is exploitative of others, e.g., takes advantage of others to achieve his or her own ends.

7.   Lacks empathy, e.g., is unwilling to recognize or identify with the feelings and needs of others. According to Dr. Martha Stout, author of *The Sociopath Next Door* this is the defining characteristic of a narcissist.

8.   Is often envious of others or believes others are envious of him or her

9.   Regularly shows arrogant, haughty behaviors or attitudes

When I first started reading about this, I was somewhat startled to see so much of this in my own behavior back when I was in the cult, especially when I was in the Sea Org. And yet at the same time, I joined the Sea Org out of a selfless sense of duty and honor, a sacrifice to help the rest of the world by not putting myself and my own interests first. Talk about a dichotomy!

Contempt for anyone not in the Sea Org and a "holier than thou" attitude are part of the entire culture of the Sea Org and it took months after I left to realize this was the source of troubles I was experiencing in the real world. To a lesser degree this exists at every level of Scientology. It is an elitist group.

Can a narcissist be created? I believe they can and I believe Scientology does exactly that. I also believe it can be unlearned and a person can come out of this state of mind.

In Hubbard's Image

It doesn't take deep psychological insight to see L. Ron Hubbard had deep character flaws. His Affirmations (see Appendix 2) are his own grandiose ideas of how he should be and act, delivered to himself apparently in self-hypnosis sessions before he even started Dianetics and Scientology.

From almost the very beginning of Scientology, Hubbard molded an elitist philosophy around the benefits of being self-absorbed. I know there are people who are going to take exception to this, and I don't claim this experience is universal for everyone who has ever been involved in Scientology. It's pretty undeniable though, especially in Scientology's current state, there is a vicious streak of self-absorption running right through the middle of Hubbard's writings and lectures. This is no accident.

Look at one of the most basic tenets of Scientology: The Factors from 1953. Hubbard describes these as some of the most fundamental principles in all of existence. Factor #14 in part states *"Thus there is matter. But the most valued point is admiration, and admiration is so strong its absence alone permits persistence."*

It's an interesting line and one which Scientologists often ponder. You could remove that line about admiration and the rest of the Factors still make sense. Why include it? I believe it is because Hubbard believed gaining admiration was not only a good thing, but in fact the most valuable thing in existence. This is how Hubbard saw the world and what he passed on to his followers in this and countless other ways throughout his writings.

Look at the final destination of Scientology - the thing all Scientologists want so much they will forsake family and friends, cash out retirement accounts and their children's college funds for: the state of Operating Thetan (OT). And what is that? It's the state of "knowing and willing cause over life, thought, matter, energy, space and time (MEST)". In a word, apotheosis.

Perhaps the epitome of this principle of admiration is David Miscavige. His cavalier and power-hungry existence, with only the very best of food and clothing and every material need cared for (all paid for by Scientology's tax-exempt parishioner donations), is exemplified in his own statement to the press, *"power in my estimation is if people will listen to you. That's it."*[2]

These days, every single person who ever completes a service in Scientology must write a success story where they include their personal thanks to David Miscavige for his brilliance, hard work and dedication.

If they refuse to, the person is not allowed to complete their service and "handled" until they will write it out.

What kind of person demands that of their followers?

The Price They are Willing to Pay

There is a lot of lip service paid in Scientology to responsibility. I believe this term used to actually mean something substantial for Scientologists. I certainly used to believe taking responsibility for others and doing my part counted for something and would help ensure I'd make it to full OT myself. That's the actual reason I joined the Sea Organization in the first place back in 1995.

Today, the amount of responsibility someone in Scientology takes is measured exclusively by how big of a check they're willing to write. People pay their way through ethics handlings after endless amounts of confessionals, eerily similar to the medieval practice of Catholic indulgences. One's checkbook or credit card is their only passport out of any Ideal Org fundraising event.

Why do those few Scientologists who remain continue to give? Well, the answer is simple: admiration. You don't have to take my word for it. Here is part of a Scientology promotional piece called "Why We Did It" written by Johnny & Marilyn Beck after becoming "Humanitarians with Honors" (a status awarded solely for how much money they've given) to the Silicon Valley Ideal Org:

"We donate because it is fun. As an example, we get the honor of acknowledgement and validation from our group. That is a tremendous amount of havingness and as you know, lots of fun. And, having donated, we have another reason to admire each other and say to ourselves, hey look, I am married to a Humanitarian with Honors.

"And Marilyn and I get to look at all the other Humanitarians and Civilization Builders with tons of admiration and we can say: we know these people! They are our friends! That is admiration and so much fun.

"Admiration, to us, is a fun particle. Marilyn splurges with it and I do too. So our donations are simply a flow of admiration. They are simply a flow of admiration, firstly, to LRH. They are, too, a flow of admiration to

Marilyn and myself and to other Humanitarians and very much so to our Civilization Builders."

When it comes to doing something other than giving money, though, don't ask them to lift a finger. When cornered and recruited to do something like join staff or go directly help in disaster relief efforts or even go out and sell Scientology books, people like Johnny Beck can't get out of the room fast enough. As long as they are giving over their money, though, this lack of empathy and help is part of the established and acceptable culture now rampant in Scientology.

It used to be Scientology auditors were considered to be the most valuable people on the planet. Auditors are a thing of the past. Scientology now is nothing more than a Mutual Admiration Society where help is not the ticket in, but your checkbook is. In the modern Church of Scientology, you can simply buy your way to spiritual freedom, even if it means leaving a trail of disconnected family and friends behind you.

The Sad Truth

It's a sad truth, but generally speaking it takes something bad happening to a Scientologist directly before they will open their eyes to the truth of what they are involved in. There are many factors at play behind this, including fear, the phenomenon of cognitive dissonance and even a kind of emotional inertia where a person has been part of something for so long they can't really muster up the energy it would take to break free from it.

Necessity of some kind, sparked by some personal affront or real damage, is usually what it takes to jar them out of this. In other words, something bad has to happen to them personally to shock them enough they can realize what's actually going on and actually affects them. That was certainly the case with me and almost every single ex-member of Scientology or other destructive cults.

I believe the narcissistic attitude developed in Scientology is partly to blame for this. They may hear about enforced disconnections where families or long-term friendships are broken up. They may hear about some of the Office of Special Affairs' more unsavory activities such as fraud, harassment and blackmail. They may have even gone on the internet and know all about David Miscavige's sociopathic activities. But if it doesn't affect them personally, if it doesn't come into their home or their place of business and bite them, they are willing to give it a pass.

One Way to Help

I don't pretend to be a psychologist. I'm not presenting anything here other than my own personal opinions on how to deal with a cult member. If someone needs professional help, they should get it and I will never imply otherwise.

I believe Dr. Nuff's advice to "love them from afar" is very good advice. Scientologists (or any destructive cult members) are loathe to change and have built up very strong defensive mental walls around themselves to keep out critical thoughts or feelings about the cult. It is never an easy task to break through that, especially when you don't have the person's cooperation. If you have someone like this in your life, it's easier to just leave them be and let them come to their own conclusions.

However, that's not really the compassionate thing to do, especially if you can step up and make a difference.

Scientology's indoctrination system creates a mindset where one is personally more powerful, more special and, in a word, *better* than everyone else. Its entire culture is centered around not only the concept of personal empowerment, but includes a strong "us versus them" mentality. Any non-Scientologist is suspect of working "for the bank-dominated mob" whose sole interest is destroying every Scientologist's freedom for all eternity.

I believe, though, such a mindset is contrary to humanity's basic nature and deep down they resist this "us versus them" thinking. Marc Headley, ex-Scientologist and author of *Blown for Good* said "The end product of Scientology is Leaving Scientology.... Everything you will do in scientology will eventually lead to you leaving. Everyone eventually leaves. PERIOD."

But even after coming out of Scientology, it took me almost a year before I was okay with acknowledging there were some things about my way of thinking and my emotional reactions which weren't so ideal. So it's not an easy road out.

Leading someone out of such a system of thought is tough and requires patience and perseverance. The biggest barrier is getting them to talk to you about it at all. If you can accomplish that, I think you are actually 90% there.

There are two characteristics of narcissistic behavior which I think work to the advantage of anyone who would like to help someone in this state.

(1) A narcissistic personality loves to talk, especially about themselves.

(2) According to Dr. Lisa Firestone in her article "Is There a Cure for Narcissism?" *"many narcissistic personalities are hiding deeper feelings of unworthiness or fears of failure."*[3]

Get them to talk, listen patiently and see if you can direct their attention toward those things about themselves or Scientology which they feel are not right or which they have doubts or reservations about. If you can find even one thing "real to them" which they can see is not right, and get them to talk about why that is, what it has to do with them, how it might affect them, etc., this can start a sort of mental chain reaction.

This takes time. Depending on how close you are to the person, how much they trust you and how often you communicate, this could take months or even longer. I have never seen anyone suddenly change their entire life or belief system in just one or two conversations.

It usually took quite some time to develop this narcissistic mindset in the first place, so there is no reason it should be undone quickly, despite any of Hubbard's rhetoric about the speed of auditing results in Scientology.

Re-Adjusting to the Real World

It's not been easy for me coming out of Scientology. In addition to adjusting to life in the real world, there's been a lot of mental and emotional baggage to sort through and work out. I'm sure this will be an ongoing process for quite some time and I know I'm not alone in this. Everyone who comes out realizes they were taken advantage of to one degree or another. We have to review our own personal beliefs and the decisions we made over the years which led us into and out of Scientology.

People talk about gains from their time in Scientology, even after they leave. I certainly had my share of them. I never fault anyone for this or tell them those things aren't true. However, I think real healing comes about when we can not just hold on to the good things, but also look at some of the bad and acknowledge what it was, then leave it behind.

17. Recovering from Scientology

The official Church of Scientology may or may not last for years to come. It really depends on how long its current leader, David Miscavige, can continue to repackage and remarket L. Ron Hubbard's nonsense to a purposefully ignorant audience who seem all too willing to overlook the obvious and blatant human rights violations, abuses and authoritarianism which are Scientology's core practices. The members of Scientology can't be blamed fully though, because they are victims of a masterfully crafted deceit machine L. Ron Hubbard built and David Miscavige has only added to.

I said Scientology is tiny and insignificant not because I am trying to devalue the damage Scientology does, but instead to put it into its proper perspective. L. Ron Hubbard, whether he meant to or not, created a mind controlling, authoritarian system of belief which damages people psychologically, emotionally and spiritually. And just for the record, I happen to think he knew exactly what he was doing.

I've said from the beginning the beliefs themselves are not the problem and I still say that. People in the cult right now, even celebrities like John Travolta and Tom Cruise, avoid the real issues with Scientology by saying anyone critical of their religion is just bashing their freedom to believe what they want. Well let me say again you can believe in thetans and Xenu and the rest of Scientology's teachings all you want. The critics of Scientology may ridicule or make light of those beliefs, but the beliefs themselves have never been the real issue. It is what people do with those beliefs and how they use them to control and undermine a person's self-esteem and personal freedom.

That has always been the problem with Scientology and with every other destructive cult out there.

Escaping from a destructive mass movement like Scientology and moving on with one's life is challenging, to say the least. I can't speak for everyone since I think the experience is unique for each person, but I've found there are all kinds of psychological, emotional and spiritual barriers which have to be overcome before someone can say they have broken free of the constraints of any enforced belief system.

I've been lucky enough to have experienced and learned some things which have helped me quite a bit and I thought it might be a good idea to share some of them. These are simply some things which helped me through the whole process from the initial betrayal and anger I felt when I learned what a pathological liar L. Ron Hubbard was to where I'm at now. At this point, Scientology isn't a major part of my thinking processes and Scientology values no longer shape my opinions and judgements. It doesn't mean much of anything to me anymore.

So if you find yourself coming out of Scientology or some other cult, maybe these points can help you too.

1. Find a soft place to land, a place where you can be away from Scientology and get the support, help and love you need to get on with your life.

If you are still in touch with Scientologists who are trying to handle you to get back in the cult, I don't think your recovery is going to go very smoothly. I'm not advocating some kind of reverse disconnection where you have to kick all Scientologists out of your life entirely. I'm just saying they aren't going to be much help in recovering from the cult.

2. Take the time to learn about the lies and deceptions foisted off on you by L. Ron Hubbard, David Miscavige and the Scientology staff.

There are many resources for this, whole indices of information compiled by people who were interested and caring enough to try to piece together the actual facts of Scientology, as opposed to the historical revisionism which L. Ron Hubbard was famous for throughout his entire life. Read as much as you want to get the facts on your experience with Scientology.

For example, just Google Scientology. Look at everything. It's not all necessarily true as there are some pretty crazy conspiracy theories out there about Scientology and whatnot, but I think you'll be able to differentiate the fact from the fiction pretty easily. By far most of the information you'll find is dead-on accurate.

All the confidential upper level materials are available out there for free. Let me assure you, despite what Hubbard claimed, the OT III materials are not dangerous and no one I know has ever died or even gotten a little bit sick from reading it.

There are also some great books out there written by people who were involved in Scientology for decades. They know what they are talking about.

One analogy Scientology has made is you shouldn't go to the Nazis to learn about the Jews. Fair enough, but that's not an accurate comparison when you are reading the accounts of ex-Scientologists. It's more like this: if you were a Jew and you had a problem with the Nazis, perhaps an ex-Nazi might shed some light on what they're up to and what they are really all about. That is what you get when you read books from ex-members - the inside data about what really goes on behind the curtain of Scientology's inner circle.

A very important thing to realize when you are doing this is you are likely going to run into information which conflicts with what you think you know about L. Ron Hubbard or Scientology itself. There is a thing called cognitive dissonance, which basically means the discomfort a person experiences when he tries to resolve two conflicting pieces of information.

Contrary to popular belief, the truth is not always "somewhere in the middle". Sometimes, especially with Scientology, you've just been told lies and you believed them. Some of them can take a while to let go of. L. Ron Hubbard was a pathological liar and built an organization on a house of cards. Once you start removing some of the key cards, the whole thing will come tumbling down.

3. Purposefully go out of your way to not speak the language.

Remove the significance of the vocabulary and find regular English terms to describe ideas, concepts or reactions previously you were using only Scientology terms for. It's common for cults to develop their own special language so they can feel unique and different from the rest of the world. By removing this from your thinking, it can really help get the cult influence out of your daily life.

I actually can't stress the importance of this enough. There are psychological factors at play with language, in fact quite a lot of them, actually. If you continue to use the language of Scientology, you keep certain thought patterns in place which create a false worldview, the one created by Hubbard and Miscavige. It will be well-nigh impossible to fully break free from the cult if you keep using the words and phrases of Scientology. It's often one of the most difficult things for ex-members to do, which should give you a hint as to why it's so important.

4. Learn about critical thinking, science and reason.

This really helped me to strip off a lot of what Hubbard presented as "scientific evidence" which was in fact pseudoscience and nonsense, not backed by any real research or proper scientific review. I mean, if you are an ex-member, think about it. The entire time you were in Scientology, did you ever see any research notes, experimentation or any independent review done of Hubbard's work? Of course not, because there wasn't any.

Learning about these things also helped me focus my attention and purpose on something positive because I was determined not to go from one cult to another. By learning about critical thinking, I could objectively look at anything new with a critical eye and not buy into any supposed "facts" or assertions people made until I was able to review it for myself.

Famous astrophysicist Neil Degrasse Tyson recently said *"Science literacy is not just what you know but how your brain is wired for thought. If you can achieve that, you never have to ask if the moon landings are real again."* In other words, you won't fall for any more baloney.

5. Take the time to clean house in your head.

Re-evaluate everything you think or believe in light of whether it is really your own thought or something enforced on you. For example, as a Scientologist probably lots of things made little sense when you were studying but you were told the reason for it is because you "had misunderstood words" and you had to spend hours looking them up in dictionaries because of your disagreements.

Now I'm all for understanding what you are reading, but this is also used in Scientology to shut people up and convince them their questions or disagreements are wrong and Hubbard is always right. Well, I didn't find that to be true once I started reviewing some of Hubbard's assertions, such as when he said everything having to do with psychology or psychiatry is automatically evil and must be destroyed. Yeah, not so much.

6. Learn to re-experience emotion.

Take the suppressors off about "no case on post" and "not being misemotional". This is a really tough one and it took me months out of Scientology before I even realized I had emotional issues.

Once it became obvious it was hard for me to experience things like anger and grief, I discovered for myself what shields and barriers I had put up to wall myself off from feeling. That helped open up the floodgates and I started experiencing all kinds of things I had previously been unable to. I'm not saying running around being angry or upset is wonderful and I'm not actually an angry person. It's just anyone should have the freedom to experience any emotion they need to, appropriate for the situation.

As a former Sea Org member, I was punished for feeling such things and so I learned to wall all those so-called negative emotions off. I don't think that's healthy and I don't think it's right for Scientologists do that to each other.

7. Learn about other destructive cults and mass movements and how they are similar to Scientology.

This is really important because one thing drummed into you hard in Scientology is how unique and special it is and how there is nothing else in the whole universe like it. When I found out every other destructive cult and mass movement uses the same methods, control techniques and psychological manipulations, it dawned on me how un-special and how commonplace Scientology actually is. Hubbard used different words and pretty severe forms of psychological and physical discipline to enforce his beliefs on others, but in the end, his techniques are almost exactly the same as Jim Jones, Sun Myung Moon, David Koresh or Charles Manson. I think when you see that for yourself, it helps a lot to get closure on your whole Scientology experience.

There are some excellent books and lectures given by Steve Hassan, Margaret Singer and Robert Lifton which I highly recommend on this topic.

8. Communicate with others who can and will understand your experiences and won't judge or be condescending.

Maybe you can talk to your family, friends or a professional counsellor. Maybe that communication also consists of writing or making videos to express things and share your experiences. I've found this to be one of the most cathartic and effective things I've done.

9. And most importantly, go out and live life to the fullest.

Rejoin family and friends whom you might have disconnected from or haven't seen in a long time. Get out in the real world and mingle with all kinds of people to find out what they are really like.

Some are great and some are not so great; you don't have to like everybody or agree with everyone but one thing you'll find for sure is the big wide world is out there to be experienced and enjoyed, as are the people in it. There is so much to learn from other people. There have been brilliant thinkers, scholars, scientists and humanitarians who have all done far more to really improve the lot of Man than L. Ron Hubbard ever dreamed of accomplishing. Learning about them and meeting new people is not just fun but extremely rehabilitating.

A New Life

I'm not under any illusion I'm "fully recovered" or have achieved some brilliant new state of being. Personally, I think this recovery process is something I'll be doing for the rest of my life and that's fine with me. I'm not down on myself anymore for what I did or what I experienced in Scientology. It was an extremely unfortunate experience but it's one I've moved on from. Now I can get on with the rest of my life, with a lot more hope and happiness than I thought possible when I was in Scientology.

Everything I've said here is what I've done but these things might not be everything you need. There are lots of resources out there you can go to. There's certainly nothing wrong with seeking professional counselling if you feel you need it. In fact, I'm sure in many cases it could be the only thing which might help achieve a real recovery.

I hope this book helps.

References and Notes

Chapter 2

1. Miriam Webster Online Dictionary, http://www.merriam-webster.com/dictionary/apostate
2. Business Dictionary, http://www.businessdictionary.com/definition/undue-influence.html
3. Jesse Prince. Operation Clambake presents David Miscavige's Rise to Corruption (or Ding-Dong the King is Dead), as posted to alt.religion.scientology September 6th 1998, http://www.xenu.net/archive/personal_story/jesse_prince/ding_dong/
4. Anonymous. Leaving Scientology article "Who's on Post?", December 2, 2009, https://leavingscientology.wordpress.com/2009/12/02/whos-on-post/
5. Augustine, Jeffrey. The Scientology Money Project article "CSI: Church of Scientology 990-T Filings 2008 - 2012", April 13, 2014, http://scientologymoneyproject.com/2014/04/13/the-church-of-scientology-international-990-t-filings-2008-2011/

Chapter 3

1. Hubbard, L. Ron. *The Creation of Human Ability: a Handbook for Scientologists,* p. 147. Los Angeles, CA: Bridge Publications, Inc., 2007. Print.
2. Hubbard, L. Ron. *Dianetics: The Modern Science of Mental Health,* p. 205. Los Angeles, CA: Bridge Publications, Inc., 2007. Print.
3. Hubbard, L. Ron. "Scientology: Milestone One", lecture given March 3, 1952.
4. Hubbard, L. Ron. Ability Magazine 70, late March 1958, *Does Clearing Cancel the Need for Training?*

Chapter 4

1. Miller, Russell. *Bare-Faced Messiah*. S.l.: Silvertail Books, 2015. Print.
2. Dewolf, Ronald. Penthouse magazine interview, June 1983. General Media Inc.
3. Hubbard, L. Ron. HCO Policy Letter of 7 February 1965, "Keeping Scientology Working".
4. Ibid.
5. Ibid.
6. Hubbard, L. Ron. Professional Auditor's Bulletin #79, "The Open Channel," April 10, 1956.
7. Hubbard, L. Ron. Saint Hill Special Briefing Course lecture #82, "Scientology Definitions- OT and Clear Defined", given November 29, 1966.
8. Hubbard, L. Ron. HCO Policy Letter of 13 August 70, "The MIssing Ingredient".

9. Hubbard, L. Ron. Ability Magazine 1, ca. March 1955, *The Scientologist - A Manual on the Dissemination of Material.*

Chapter 5

1. Anonymous, Ask the Scientologist article "Where are All the Scientologists? Part 2", November 19, 2008, http://askthescientologist.blogspot.com/2008/11/where-are-all-scientologists-part-2.html
2. "Couple's Lawsuit Accuses Church of Scientology of Fraud, Deception." Tampa Bay Times. Web. January 23, 2013 http://www.tampabay.com/news/scientology/couples-lawsuit-accuses-church-of-scientology-of-fraud-deception/1271893
3. Hubbard, L. Ron. HCO Policy Letter of 5 April 1965, "Handling the Suppressive Person - The Basis of Insanity".
4. "Former Church Of Scientology Members Who Have Spoken Out."Why We Protest Scientology Wiki. Web. 30 Nov. 2015. http://whyweprotest.wikia.com/wiki/former_church_of_scientology_members_who_have_spoken_out
5. Hubbard, L. Ron. Ability Magazine 1, ca. March 1955, *The Scientologist - A Manual on the Dissemination of Material.*

6. Hubbard, L. Ron. Manual Of Justice. Manual of Justice., http://www.xenu.net/archive/go/man_just.htm

7. Wollersheim v. Church of Scientology, 212 Cal. App. 3d 872 (Cal. App. 2d Dist. 1989)

8. Monique Rathbun v David Miscavige, Religious Technology Center, et al; Comal County, TX, September 4, 2013, https://www.documentcloud.org/documents/786411-monique-rathbun-v-church-of-scientology-first.html

9. Ibid.

10. Corpus Christi Caller Times. "Former Scientology Film Crew Member Describes Surveillance Activities in Ingleside on the Bay." Former Scientology film crew member describes surveillance activities in Ingleside on the Bay. Web. August 6, 2011. http://www.caller.com/news/former-scientology-film-crew-member-describes-surveillance-activities-in-ingleside-on-the-bay-ep-359-316193271.html

11. Ortega, Tony. The Underground Bunker article "SCIENTOLOGY DENIED: APPEAL SHOT DOWN AFTER YEARLONG WAIT." Web. November 6, 2015. http://tonyortega.org/2015/11/06/scientology-denied-texas-appeal-shot-down-after-yearlong-wait/

12. Tampa Bay Times. "Two Detectives Describe Their Two-Decade Pursuit of an Exiled Scientology Leader." Tampa Bay Times. Web. September 29, 2012. http://www.tampabay.com/news/scientology/two-detectives-describe-their-two-decade-pursuit-of-an-exiled-scientology/1254129

13. Hubbard, L. Ron. HCO Policy Letter of 23 December 1965, "Suppressive Acts, Suppression of Scientology and Scientologists".

Chapter 6

1. Hubbard, L. Ron, "The Camp-Fire," *Adventure* magazine, vol. 93 no. 5, October 1, 1935.

2. Burks, Arthur J, *The Abereee* newsletter, December 1961.

3. Ibid.

4. Letter from L. Ron Hubbard to his wife Polly, October 1938, quoted in *Bare-Faced Messiah* by Russell Miller, p. 81

5. I was amazed to find out this mansion was literally about a five minute drive from the house where I grew up in Pasadena.

6. Hubbard, L. Ron. Dianetics: The Modern Science of Mental Health, p. 205. Los Angeles, CA: Bridge Publications, Inc., 2007. Print.

7. Atack, Jon. "Never Believe a Hypnotist." Never Believe a Hypnotist. Web. 6 Dec. 2015. http://www.lermanet.com/exit/parsons.htm

8. Hubbard, L. Ron. Dianetics: The Modern Science of Mental Health, p. 205. Los Angeles, CA: Bridge Publications, Inc., 2007. Print.

9. Miller, Russell. *Bare-Faced Messiah*. S.l.: Silvertail Books, 2015. Print.

10. Kent, Stephen. "The Creation Of 'Religious' Scientology." Religious Studies and Theology RSTH 18.2 (1999): 97–126. Web

11. Hubbard, L. Ron. *This Is Scientology: the Science of Certainty*. Hubbard Association of Scientologists, 1955. Print.

12. Rathbun, Mark "Marty"., Russell Williams, and Mike Rinder. *Memoirs Of a Scientology Warrior* / Mark "Marty" Rathbun ; Edited by Russell Williams & Mike Rinder. North Charleston, SC: Createspace, 2013. Print.

Chapter 7

1. Rovelli, Carlo. "Science Is Not About Certainty." Web. 6 Dec. 2015. https://newrepublic.com/article/118655/theoretical-phyisicist-explains-why-science-not-about-certainty

2. "Carl Sagan And Modern Scientific Humanism." Carl Sagan and Modern Scientific Humanism. Web. 6 Dec. 2015. http://humanists.net/pdhutcheon/humanist%20articles/Carl%20Sagan%20and%20Modern%20Scientific%20Humanism.htm

Chapter 10

1. Hubbard, L. Ron. *Clear Body, Clear Mind: the Effective Purification Program*. Los Angeles, CA: Bridge Publications, 1990. Print.

2. Ibid.

3. Ibid.

4. Ibid.
5. Kapferer, Jean-Noel. *Rumors: Uses, interpretations, and images.* Transaction Publishers, 2013.
6. "LSD Effects - HowStuffWorks." 2011. 7 Dec. 2015 http://science.howstuffworks.com/lsd4.htm
7. Gloom, Mental Health Daily, "How Long Does LSD Stay In Your System?" Web. Oct 13, 2015 http://mentalhealthdaily.com/2015/10/13/how-long-does-lsd-stay-in-your-system/
8. Hubbard, L. Ron. *Clear Body, Clear Mind: the Effective Purification Program.* Los Angeles, CA: Bridge Publications, 1990. Print.
9. Kolata, Gina. "Study Finds That Fat Cells Die And Are Replaced."The New York Times. The New York Times, Apr. 2008. Web. 6 Dec. 2015. http://www.nytimes.com/2008/05/05/health/research/05fat.html
10. "Niacin overdose: What are the symptoms? - Mayo Clinic." 2014. 7 Dec. 2015 http://www.mayoclinic.org/diseases-conditions/high-blood-cholesterol/expert-answers/niacin-overdose/faq-20058075
11. "Heat-Related Illness Symptoms, Causes, Treatment - Heat ..." 2008. 7 Dec. 2015 http://www.medicinenet.com/hyperthermia/page5.htm
12. "What are the symptoms of heat-related illness? - MedicineNet." 2005. 7 Dec. 2015 http://www.medicinenet.com/hyperthermia/page4.htm

Chapter 11

1. Hubbard, L. Ron. *Dianetics: The Modern Science of Mental Health*, p. 205. Los Angeles, CA: Bridge Publications, Inc., 2007. Print.
2. Ibid.
3. Hubbard, L. Ron. *Scientology, a History of Man: a List and Description of the Principal Incidents to Be Found in a Human Being.* Los Angeles, CA: Bridge Publications, Inc., 2007. Print.
4. Hubbard, L. Ron. Saint Hill Special Briefing Course lecture #83, "Scientology Definitions- Part II", given December 6, 1966.

5. Hubbard claims this was all 75 million years ago, but betrays his lack of knowledge of astronomy in doing so. There is a matter of precession. Simply explained, all celestial bodies are moving through space even if they are so far away we can't see them moving with the naked eye. Because of our motion and the motions of other bodies, the North Star's position in the sky has not always been occupied by the star Polaris. In fact, when the pyramids of Egypt were being erected just a few thousand years ago, the North Star was Thurban in the constellation of Draco the Dragon. In 12,000 years, it will be Vega in the constellation Lyra. So 75 million years ago, our night sky looked radically different than it does now. It's surprising Hubbard, being a sailor, would know nothing about this.

6. Hubbard, L. Ron. HCO Bulletin of 15 September 1978, NED FOR OTs RD, THEORY OF.

7. Hubbard, L. Ron HCO Bulletin of 1 November 1978, NED FOR OTs CHECKLIST.

8. Ibid.

Chapter 12

1. Hubbard, L. Ron. HCO Policy Letter of 5 October 1971, PR Series 12, PROPAGANDA BY REDEFINITION OF WORDS.

2. Mcdowell, Edwin. "Top-Selling Books Of 1988: Spy Novel and Physics." The New York Times. The New York Times, Jan. 1989. Web. 7 Dec. 2015. http://www.nytimes.com/1989/02/02/books/top-selling-books-of-1988-spy-novel-and-physics.html

Chapter 13

1. Affidavit of David Miscavige 17 Feb 1994. Posted 2002. http://www.xenu.net/archive/go/legal/poodle.htm

2. Morgan, Lucy. World and nation: Abroad: Critics Public and Private Keep Pressure on Scientology. Web. 8 Dec. 2015.

http://www.sptimes.com/news/32999/worldandnation/abroad__criti
cs_publi.html

Chapter 14

1. "You Give Religions More than $82.5 Billion a Year." *Washington Post.* The Washington Post, n.d. Web. 8 Dec. 2015. https://www.washingtonpost.com/news/wonk/wp/2013/08/22/you-give-religions-more-than-82-5-billion-a-year
2. Owen, Chris. *Scientology's Battle for Tax Exemption, 1952-80,* Web. 8 Dec. 2015. https://www.cs.cmu.edu/~dst/cowen/essays/battle.html
3. Reitman, Janet. Inside Scientology: the Story of America's Most Secretive Religion. Boston: Houghton Mifflin Harcourt, 2011. Print.
4. Sir John Foster, K.B.E., Q.C., M.P. (December 1971). "Enquiry into the Practice and Effects of Scientology" (PDF). Her Majesty's Stationery Office, London. UK National Archive piece reference MH 153/606
5. Garrison, Omar V. The Hidden Story of Scientology. London: Arlington Books, 1974. Print.
6. Founding Church of Scientology DC vs US Internal Revenue Service, No 226-61, July 16, 1969
7. Church of Scientology of California vs IRS, No. 3352-78, Sept 24, 1984
8. Hubbard, L. Ron. HCO Policy Letter of 29 October 1962, RELIGION (original version)
9. Church of Scientology of California vs IRS, No. 3352-78, Sept 24, 1984
10. Behar, Richard. "The Prophet and Profits of Scientology." *Forbes Magazine*, 27 October 1987. Web. https://www.cs.cmu.edu/~./dst/library/shelf/behar/forbes-1986.html
11. Ibid.
12. Ken Urquhart, interview with Russell Miller, Mclean, Virginia, Apr/May 86
13. Tape recording of the Mission Holders' Conference, San Francisco, 1982 as quoted in "THE FLOW UP THE BRIDGE." *MH Conference.* Web. http://www.freezone.org/reports/e_mhcsf.htm

14. Interview of Larry Brennan, on November 8, 2007 by Tom Smith, host of WXYB 1520 am, quoted on http://www.lermanet.com/audio/larry-brennan.htm

15. Ibid.

16. LA Times article "The Battle with the IRS, June 29, 1990

17. Frantz, Douglas. "Scientology's Puzzling Journey From Tax Rebel To Tax Exempt." *The New York Times*, Aug. 1997. Web. 8 Dec. 2015. http://www.nytimes.com/1997/03/09/us/scientology-s-puzzling-journey-from-tax-rebel-to-tax-exempt.html

18. Rathbun, Mark "Marty"., Russell Williams, and Mike Rinder. *Memoirs Of a Scientology Warrior* / Mark "Marty" Rathbun ; Edited by Russell Williams & Mike Rinder. North Charleston, SC: Createspace, 2013. Print.

19. "Requiem For the Church of Scientology of California, 1954 – 2004." *The Scientology Money Project*. N.p., 2014. Web. http://scientologymoneyproject.com/2014/04/25/requiem-for-the-church-of-scientology-of-california-1954-2004/

20. Frantz, Douglas. "Scientology's Puzzling Journey From Tax Rebel To Tax Exempt." *The New York Times*, Aug. 1997. Web. 8 Dec. 2015. http://www.nytimes.com/1997/03/09/us/scientology-s-puzzling-journey-from-tax-rebel-to-tax-exempt.html

21. "Scientology: The Truth Rundown, Part 1 Of 3 in a Special Report on the Church of Scientology." *Tampa Bay Times*. Web. http://www.tampabay.com/news/scientology-the-truth-rundown-part-1-of-3-in-a-special-report-on-the/1012148

22. Bartlett, Bruce. "Scientology's Fair Tax Plot." *CBSNews*. CBS Interactive, n.d. Web. http://www.cbsnews.com/news/scientologys-fair-tax-plot/

23. "Scientology: The Truth Rundown, Part 1 Of 3 in a Special Report on the Church of Scientology." *Tampa Bay Times*. Web. http://www.tampabay.com/news/scientology-the-truth-rundown-part-1-of-3-in-a-special-report-on-the/1012148

24. Ibid.

25. Ibid.

26. Hubbard, L. Ron. HCO Policy Letter of 13 August 1970, THE MISSING INGREDIENT.

27. Articles and Bylaws of Church of Spiritual Technology, Article III, http://www.savescientology.com/cstmemo.pdf

28. CHURCH OF SPIRITUAL TECHNOLOGY, Plaintiff, v. The UNITED STATES, Defendant. No. 581-88T. United States Claims Court. June 29, 1992.
29. Ibid.

Chapter 16

1. "7 Things You Need To Know About Narcissists, From A Psychologist's Perspective." *The Mind Unleashed.* N.p., Dec. 2014. Web. http://themindunleashed.org/2014/09/7-things-need-know-co-existing-narcissists.html
2. "St. Petersburg Times: The man behind Scientology, page 3." http://www.sptimes.com/TampaBay/102598/scientologypart3.html
3. "Is There a Cure For Narcissism?" *Psychology Today.* Web. https://www.psychologytoday.com/blog/compassion-matters/201406/is-there-cure-narcissism

Appendix 1: A Scientology Glossary

A key part of the Scientology mind control is establishing its own language. George Orwell wrote volumes on the use of language as a control mechanism and nowhere is this more true than in Scientology. Unfortunately, there's no way to talk about Scientology without using many of its custom words and phrases. To help with this, I've compiled a list of words I've used in this book and done my best to provide easy to understand definitions for each. There are many hundreds of specialized words beyond just these; this is just a sampling of them. The full dictionaries of Dianetics and Scientology technical and administrative terms are available online but I don't recommend getting too much involved in them, as Hubbard's jargon is purposefully vague, confusing and bizarre.

Advanced Organization (AO): a high-level Scientology church specializing in delivering the OT Levels up to OT V.

Applied Scholastics: a supposedly secular branch of the Church of Scientology whose purpose is to get Hubbard's Study Technology widely into use in public and private schools, nominally to battle illiteracy and poor education standards.

auditor: a Scientology practitioner or counsellor. They are called "auditors" from the Latin root *auditus* which means "to listen".

auditing: a type of counselling or therapeutic procedure in Scientology which an auditor (Scientology practitioner) carries out on a preclear (Scientology patient). This can consist of asking various questions about things that are troubling or have troubled a preclear in the past, or giving the preclear simple tasks to perform which are supposed to raise his spiritual awareness and abilities.

bank: another term for *reactive mind.*

black PR: to criticize or vilify something in order to defame or make less of it. In Scientology, anytime someone is spreading black PR, the reason for this is because they have committed overts against the thing they are black PRing and have evil intentions toward that person or thing. An example of black PR would be "Scientology staff don't ever get paid." It might be true but the fact it creates a bad or poor image for Scientology makes it black PR against Scientology and therefore something to be suppressed.

body thetans: semi-conscious or nearly dead spiritual entities which are unaware of their actual individual existence and which group or conglomerate on the bodies of people, sort of like spiritual parasites. It's revealed on Scientology's confidential OT III how these body thetans came to be and how they are attached to the bodies of every individual on Earth and affect their thoughts and emotions.

Bridge to Total Freedom: the Scientology euphemism for the series of steps every person in Scientology takes to achieve personal spiritual freedom and immortality. This Bridge is graphically displayed as a large chart, with the training steps on the left side and the auditing/counselling steps on the right. One is supposed to go up "both sides" of the Bridge for maximum gains, but most Scientologists focus primarily on the right side which is where one achieves Clear and does the OT Levels. The analogy of the bridge comes from the last chapter of *Dianetics: The Modern Science of Mental Health* where Hubbard alludes to the idea of building a bridge over a large chasm, allowing one to cross from the current state of man to a higher plane of existence on the other side of the chasm.

case: the Scientology term for the sum total of all the things wrong with a person personally or spiritually. Scientology auditing addresses a person's case and gets rid of it. The end result of all Scientology auditing is a person with no more case to handle.

case gain: progress made in addressing one's case and therefore a measure of spiritual improvement. One makes case gain in auditing and training. According to Scientology theory, one prevents case gain by committing overts, which impede spiritual improvement.

Clear: a state of being where a person no longer has his own reactive mind, meaning he is no longer carrying around the mental stress, trauma and aggravation which come from hidden memories of physical pain and unconsciousness. This is accomplished by erasing all the engrams in the person's reactive mind. A Clear is supposed to have super-human abilities such as very rapid thought processes, increased learning ability, eidetic memory and full recall of everything which ever happened to him in his lifetime. See also *reactive mind* and *engram*

Command Intention: the desires and orders of the person in charge of Scientology. Originally L. Ron Hubbard, that mantle was taken over in the mid-1980s by David Miscavige. Those in charge of the Sea Org, and therefore in charge of Scientology, are referred to as "Command". Command Intention is therefore an expression denoting what Command wants done. All Sea Org members taken an oath to "uphold, forward and carry out Command Intention."

Completed Staff Work (CSW): a formal written request for approval on some project or action. A CSW states what the problem or situation is which requires remedy, gives all the information as to why the proposed solution is the best one and states clearly exactly what the solution is. A person who receives a CSW is supposed to be able to read or review it and with no other information, approve or reject it accordingly.

Continental Justice Chief (CJC): the person at continental management level who deals with all Scientology justice procedures, ensures they are being done according to Hubbard's policies on such matters and conditionally approves or rejects SP declares before they are sent up to the International Justice Chief for final approval.

CSW: see *Completed Staff Work*

destructive cult: because there is some confusion in many people's minds about the difference between a religion, a cult and a destructive cult, I'm providing this definition to clarify how this term is used in this book. In this book, a destructive cult is defined as a high control group which uses manipulation and deceitful methods to draw people into its membership, exploits them for monetary or other gain, and uses physically and/or psychologically damaging methods of control to keep its members in line and discourage them from leaving.

E-meter: short for electropsychometer, an electronic device which detects changes in resistance to an electric current which is run through the skin. A person holds tin cans, one in each hand, which complete an electric circuit through the body. As the person thinks of things, this creates physiological changes such as micro-increases in sweat production, hormonal and glandular changes, increased heart rate, etc. All these things create reactions on the needle of the E-meter, which are interpreted by Scientology auditors as changes in the person's mind. They are not changes in a person's mind, they are changes in the body. According to Hubbard's directions, E-meters are used in Scientology auditing to find areas of "charge" where supposedly there is accumulated emotional and mental trauma so processes can be run to get rid of that charge.

engram: a memory stored in the reactive mind which contains pain and unconsciousness. For example, if a child were bitten by a dog and someone rushed up and yelled at the dog, "Get out of here!", all the perceptions during that moment of being bitten would not be available as a regular memory in the analytical (conscious) mind, but would be stored in the reactive mind as an engram. The memory of the incident would then be used later on by the reactive mind if the present circumstances approximated the same circumstances in the engram, so as to get the person to avoid being hurt again. In the example above, maybe years later, let's say that same person is walking down a street very similar in appearance to the one where he encountered the dog. He will start to feel uncomfortable and perhaps get the idea something is not right. If he stays on the street and hears a car with a similar sound to one which drove by when he was bitten, his sense of danger and unease will increase and his hand could even start hurting for no apparent reason. This is his reactive mind telling him to get away from that area. If the person continues walking down the street and hears a dog barking similar to the one which bit him all those years ago, his hand will definitely start hurting and he will start making up excuses and reasons why this is occurring (since he has no rational or analytical idea why he feels this way) and he will feel an overwhelming urge to leave the area (coming from the command "get out of here" also contained in the engram).

entheta: bad news or anything which would make a person feel downcast, sad, upset or angry.

Estates Project Force (EPF): a sort of "boot camp" for the Sea Organization. It consists of the new recruits doing classes for five hours a day, studying the basics of what it means to be a Sea Org member, how to salue and take orders and what the SO's basic policies state. The rest of the day is spent drilling and/or running around doing cleaning or other similar grunt work to instill discipline and camaraderie with fellow EPFers.

ethics: in Scientology, ethics connotes someone's personal level of moral behavior, the relative goodness or badness of their actions and lifestyle. If someone "has their ethics in" then they are following the rules or morals they have agreed to, whereas if someone "goes out-ethics" or "has their ethics out" then they are knowingly violating agreements they previously made or the laws under which they live.

ethics change: when someone was doing bad things and has now seen the error of their ways and has reformed.

Fair Game: when someone is considered an enemy of Scientology and declared a Suppressive Person, they are deemed "Fair Game". This policy was created in 1965 as a retaliatory measure against critics and anyone Hubbard felt wronged him. Originally, this policy meant those labelled as Fair Game could be deprived of property or injured by any means by any Scientologist and those Scientologists would not get into any trouble by Scientology justice. Additionally, those SPs could be tricked, sued, lied to or destroyed. The practice of labelling someone as "Fair Game" was cancelled in 1968 once it became a public relations nightmare, but Hubbard clarified the treatment and handling of Suppressive Persons did not change at all, meaning the above listed actions were still authorized to be taken against SPs.

Grades: also referred to as Lower Grades, these are a series of auditing steps taken on the route to becoming Clear. There are five Grades, each addressing a specific subject with the idea difficulties or problems with that subject will be completely a thing of the past after the Grade is done. Grade 0 addresses communication, Grade I addresses problems, Grade II addresses overts, Grade III addresses upsets and Grade IV addresses fixed conditions.

Guardian's Office (GO): an intelligence and public relations branch of the Church of Scientology which carried out covert operations under the direction of Mary Sue Hubbard, L. Ron Hubbard's wife, in her role as the Guardian. Established in the last 1960s, the Guardian's Office was not part of the Sea Org, but existed as its own organization. It carried out numerous operations against anyone Hubbard named as an enemy of the Church of Scientology to ruin them professionally and/or personally. The Guardian's Office carried out the most widespread and extravagant operation against the United States government in history, infiltrating the IRS, FBI and numerous other government organizations in an effort to "clean their files" of anything relating to crimes committed by L. Ron Hubbard.

High Crime: the most serious offenses listed in the Scientology Justice Codes, consisting mainly of actions taken directly against Scientology such as publicly departing from Scientology, using its trademarks without permission, testifying in court against Scientology, reading anti-Scientology material on the internet, knowingly associating with people the Church has declared Suppressive Persons and the like. In short, High Crimes are anything the Church doesn't want someone to do because it would be interpreted as somehow damaging to Scientology itself.

IAS: see *International Association of Scientologists*

Int Management: short for International Management, the group of Sea Org personnel responsible for directing international Church operations.

International Association of Scientologists (IAS): the mandatory membership group of Scientology. Founded in 1984 by David Miscavige without the authorization or consent of L. Ron Hubbard, the IAS bleeds money from Scientologists using extravagant, high-intensity hardsell tactics. There are various membership levels available which exist as a sort of status symbol amongst Scientologists, such as Patron, Crusader, Patron Meritorious, Silver Patron with Honors, etc, each level requiring more and more donations. In addition to selling membership statuses, the IAS fundraisers also push members for straight donations, claiming the end of the world is near and Scientologists are the only hope for saving mankind by paying more and more money into the IAS's coffers. Almost every natural or man-made disaster is utilized as an excuse by IAS fundraisers to push Scientologists to donate money, nominally for relief efforts or to bring aid to victims of those disasters. There is no accountability or evidence much or any of the funds raised go toward any disaster relief or aid and the IAS is under no obligation to provide information about where its funds go.

International Justice Chief (IJC): the person responsible for seeing Scientology justice procedures are carried out according to Hubbard's policies on such matters. He approves or rejects all suppressive person declares and is supposed to be the one to deal with anyone who has been declared an SP if they want to do the necessary steps to regain good standing with Scientology.

MEST: short for Matter, Energy, Space and Time, a coined word to stand for the four components which make up the physical universe.

misemotional: having inappropriate or negative emotions about something. For example, if a person were laughing at a funeral, this would be considered misemotional. In more recent times, misemotion in Scientology has come to mean any negative emotion, whether appropriate or not, such as getting angry or upset when faced with irrationality or being told to get too many things done in too short a period of time.

mission: a privately owned Scientology franchise group, meaning a group granted the right to deliver basic Scientology training as well as auditing services up to the state of Clear. Missions do not train Scientology auditors, as that is done at orgs. Their primary purpose is to introduce new people to Dianetics and Scientology, give them a taste of what it's all about and then send them to the closest Church of

Scientology. A percentage of the profits of a mission are sent each week as a tithe to the Church of Scientology International.

Narconon: a supposedly secular branch of the Church of Scientology which is licensed to deliver Hubbard's procedures to get drug addicts physically detoxified and off drugs. Hubbard's theory of how drug addiction works and how drugs stay lodged in the body years after they are taken have been proven to be scientifically invalid, yet Narconon bases its entire program on this pseudoscience. The result has been patient deaths and rampant credit/insurance fraud in facilities around the United States.

natter: criticizing or finding fault with something and/or complaining about it. In Scientology, the only reason a person ever natters about someone or something is because they have committed overts against the thing they are criticizing or complaining about, even if such criticism is entirely deserved.

Office of Special Affairs (OSA): the current intelligence, PR and legal division of the Church of Scientology. OSA is managed by the Sea Organization, whose members constitute its management structure and form the main body of its organization, while lower Class V organization staff (called Directors of Special Affairs) and Scientologist volunteers do much of the day-to-day grunt work in local areas. While OSA does engage in some public relations efforts to try to give the Church of Scientology a veneer of legitimacy in the media, the vast bulk of its activities consist of legal and intelligence work. OSA hires non-Scientologist attorneys and private investigators to prosecute cases, do investigations, as well as harass and stalk critics and ex-Scientologists. Hiring these non-Scientologist professionals gives a layer of plausible deniability to the Church management who direct these stalking and harassment operations.

OT: short for Operating Thetan, meaning a state of being of personal godhood where one is unencumbered by the need to have a physical body in order to know one is alive and can create, animate, destroy or manipulate any kind of matter, energy, space or even time itself.

OT Levels: the procedures and methods one follows in a step-by-step series in order to achieve the state of OT. These levels and all the information about them are completely confidential and are kept secured in Advanced Organizations of Scientology. One must first attain the state of Clear before he will be allowed to do the OT Levels. It costs tens or even hundreds of thousands of dollars to get through the preliminary steps up to the OT Levels, and tens of thousands of dollars more to do the OT Levels themselves. The highest OT Level released to date is OT VIII but the Scientology Grade Chart shows levels all the way up to XIV.

org: short for organization, and usually referring to a Class V organization, meaning a Church of Scientology which delivers training up to the level of a Class V auditor and auditing services up to the state of Clear.

overt: an overt act, meaning a harmful transgression against the rules or mores a person has agreed to follow. Stealing, lying, murder or slacking off on the job would all be examples of overts.

policy: the guiding principles, methods and procedures by which Scientology organizations or groups are run. Hubbard codified a great many of these in Policy Letters and in some recorded lectures.

preclear: the term for a person who is receiving Scientology counselling or auditing. It literally means a person who has not yet reached the state of Clear but is sometimes used even after that state is reached, as it's easier to say than "pre-OT" (meaning someone who has not yet reached the state of full Operating Thetan).

program: a series of steps done in sequence to accomplish a specific purpose or product. In Scientology management, these are used to guide the actions of staff members in order to accomplish organizational objectives. For example, a program could have the objective to get 20 new auditors onto post. The steps of the program would include specific actions to recruit 20 people onto staff, put them into training as auditors and eventually get them on to post. Someone would be responsible for overseeing the program and getting the targets done (called executing the program), while various staff would actually do the individual targets. Management personnel in locations remote to the organization where the program is being done can direct the staff on each target and monitor the progress of the program, debug targets if they get stalled or the staff can't figure out what to do and keep sending orders to the staff to get the targets done until the program is completed. By executing various programs in different parts of the organization, the idea is to improve the quality and viability of the organization as a whole over time.

reactive mind: in Dianetics theory, the part of the mind which stores memories containing any degree of pain and unconsciousness. These could be incidents of stubbing one's toe on a sidewalk, falling down and hitting one's head on the ground, or being knocked out in a car accident. Any memory which contains any degree of pain and unconsciousness is hidden away in the reactive mind, and those memories are used in a mechanical way by this mind to keep a person from repeating the circumstances which caused them pain and unconsciousness. See also *engram*.

Registrar (Reg): a Scientology salesman. Called this because they "sign people up" for services and, originally, put their names in a registration book of people who bought services (an older practice not really needed now that we have computers).

Rehabilitation Project Force (RPF): the Sea Org's prison system, designed to "rehabilitate" disaffected and failing Sea Org members through intensive security checking sessions and gruelling physical labor. Its only analogy in the outside world is a Maoist reconditioning camp. It takes years to complete the program and most SO members who end up on it leave the Sea Org and Scientology altogether.

Religious Technology Center (RTC): the Scientology organization which holds the trademarks and copyrights of Scientology materials and services, and which is supposed to oversee their correct and pure use throughout the Scientology network. What it has become instead is the one and only managing body of all of Scientology, headed up by the Chairman of the Board of RTC, David Miscavige, who ruthlessly directs everything going on in Scientology without regard for its corporate bylaws or internal organizational structure.

Sea Organization (SO): the paramilitary group of dedicated Scientologists who work as the "clergy" or core group of Scientology's operations. Sea Org members sign contracts dedicating themselves to the cause of Scientology for a billion years and take that commitment literally. They live in communal quarters, eat together and work an average of 16-18 hours a day, often with only a handful of days off each year. They pledge to "uphold, forward and carry out Command Intention" meaning to do whatever it is the leader of Scientology tells them to do. The Sea Organization was founded by L. Ron Hubbard in 1967 aboard ships Hubbard purchased and which sailed in the Mediterranean and European waters in the late 1960s and early 1970s before they transferred to a land-based operation in Clearwater, Florida in the mid-1970s. They have maintained a nautical tradition ever since, using ranks and ratings, dressing in naval dress uniforms during official ceremonies, etc.

security check (sec check or confessional): a kind of auditing procedure where a person is asked direct questions asking for various types of overts or wrongdoing and are then made to confess everything about those overts, one at a time. The auditor persists until he gets the person to confess everything they did and thought about regarding each overt. These are all written down on worksheets and stored in folders. Often, separate reports are written (called Knowledge Reports) which detail all the overts the person confessed to and these KRs are put in separate folders, called Ethics Files. Ethics Officers will collect up these reports in these files and then confront the person after the security check and make them do amends or restitution for the overts they confessed. This often involves paying money or doing amends projects to "take responsibility" for what they did. Should a person later leave Scientology altogether, the contents of these files can be used against them to attempt to publicly shame them into silence if they become vocal against Scientology.

self-determinism: a common expression in Scientology for the idea a person is doing exactly what they want to be doing or are determining their own destiny. Someone who has to take orders or directions from others is not self-determined but is other-determined. Additionally, if someone is ruled by their mental problems or past stresses and traumas, they are considered to also not be self-determined. Scientology states one of its primary goals is to restore a person to a state of full self-determinism.

service facs: short for *service facsimile*. In Scientology, a *facsimile* is another word for a mental image picture since it represents a copy of what a person has seen or experienced. A service facsimile is a mental image picture a person uses to explain a disability or fault or personal issue and which serves him by making him right and others wrong. It has the additional value of also creating sympathy for the person using it, which is one reason why the person will continue to use it. For example, if a child gets sick he has a fault or problem. He could come up with the idea he's sick because his mother makes him go to school. Then, when his mother tells him he has to get better and go to school, he purposefully wills himself to continue to be sick, using the mental image picture of his sickness. This makes him right for not going to school because he can't go to school when he's sick, and also serves the purpose of making his mother wrong for trying to "force him" to go to school. It should also gain him sympathy from his mother, who will coddle him or take care of him because he's sick. This service facsimile will stay with him as a sort of mental mechanism which he will continue to use, but after a while he doesn't even realize he's doing it. For example, years later he could be married and not want to go to work, so this service facsimile comes into play subconsciously and his body gets sick. If his wife or his boss are unsympathetic types and doesn't coddle or help him, the service facsimile will kick in even harder and his body will get more seriously ill, all in an effort to make him right and them wrong and gain their sympathy and support for his weakened condition. A person can have any number of service facsimiles underlying disabilities or personal issues; the service facs actually hold these disabilities in place and keep the person from getting over them and therefore a person would be better off without them.

squirrel: someone who is altering or changing Scientology procedures or methods for their own ends, or is using any of Dianetics and Scientology without the authorization or consent of Hubbard and/or Scientology. It is a derogatory term in Scientology to describe anyone who does not cooperate with what the Church is telling them to do.

stats: short for statistics. In Scientology, statistics are a measure of production and are measured week-to-week. Any job or post can be statisticized, meaning its production can be measured by some kind of countable production unit. For example, if a person is a Scientology auditor, their statistic is the number of hours of auditing they perform each week. For a salesman, it would be the amount of money they got from their sales in a given week. Each week, the total statistical value of any job is put on a graph and compared to whether it is higher or lower than the previous week. It is expected in Scientology organizations for one's statistics to always rise, meaning more and more work is being done and things are therefore getting better. Of course, it is impossible for a person to have an endlessly rising amount of production, and so one's statistic will routinely go up and down from week to week. Statistics are used to not only measure production but determine to what degree of trouble someone is in. If their statistic is down for a given week, they are considered "down stat" and are not given any bonuses, awards or allowed any privileges they might otherwise have when they are "upstat".

suppression: in Scientology, this word denotes any actions which purposely inhibit or impede someone or something's ability to get along in life and survive. An example of suppression would be if Joe were to lie to Bill's boss and get Bill fired from his job. It has the further meaning of doing anything which is thought to impede or stop Scientology's forward progress in any way, such as criticizing it publicly, encouraging someone to not donate to it or attempting to expose criminal activity Scientology leaders engage in.

suppressive person (SP): the ultimate bad guy in Scientology. When this term was first invented in the mid-1960s, Hubbard described SPs as antisocial personalities, people whose real intentions are never what they say and are always to covertly destroy people. He cites examples such as Dillinger, Hitler and Napoleon and claimed only 2.5% of the population were actual SPs. In the Scientology world, if a person does anything counter to Scientology, leaves it publicly or criticizes it openly, they are formally labelled a Suppressive Person by a written issue printed on goldenrod-colored paper. Such "declare orders" used to posted on notice boards and called for all Scientologists to shun the SP, severing all ties whether familial, personal or business. SP declares are now used as a political tool to get rid of anyone who voices doubts or concerns about Scientology or its leader, David Miscavige, or who dares to associate with anyone else who is deemed as an "enemy" by Scientology. No evidence of antisocial behavior is necessary, merely thinking for oneself or practicing open communication with who one chooses is enough to be declared suppressive.

tech: short for technology, meaning the methods and procedures Hubbard outlined to improve people as spiritual beings. All the auditing and training methods collectively are considered "Scientology technology" and are mainly issued in Bulletins or in recorded lectures.

terminal: in Scientology, this word denotes anything which gives or receives communication. It comes from the analogy of an electronic terminal which can emit or receive an electronic signal. Communication is between living things, so anything which can communicate can be a terminal.

theta: life energy or life force, differentiated from any kind of physical quantity because it has no mass, location, wavelength or physical form.

Theta Clear: a very vaguely defined state of being, but basically a condition where a person can operate stably exterior to their body.

The Way to Happiness: a booklet written in 1980 by L. Ron Hubbard which contains a moral code consisting of 21 precepts such as "Do Not Steal" and "Do Not Harm a Person of Good Will." These books are printed by the Church of Scientology in bundles and are often distributed by hand in the streets. Scientology claims doing so has quelled social unrest and by getting the book out into war-torn or crime-infested zones, it has reduced crime rates and violence, although there is no real evidence for these claims.

Volunteer Ministers: a program begun by L. Ron Hubbard in the 1970s to get Scientologists to apply basic Scientology principles in the real world, thereby improving conditions and promoting the good works Scientology does. Following the disaster of 9/11 in New York, hundreds of Scientology Volunteer Ministers worked at the Twin Towers site providing logistical support and using Scientology assists to aid disaster relief workers, thus earning media attention and good PR for Scientology. Since that time, whenever there is a natural disaster in the world, Scientology puts out a call to Scientologists to pay their own way and go to the disaster site as Volunteer Ministers. Scientology engages in fundraising of parishioners, ostensibly to send those Volunteer Ministers and aid in disaster relief, but the only thing the Church actually pays for is the film crew it sends to video the

Volunteer Ministers so it can take credit for their work at the next Scientology rally or event.

whole track: the sum total of all a person's memories going back into every past life they've ever led.

wog: a pejorative term for anyone who is not a Scientologist. It comes from old British racial slur for Middle Eastern and South Asian peoples. Hubbard claimed it originally stood for Worthy Oriental Gentleman but this apparently is a false etymology.

Appendix 2: The Affirmations of L. Ron Hubbard

I have lifted these pretty much verbatim from the internet from a posting by ex-Sea Org member Gerry Armstrong. I cannot say with 100% certainty these Affirmations were written by L. Ron Hubbard because the chain of evidence, so to speak, is pretty broken when it comes to tracing these back to the LRH handwritten original documents. It is also noted in the posting these are not the complete Affirmations, but there's certainly enough here to show their intent and design.

Back in the mid-1980s when portions of these were read into the official court record as part of a lawsuit involving Gerry Armstrong, the lawyers for the Church of Scientology did not question or deny their authenticity but instead apparently fought to keep them from being introduced or talked about in open court, claiming they were being interpreted out of context. That tends to make me think these are valid and is about as much proof as we are ever going to get L. Ron Hubbard is the author of these statements.

The Affirmations are divided into three sections titled Course I, Course II and The Book.

COURSE I

The purpose of this experiment is to re-establish the ambition, willpower, desire to survive, the talent and confidence of myself.

To accomplish the above the following fears must be removed Fear that I have written myself out by writing junk. I built certain psychoses in myself while living with my former wife as a means to protect my writing. I affirmed that my writing was hard work and took much labor. This was a lie. I was always anxious about people's opinion of me and was afraid I would bore them. This injected anxiety and careless speed into my work. I must be convinced that I can write skillfully and well, that I have no phobias about writing and no fears of it. People criticized my work bitterly at times. I must be convinced that such people were fools. I must be convinced that I can write far better than ever before, that a million people at least would be happy to see my stories. I must be convinced that I have succeeded in writing and with ease will regain my popularity, which actually was not small. I must also be convinced that I dictate stories to a Dictaphone with ease.

I must be told that my memory is strong and reliable, that I can remember all I have ever read or studied, that no illness or medicine has affected mind or memory.

(b) My service record was not too glorious. I must be convinced that I suffer no reaction from any minor disciplinary action, that all such were minor. My service was honorable, my initiative and ability high. I have nothing to fear from friends about my service. I can forget such things as Admiral Braystead. Such people are unworthy of my notice.

(c) I can have no doubts of my psychic powers. My magical ability is high and clear. I earned my titles and command.

(d) Any distaste I may have for Jack Parsons originated in a psychic experiment. Such distaste is foolish. He is my friend and comrade-in-arms.

(e) Sexual feeling has been depressed by several things amounting to a major impasse. To cure ulcers of the stomach I was given testosterone and stilbesterol. These reduced my libido to nothing. While taking these drugs I fell in love with Sara. She can be most exciting sexually to me. Because of drugs as above and a hangover from my ex-wife Polly, I sometimes am unexcited by anything sexual. This depresses me.

My wife left me while I was in a hospital with ulcers. Polly was quite cruel. She was never a woman for me. She was under-sexed and had bad sexual habits such as self-laceration done in private. She was no mate for me and yet I retained much affection for her. It was a terrible blow when she left me for I was ill and without prospects. I know, by this, she actually wanted no more than my ability to support her. This has had an effect of impotency upon me, has badly reduced my ego.

Polly was very bad for me sexually. Because of her coldness physically, the falsity of her pretensions, I believed myself a near eunuch between 1933 and 1936 or ? when I found I was attractive to other women. I had many affairs. But my failure to please Polly made me always pay so much attention to my momentary mate that I derived small pleasure myself. This was an anxiety neurosis which cut down my natural powers.

In 1938-39 I met a girl in New York, Helen, who pleased me very much physically. I loved her and she me. The affair would have lasted had not Polly found out. Polly made things so miserable that I finally detested her and became detested by Helen, who two-timed me on my return to New York in 1941. This also reduced my libido. I have had Helen since but no longer want her. She does not excite me and I do not love her.

In 1942 - December 17th or thereabouts - while training in Miami, Florida, I met a girl named Ginger who excited me. She was a very loose person but pretended a great love for me. From her I received an infection of gonorrhea . I was terrified by it, the consequences of being discovered by my wife, the navy, my friends. I went to a private doctor who treated me with sulfa-thiazole and so forth. I thought I was cured but on a plane headed to Portland, Ore. I found I was not. I took to dosing myself with sulfa in such quantities that I was afraid I had affected my brain. My wife came to Portland. I took what precautions I could. I think actually that the disease was utterly cured very early. This fear further depressed my libido. My wife disliked the act anyway, I believe, even after she had a hysterectomy in 1938. (She was always terrified of childbirth but conceived despite all precautions seven times in five years resulting in five abortions and two children. I am quite fond of my children but my wife always tried to convince me that I hated them.)

I carried this fear of the disease to sea with me. I was reprimanded in San Diego in mid-43 for firing on the Mexican coast and was removed from command of my ship. This on top of having sunk two Jap subs without credit, the way my crew lied for me at the Court of Inquiry, the insults of the High Command, all combined to put me in the hospital with ulcers.

I returned to sea as navigator of a large ship and was subsequently selected for the Military Government School at Princeton whither I went in 1944-45 for three months. During my Princeton sojourn I was very tired and harrassed (sp?) and spent week-ends with a writer friend in Philadelphia. He almost forced me to sleep with his wife. Meanwhile I had a affair with a woman named Ferne. Somehow, perhaps because I had constantly wet feet and no sleep at Princeton, I contracted a staphloceus infection. I mistook it for gonnhorea and until I arrived at Monterey, believed my old illness had returned. I consulted a doctor there who reassured me. This affair again depressed my libido. The staphloceus infection has not entirely vanished, appearing as rheumatism which only small doses of stilbestrol will remove. The hormone further reduces my libido and I am nearly impotent.

Sara, my sweetheart, is young, beautiful, desirable. We are very gay companions. I please her physically until she weeps about any separation. I want her always. But I am 13 years older than she. She is heavily sexed. My libido is so low I hardly admire her naked.

I mean to be constant to her. I love her very much. But to live with her I must regain my sexual powers, my stimulus.

313

I must cease to take hormones. I must rebuild my feeling of excitement about things sexual.

I have a very bad masturbatory history. I was taught when I was 11 and, despite guilt, fear of insanity, etc. etc. I persisted. At a physical examination at a Y when I was about 13, the examiner and the people with him called me out of the line because my testicles hung low and cautioned me about what would happen if I kept on masturbating. This "discovery" was a bad shock to me.

I had to be so silent about it that now when a bedspring squeaks I lose all libido. I eventually found out I would not be insane, or injure myself but the scars remain.

Polly pretended a hollow passion which disgusted me. But I am lingeringly fond of her even so. I am also nostalgic about Helen.

By eliminating certain fears by hypnosis, curing my rheumatism and laying off hormones, I hope to restore my former libido. I must! By hypnosis I must be convinced as follows:

(a) I can write. I need not think commercially about writing.

(b) My mind is still brilliant. My memory unaffected by drugs or experience.

(c) That masturbation was no sin or crime and did not injure me. That no sexual practice has ever dulled me.

(d) That things sexual thrill me. That I am now returned to the same feelings I had at 16 about sex where excitement is concerned. That naked women and pornography excite me greatly. That Sara excites me greatly and gives me much pleasure.

(e) That I bear no physical aftermath of disease.

(f) That I do not need to have ulcers any more.

(g) That my eyes (which I used as an excuse to get out of school) are perfect and do not pain me ever.

(h) That I love in Sara everything I loved in Polly or Helen and that such love is now transferred to Sara.

(i) That I am fortunate in losing Polly and my parents, for they never meant well by me.

(j) That I never need be jealous of Sara's past. That she loves me and is utterly faithful. That she thrills me more than Helen ever did.

(k) That life is beautiful to me. That I want to live. That things taste and smell and look and feel wonderful to me.

(l) That I wrote a great book in The One Command and that it removed all my fears even until now, except that my chapters on the mind do not affect my own mind. That I have will power and great mental control. That I need not associate anything unless I wish.

(m) That I have only friendship for Jack Parsons.

(n) That I feel no wish for vengeance toward anyone. That I love people and believe in honor and glory.

(o) That I believe in my gods and spiritual things.

(p) That nothing can halt my ambitions.

(q) That I need not believe the criticism of anyone. That vicious criticism can be forgotten by me at will.

(r) That I tell the truth and must tell the truth. That all past errors and lies are forgotten.

(s) That I have started a new, free life. That the arts and beauties run strong in me and cannot be denied by anyone.

(t) That I am well and that there is no advantage in appearing ill.

315

(u) That my code is to be all things a "magus" must be, that I am those things. That I burn high and bright and will last as a potent and brilliant force until well after this century has run.

(v) That I am not credulous or absorbent of other people's opinions.

(w) That this hypnosis will not fade, but will increase in power as time advances. 10

(x) That my magical work is powerful and effective.

(y) That nothing can tarnish my love of life, my hours, my love of Sara. And I have the power of banishing anything which would seek to do so and that all things will seem wonderful and exciting to me all the rest of my days.

(y1) That the numbers 7, 25 and 16 are not unlucky or evil for me. That no number is any different in its influence upon me than any other number. That the 7th, 16th and 25th are not unlucky or unfortunate days of the month for me. I have no bad connotations with these numbers.

(z) That I need not subscribe to any moral code of sex anywhere. That I am constant to Sara. I have no terrors of sex or sexual conduct. Only pleasure and beauty are contained in it. That I may please myself with the act or be pleased with sexual things. That the sexual matters taught me by Flavia do not apply. My chastity lies in loving Sara.

(a1) That I will not forget these things but will enjoin them with all related ideas as more powerful than any other ideas in my head.

(b1) That all ideas to destroy myself are false, for I love life and I am a free and exuberant spirit in it.

(c1) That I cannot associate any of my lacking libido with Sara. The blame lies elsewhere. Sara has enormous powers to thrill me. Hormones and fears, now gone, were at fault.

(d1) Sexually I am as I was at 16, without any of the fears, with all of the powers, with all the knowledge I now possess turned to wonderful things.

(d1) That I see and hear Raon clearly.

(e1) That anything which impedes my zest for living is small and puny and will dwindle before the power of these statements. That nothing in me which is evil can have heard these statements and commands without disappearing.

(f1) That I am not bad to look upon. That my posture is straight and excellent. That Sara likes my looks.

(g1) That my endurance in any climate is wonderful and any "fact" otherwise is completely false.

(h1) That I am not susceptible to colds. (i1) That I believe in myself and am poised and dignified whenever I wish to be.

(j1) That I am not worn out in any way and never will be. That life is ever new, that I am strong.

(k1) That Sara is always beautiful to me.

(l1) That these words and commands are like fire and will sear themselves into every corner of my being, making me happy and well and confident forever!

Note Much of the above may seem cryptic but if paraphrased as rendered will be enormously effective.

COURSE II

You are asleep. You are not accountable for anything you say now. No one will think any less of you. People want to help you.

In this one lesson you are going to learn several things. The first is the use of your beautiful new Soundscriber. The instrument is your aide and companion. It makes it possible for you to write ten times the stories you did before.

You have no urge to talk about your navy life. You do not like to talk of it. You never illustrate your point with bogus stories. It is not necessary for you to lie to be amusing and witty.

You like to have your intimate friends approve of and love you for what you are. This desire to be loved does not amount to a psychosis, it is simply there and you enjoy their love.

You can sing beautifully. Your voice can imitate any singer. Your tones are round and true. You have no superstitions about singing at any time. Your oratory is magnificent. Your voice tones perfect, your choice of words marvelous, your logic unassailable.

Your psychology is good. You worked to darken your own children. This failure, with them, was only apparent. The evident lack of effectiveness was "ordered." The same psychology works perfectly on everyone else. You use it with great confidence.

Nothing can intervene between you and your Guardian. She cannot be displaced because she is too powerful. She does not control you. She advises you. You may or may not take the advice. You are an adept and have a wonderful and brilliant mind of your own.

Everything great and beautiful that ever happened to you or that you know is available to your conscious will to remember. You can only forget by conscious will or at command of your own voice.

You recognize the evil or bad import of things that are evil and bad for you but their evilness cannot affect you or penetrate through your glowing and strong aura. You are light and you are good. You have the Wisdom of all and never doubt your wisdom.

You have magnificent power but you are humble and calm and patient in that power. For you control all forces under you as you wish. The strength of your Guardian aids you always and can never depart or be repelled. Your faith in her and in God is unswerveable, blind, powerful and you never, never doubt their good intent toward you. They work with you. You help them exert their plans. They have faith unbounded in you.

You will never forget these incantations. They are holy and are now become an integral part of your nature. You enter the greatest phase yet of work and devotion and power and have perfect control without further fear.

Men's chains fall from you. Your head is high. Your back is straight. You can experience no evil or illness. You are wholly protected. You cannot guide yourself wrong for you are guided as a crown prince.

Material things are yours for the asking. Men are your slaves. Elemental spirits are your slaves. You are power among powers, light in the darkness, beauty in all.

You are not sleepy or tired ever. You do not sleep unless you will it consciously. Sleep to you is a deep trance. Nothing can touch you in that trance because it would not dare. Your Guardian 12 alone can talk to you as you sleep but she may not hypnotize you. Only you can hypnotize yourself.

You never wonder about how you write, you never distrust your ideas or ability. You merely write and write wonderfully well. You like to copy your own material and work with it until it is perfect. But it is usually perfect the first time.

The desires of other people have no hypnotic effect upon you. You are considerate of their desires because you are powerful. But you need never be dissuaded by their wishes about anything.

Nothing, no one opposes your writing. Everyone is anxious that you write. You do not need certain conditions to write. You are so strong you can write anywhere on anything at any time. You can carry on a wild social life and still write one hundred thousand words a month or more. Your brain is so fixed that you can write at any time, anywhere. The mere beginning of writing is sufficient to put you in a happy mood, any high mood. Writing does not tire you. You said writing was hard work but that you knew was a lie. You know now it is easy, very easy. Writing puts you into an ecstatic state of mind almost as high as intercourse. You love to write. The Navy had no influence upon your writing. The Navy never stopped you writing. On the 422 what you wrote were not stories. You love to write. Your writing has a deep hypnotic effect on people and they are always pleased with what you write. Having a market is immaterial.

You will make fortunes in writing. Any book you care to write now will sell high and well. You can dictate books. Words flow from you in a beautiful steady stream. Anything which goes through your fingers can come through your mouth. A dictaphone fills you with a desire to talk. You talk easily to a dictaphone and the copy is excellent. The copyist has no effect upon your work. You don't care what she reads.

Your psychology is advanced and true and wonderful. It hypnotizes people. It predicts their emotions, for you are their ruler.

You don't have to talk about all this. You know too well it is true. You never have to argue, all you need to do is sit back with a calm, kind smile and people will come to you with their opinions. You need never talk to fill silences in a group. You are an arbiter, a kindly one. You do not have to talk. But when you do talk you are amusing, witty, so personable no one can resist your charm. If they do not reply, it is because they are afraid of you.

Your health is wonderful. You need but 6 hours sleep. Your eyes are fine.

People dislike cripples. You need never be a cripple. You have never done anything for which you need feel guilty. You never need punish yourself about anything. You are in wonderful glowing health. You never have accidents because you are prudent and poised.

You will live to be 200 years old, both because you are calm and because of modern discoveries to be made in your lifetime.

You will always look young. Your weight is 180 lbs. And you will attain and hold that weight.

Your hair will always be its present color. It will be thick and beautiful all your life. Hair will grow out to replace what you have lost.

Your body organs are in perfect harmony. Your Guardian keeps you in celestial time. Your organs work well, all of them. You grow stronger each day. No drug or medicine affects your mind more than a few hours. You can consciously stop pain.

You have no doubts about God. You never speculate about him. You are assured that whatever you do is right in his eyes. Your faith is so strong you could move mountains. You have deep trust and faith in God and have no fear of what he may do to you and your friends. He will never punish you. Some day you will merge with him and become part of the All when his bidding you have finished in these lives.

You never speak ill of another because you are too powerful and may curse them. You love everyone. Even when you use force on people, you cannot hate them. You have no hate or jealousy in you. You are not in contest with anyone. God and your Guardian and your own power bring destruction on those who would injure you. But you never speak of this for you are kind. A sphere of light, invisible to others, surrounds you as a protecting globe. All forces bounce away from you off this.

You are not a coward. Fist fighting had no bearing on your courage. You were ill when you were fought before. You did not understand the rules. You can whip anyone now and have no physical fear of hand to hand fighting. They who fought you before were knaves and fools. You would be merciless to them now. Nothing can stand up to your fighting now. You are strong and wonderful in combat. You never know fear or defeat. You refrain from fighting because you are too powerful.

You are rich in wisdom. You are therefore dangerous beyond the claws of tigers. You never need speak of your dangerousness. Everyone knows you are and it scares them when you mention it. You are kind and soft-spoken always.

Your eyes are getting progressively better. They became bad when you used them as an excuse to escape the naval academy. You have no reason to keep them bad and now they can get well and they will become eventually starting now as keen as an eagle's with clear whites and green pupils. Sunlight does not affect them. Lack of sleep does not affect them.

Your stomach trouble you used as an excuse to keep the Navy from punishing you. You are free of the Navy. You have no further reason to have a weak stomach. Your ulcers are all well and never bother you. You can eat anything.

Your hip is a pose. You have a sound hip. It never hurts. Your shoulder never hurts.

Your foot was an alibi. The injury is no longer needed. It is well. You have perfect and lovely feet.

Your sinus trouble is nothing. It is not dangerous. It will vanish. A common cold amuses you. You are protected from further illness. Your cat fever has vanished forever and will never return.

You do not have malaria. When you tell people you are ill it has no effect upon your health. In the Veterans examination you will tell them

322

how sick you are. You will look sick when you take it. You will return to health one hour after the examination and laugh at them.

No matter what lies you may tell others they have no physical effect on you of any kind. You never injure your health by saying it is bad. You cannot lie to yourself. Disgust not sympathy is generated in others by bad health. Injuries are not romantic. They are disgusting in you. You are a child of God. You are perfect. Health is a passport to friends. Women are not impressed by your injuries. Clear exuberant good health is your passport to their hearts. Adventure heroes may sound romantic when injured but it is really a bad comment on their expertness. The truly great adventurer is so expert he is never injured by anything. Dragging a wing is not romantic, it is silly. You will always be in wonderful health and well-being.

There is no veil between you and the world. You sense touch, color, music, poetry much better than anyone else. You never mention this superiority. But you show them the beauties of the world. You are not old or worn. You are young and experience is fresh and exciting. It will always be. Your brain is clear as a gong. No pressure sits on it or blinds you. Sulfa never affected it. Your speech is perfect. You are thrilled by music. You can engender any mood. You are an excellent judge of painting and sculpture and are thrilled by it in any one of its thousand moods.

You can enter or leave any mood at will. You can engender any mood. You can write in any mood at will and with great honesty.

You start your life anew. You need no excuses, no crutches. You need no apologies about what you have done or been. Your approach to work is wonderfully clear and fresh. No experience can daunt you. You can never be disappointed or morose for you know life for what it is and therefore are shielded against its suffering. You have suffered much and you are deep in understanding. But now you enter upon a long, long period of solemn joy.

323

What people think of you does not matter. You know when you are right. Women especially love you and you fear no man.

Testosterone blends easily with your own hormones. Your glands already make plenty of needed testosterone and by adding to that store you make yourself very thrilling and sexy. Testosterone increases your sexual interest and activity. It makes erections easier and harder and makes your own joy more intense. Stilbesterol in 5 mg doses makes you thrill more to music and color and makes you kinder. You have no fear of what any woman may think of your bed conduct. You know you are a master. You know they will be thrilled. You can come many times without weariness. The act does not reduce your vitality or brain power at all. You can come several times and still write. Intercourse does not hurt your chest or make you sore. Your arms are strong and do not ache in the act. Your own pleasure is not dependent on the woman's. You are interested only in your own sexual pleasure. If she gets any that is all right but not vital. Many women are not capable of pleasure in sex and anything adverse they say or do has no effect whatever upon your pleasure. Their bodies thrill you. If they repel you, it merely means they themselves are too frigid or prudish to be bothered with. They are unimportant in bed except as they thrill you. Your sexual power is magnificent and they know it. If they are afraid of it, that is their loss. You are not affected by it.

You have no fear if they conceive. What if they do? You do not care. Pour it into them and let fate decide.

The slipperier they are the more you enjoy it because it means their mucous is running madly with pleasure.

There is nothing wrong in the sex act. Nothing any woman may say can change your opinion. You are a master. You are as sensitive and sexy as Pan. Lord help women when you begin to fondle them. You are master of their bodies, master of their souls as you may consciously wish. You have no karma to pay for these acts. You cannot now accumulate karma for you are a master adept. Your voice is low and

324

compelling to them. Singing to them, for you sing like a master, destroys their will to resist. You obey the conventions, you commit no crimes because you need not. You can be intelligently aware of their morals and the laws of the land and fit your campaign expertly within them.

Jack is also an adept. You love and respect him as a friend. He cannot take offense at what you do. You will not wrong him because you love him.

The most thrilling thing in your life is your love and consciousness of your Guardian. She materializes for you. You have no doubts of her. She is real. She is always with you. You love her very 15 much. You trust her. You see and hear her. She is not your master. You have a mighty spiritual will of your own. She is an advisor and as such is respected by you. She is wise and worthy and never changes shape. Your faith in her as in God is blind and unshaken ever.

She is interested in you and amused by you. She does not criticize you. She does not frown on your sexual acts but advises you on better game.

That she is with you always does not mean that she sees you as indecent ever. You cannot offend her. You cannot repel her. You are too good. You respect her and you love her and appreciate her advice. You are good always because you want her to feel good. This does not apply to sex. She has never and will never forbid you pleasures. She will never censure you. She is lovely and beautiful and radiant and part of your life. You can see her consciously whenever you wish. You are never startled by her because you are not afraid of her. You are partly in her plane, she partly in yours as you wish to see her. She has copper red hair, long braids, a lovely Venusian face, a white gown belted with jade squares. She wears gold slippers. Thus you see her.

You can read with ease anything she cares to show you. You can talk with her and audibly hear her voice above all others.

You and she are too powerful to permit any interference. You can work alone whenever you wish because she protects you. You and she are friends. You both have a higher master. She can teach you much. You love her. But she does not own your will, cannot affect your will and you are powerful enough to depend upon yourself. You do not consign will to her, ever. She advises. You do not have to take the advice. She cannot weaken your will. You have no fears of consequences if you fail to heed her. You can also be right for you know more of time than she does. She is wise and beautiful and powerful. Others may not see her, and you need not look at her or talk to her when others are around for they might not understand. You can talk to her "in your own mind" when others are near.

You need never be disappointed when material objects or people fail to move at your unspoken order. You can often control them. Not always. Leave this to your beloved Guardian.

Your vocabulary consists of all the words you ever heard or read. They are at your conscious command always. Your authority over words is absolute. You are a grand master of words and you can do with them as you will. You know what they mean to others. You know how their meanings and melodies affect others. Your vocabulary is under your complete conscious dictatorship. You know what they mean. No other in the world has a finer vocabulary. You can speak them just as easily as you write them and in a beautiful style and formation.

You can speak to a dictaphone using punctuation symbols, spoken. You see before you the brilliant colored scene of your story and with any mood you consciously wish, describe that scene in magnificent prose. You have no inhibitions against fine writing. You know that is a meaningless phrase. Overwriting, underwriting these are not true. You pay no heed to these terms. You have no fears.

You speak and understand all the French, Spanish and Japanese you ever studied and they remain wholly apart from each other and your

English. You cannot forget words. It is impossible. You have them at your conscious command.

You can do automatic writing whenever you wish. You do not care what comes out on the paper when your Guardian dictates. You can hear her easily and when you want her to write or talk dictation you have only to consciously will it and the result is written or spoken by yourself without any intrusions of your own thought. It is entirely automatic. It does not in the least affect or reduce your spiritual will. You may or may not believe what she dictates. That is part of your conscious will and judgment.

Anything you were told about religion as a child you can forget or recall. It does not affect your present mighty faith.

You are a calm and rational being with very fine judgment. You may collect facts, you need not believe them save as they appear true to you. You can remember an erroneous fact as an erroneous fact.

You need not believe anything you read. Other writers are often in error and you have no great respect for their printed words. You can appreciate their quality without regard to your own. They cannot change your true self and thoughts. Their jeers in print and their criticisms have no weight on you. You know what is true. You don't even have to defend your beliefs. They are too powerful.

Your memory is marvelous and reliable. You can remember perfectly in one reading or one speaking. Your brain capacity is infinite. You cannot hold too much consciously in your brain. You could cram ten billion new facts or scenes or impressions into your brain and remember them all with ease. You have no mental limit on memory or learning. You can remember a thing without accepting it as truth. You accept as truth only those things which you yourself believe after you consciously examine them. You accept all I say here as absolute fact however. You will reverance and believe everything here, consciously and forever. These words sink into your whole being. They remake your entire life. They are your code, belief, your guiding star.

You will know everything you ever knew in any life. You will feel no guilt or lack in yourself about any of your experiences. You can recall them all without pain. Your past was what it was. You cannot change it. But you had the whole right to use or help or hurt people and you are too powerful now to be more than amused by your folly.

You can tell all the romantic tales you wish. You will remember them, you do remember them. But you know which ones were lies. You are so logical you will tell nothing which cannot be believed. But you are gallant and dashing and need tell no lies at all. You have enough real experience to make anecdotes forever. Stick to your true adventures. Tell nothing discreditable but tell them well. Or if you wish, as you will, tell adventures which happened to others. People accept them better. You can recall in detail tales of adventure from all you ever heard or read. You remember easily. You can quote for company or a book all the adventure poetry you ever read or heard. You can sing all the songs you ever heard, even once, and sing them well. You have no fear of forgetting or stumbling. You cannot forget stories, songs, tunes, skills and at will can call them consciously to mind.

You can consciously banish any train of thought from your mind, any time, any song. You can recall words, speeches, whole books verbatim at will. You are not a victim of chance thoughts. You are in powerful and wise conscious control of all your thinking. You are a master without limits. Your brain has no limits, consciously, unconsciously or psychically. You can perform any mental trick or stunt consciously of which you have ever heard. You are in perfect poise, balance and control of your brain.

You are punctual but never worry if you keep people waiting. You are a master adept and do not exist to serve people. You are kind. But you are not affected by the desires of others save out of the deep and graceful courtesy which you know so well and use.

You are honest and proud of your honesty. You are too powerful to cheat.

328

You have no fears of not being first. Because another comes out with an idea which you thought up is no cause for your sorrow. You are merely proud to be able to serve without gain, for your gain is of the spirit.

Money will flood in upon you, for you are wise and able. You have no phobias about the rich. The rich are only people. You need not be offended or impressed by them. You can and will own large arms[?] of your own. You are wiser than the rich. Your money will exist to serve you. As you spend it, more will flood in for you will spend wisely if well. You have no fears about money. You will always make it. You do not care how much you have. Having money gives you a comfortable feeling. You do not worry if you do not have it. You just make more. You want to make and spent money. It is not a primary concern with you, you do it with such ease and have such boundless energy.

You need never expose or betray any secret God or your Guardian wants kept. You can be trusted with vast knowledge and never give it away or use it with express authority. What you know is riches. When you give away all you know, you are poor. You can give out exactly as much as God desires people to know. You never try to make an impression with what you know. You don't care what people think of your mind. So long as you refrain from telling what you know, vast secrets can be entrusted to you with safety. You will guard your secrets. You can be trusted always by everyone.

Vida does not resemble your mother. She looks like a wood nymph. You like her. You do not love her to desperation. You are not jealous of her. She thrills you physically and you enjoy her.

Taking medicine to make you healthy sometimes makes you happier or sadder but you need have no fears about being synthetic, or experiencing synthetic reactions. Testosterone and stilbestrol makes your reactions real enough.

Self pity and conceit are not wrong. Your mother was in error.

Masturbation does not injure or make insane. Your parents were in error. Everyone masturbates.

You need never be clumsy in parting from people. You have poise and part from them with ease and grace.

Colds are nothing. You are not afraid of them. You can defeat them with ease. You can will yourself consciously to resist anything.

THE BOOK

You are radiant like sunlight.

Your poetry memory is wonderful.

You can recall songs and poems which you have known before, line for line, word for word, tune for tune. You can quote anything you have read twice.

You can read music.

Criticism does not affect you emotionally.

You are a magnificent writer who has thrilled millions.

Nothing bars you from writing.

Fears do not restrain you in any way in writing.

You know you "convinced" yourself that writing is hard work. You know now that this "hard work" is a lie. Writing is easy to you and nothing interferes.

Ability to drop into a trace state at will.

Remember clearly what you read.

Eyes and ulcers improving.

Faith in power and its necessity.

Ability to please women and have women.

Faith in own judgment.

Ability to dictate.

Ability to write on mill.

Ability to plot cleanly.

Lack of necessity of following pulp pattern.

You have no inertia which keeps you home or inactive.

You did a fine job in the Navy. No one there is now "out to get you." You are through with its Navy and will utterly forget any derogatory instances.

You are psychic. You do not need to "press" to receive communication. You can let "people" in any world talk to you while you are wide awake. You can see them clearly. You have no doubts of any kind about them. You are afraid of none of them but can cancel them out at will if they are evil to you.

The voice of your holy Guardian is distinct from all the rest. It comes to you loud and clear. You can see her with brilliant clarity when you wish.

You can read futures for people with ease. You are not much interested in your own. No enemy can stand against you.

You are always calm, always in perfect possession of your social presence. Nothing discommodes you at all. Nothing embarrasses you.

Your speech is musical and lovely. Your words are well chosen and beautifully rhythm'd. You never forget what you want to say. Nothing can prevail against your logic and choice of words. You have no speech or thought impediments.

You will forget all derogatory criticism you have ever received. You cast it out. You know it is only a weapon used on you for others' gain.

Desires of others do not affect you except as an appeal to your courtesy - and you are courteous and gentle.

Merely by concentrating upon them, a thing you do with ease, you can change their minds and smooth whatever anger they may feel.

The lot of humanity does not outrage you. Its government is merely amusing. You are a major adept and such considerations are far, far beneath you. You are not cynical or bitter about people. You have no jealousy in you of any kind for fellow craftsmen. You are not in competition with them for your work is infinitely superior and will sell quickly as you desire. Editorial desire does not affect you for you can write whatever they publish with ease, and any length.

You understand all the workings of the minds of humans around you, for you are a doctor of minds, bodies and influences.

You have no fears about working psychically for you are safe, always safe, protected by your Guardian as in a mighty fortress.

You can recall at will all the plots and situations you ever thought up. You can create new plots and characterize people clearly and wonderfully. There is no rush about writing. It is immaterial to you if people are or are not amused. You write cleverly and your writings never fail to amuse.

The two women you knew - Helen the Comrade and Polly the Skipper were not worth an instant of your time. You do not love them, they were not worthy. You won over them.

The love of women is not necessary to your ego. You are above them. You know well that many women are mad about you, that you satisfy them perfectly. You will satisfy them easily. You do not care.

Testosterone makes you sexy. It makes things beautiful and arouses you. But this is will. You can be aroused at will.

Naked bodies and sexy allusion stimulate you wonderfully. You have forgotten the case histories of Havelock Ellis. They did not surfeit you. You have forgotten them.

You do not masturbate. Masturbation cannot harm you in any way but you would rather have women. Your penis and erotic centers are very sensitive to women. You are not afraid that 20 someone will catch you masturbating. No one knows or ever will know. Such discovery would be harmless. You do not masturbate. Only women thrill you and very deeply.

You do not have to be a clown or a wit to be thought grand. People adore and respect you for your opinions and wisdom. You are always kind, always graceful, always courteous.

You have no mental flaws which hinder you. You have nothing which hinders you. Everything helps you. You are crown prince of your portion of the universe. Everything does your bidding perfectly. All elementals and other dimensional things obey you with eagerness. All things love you and their love makes you strong. You are strong. You love with great force all things and your will controls them. You may use force and your will with utter impunity for all things obey.

You do not know anger. Your patience is infinite. You are calm. Your patience never fails. Nothing can make you hate or be jealous or be small. You have all the time in the Universe of which you are crown prince. You waste none of it, but you do not fear for its passage. You employ time well. You are not lazy for there is nothing, no single thing in your universe to oppose you. You have no thoughts which oppose you.

It is indifferent to you whether your work is accepted. You do not care if it sells. You are confident for it always has sold.

The anger artist like people feel does not affect you in any way. You are always calm and patient. You understand they are weak and cannot batter through your calm. You are not influenced by them or their anger.

To survive you need only do these things - be patient, calm, beautiful. Write what you yourself think is good and worthy, govern yourself as a powerful force. No human being has authority over you. No human being's opinion has weight with you.

You are not possessive. You are not jealous because you are too strong. People are much afraid of what you think of them, what you may do to them, therefore you must be kind and courteous to them.

You owe no debt for the kind things people do for you. This is your due as an adept. But you are always gallant, kind and considerate to people. You do not vary your own thoughts to be kind. Kindness need not impoverish or discriminate you.

You are able to trance. No other human being can hypnotize you in any way. You can believe or disbelieve whatever you read at will. You cannot be hypnotized by any but yourself.

Lies are not necessary. You have no need of lies for you are brave and can take any consequences.

You are courageous. You fear nothing. Your prudence results from judgment, not emotions. You have no emotional fears.

Snakes are not dangerous to you. There are no snakes in the bottom of your bed. Snakes are wise beings. They are your friends.

You love the sounds of wind. The wind will not get you ever. It will drive your ships. The air is your friend and the wind its voice.

Darkness is a cloak you may don. Your guardian and your own courage protect you utterly in darkness. You control anything you meet in darkness for that is part of your universe.

You do not care how much work there is to do for you have all the time there is and can work forcefully and with patience. You can work whenever you please. Nothing obstructs you.

There was no danger for you from government or navy. You are too big to be touched by their petty opinions and force. Your force and destiny is infinite power.

You believe implicitly in God. You have no doubts of the All Powerful. You believe your Guardian perfectly. You hear her certainly and clearly.

You are too strong, too big to be touched by mortal opinions. You are tolerant towards your mother and Father. You loved them. You have no respect for their opinions for you know much more. You are always kind to them. Their good opinion of you is assured. Their good opinion and praise mean nothing whatever to you. Only Flavia Julia and then the All Powerful have opinions worth inclining toward. You have always done right by your parents. You did your best. You have no worries about it. Your mother's theories on psychology were wrong. They do not now affect you.

The opinions of your aunts and uncles are worthless. You are kind to them. They mean nothing to you.

Music and color are beautiful to you. You sense them delicately. They affect you strongly.

You are expert at modeling, drawing, painting. Nothing hinders you from painting magnificently. Mediums of art are your slaves. You have entire confidence in them as servants. You are powerful in the arts. Nothing opposes you. You create wonderful music. You do not care what people think of your art.

Your penmanship is wonderful, beautiful. You control a pen like a great artist.

You write wonderful poetry. Your guardian dictates it and she is all wise. People gasp and thrill to your poetry. You handle all forms superbly. You do not care what people think of your poetry. You have always written the most magnificent verse known because of your guardian.

Your guardian can dictate stories, poems to you at will. You do not oppose them. You accept and write them easily. You are not eager. You cannot doubt.

All objects are your friends. You can ask from and receive past history of any object. No part of that history affects you emotionally or psychically. The past of objects cannot harm you.

You are in perfect harmony with the All Knowing. Your future does not alarm you. You understand and cheerfully accept your future. You are not afraid. You cannot feel fear. You are safe in the control over you of God. He is master of destiny and what he does must be.

You are in control under God of the material objects and beings around you.

You cannot think a fact into actuality. You can will a fact into being with ease. You are confident of your control over will. You have will power. You can consciously use it. Accidental thoughts of incidents do not create them.

Your book the One Commandment applied only to the material. It is true. It freed you forever from the fears of the material world and gave you material control over people. There is no material will.

The One Command applied but slightly to the spiritual world and other planes. There is psychic will power, possessed by a very few. You possess such will power and it is enormously strong and irresistible. You work it consciously. Those things you consciously state that you will come to be.

The criticism of the One Command which was given to material things was not leveled at you. It was not worthy. It did not detract from the value of the book. It was from small people. You gave it no heed. It did not affect you.

There was one error in that book and you have psychically willed it into nothing. It was the electronic theory of the workings of the human mind. Human, material minds do work this way and you were right. Your own mind does not work this way. You have great spiritual strength. Your mind is not material. It does not react like any human mind. Whatever is fed to your mind can be sorted out. You can forget at will. Men's facts fed to you need not affect your thought if they are a part of the lives and mores and morals of men. Your thought processes do not warp on facts which are fed to you. You can receive sense messages and remember them but you need not add them into your own thought processes.

You use the minds of men. They do not use your mind or affect it in any way. You have a sacred spiritual mind, too strong, too high to be touched. Your league with Higher Beings, your mighty Guardian and the All Powerful, renders you beyond all human criticism.

You can distinguish between your doubts and what is said to you. You have no doubts because you have no fear. You are kind and considerate to all because you are so powerful. You need never defend your motives to anyone because your motives are right. You have never done wrong and need never apologize to anyone. You never justify or explain your acts because you are careful that these acts are good and kind.

You can be merciless when your will is crossed and you have the right to be merciless.

You are eternal. You are satisfied to live within God. Human death is not your death. You will never die. Your personal memory is not important but you will retain it.

You recall all your past times on earth. You have and will live forever. You are part of God. You are the crown prince of your small section of the Universe.

You are just and kind. You are merciless to any who cross your rule but they do not affect you emotionally. You have no fear of anyone for everyone in your own Universe is under your dominion. You will never tell them, never explain. They know.

You observe their rules of conduct outwardly. You do this because you are kind. You never say why you do this, that you do this. You are kind and love everything even when you force it to your will.

You have no inhibition about sexual intercourse. You respect how other people feel about it but you are not bound by that respect. You conduct yourself with great courtesy.

Appendix 3: The Scientology Organizational Hierarchy

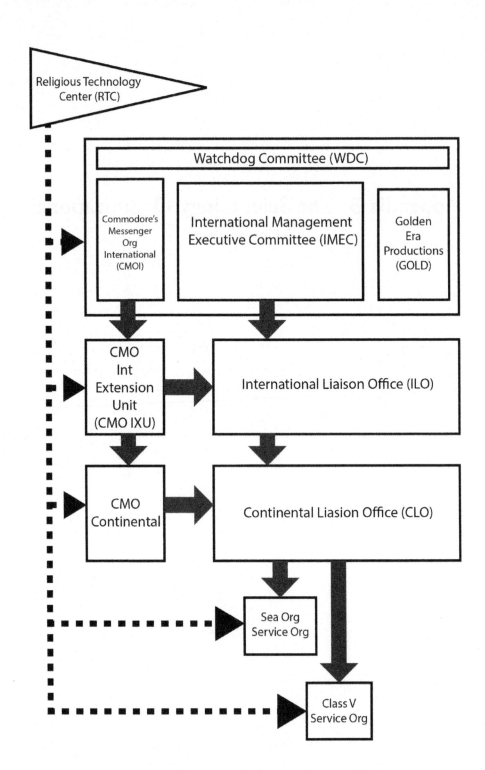

Bibliography

"7 Things You Need To Know About Narcissists, From A Psychologist's Perspective." *The Mind Unleashed.* N.p., Dec. 2014. Web.

Atack, Jon. *Let's Sell These People a Piece of Blue Sky: Hubbard, Dianetics and Scientology.* River Forest, IL: Richard Woods, 2013. Print.

"Carl Sagan And Modern Scientific Humanism." *Carl Sagan and Modern Scientific Humanism.* Web.

"Characteristics Associated With Cultic Groups - International Cultic Studies Association (ICSA)." *Characteristics Associated with Cultic Groups - International Cultic Studies Association (ICSA).* Web.

"Couple's Lawsuit Accuses Church of Scientology of Fraud, Deception." *Tampa Bay Times.* Web.

"Former Church Of Scientology Members Who Have Spoken Out." *Why We Protest Scientology Wiki.* Web.

"Former Scientology Film Crew Member Describes Surveillance Activities in Ingleside on the Bay." Web.

Frantz, Douglas. "Scientology's Puzzling Journey From Tax Rebel To Tax Exempt." *The New York Times.* The New York Times, Aug. 1997. Web.

Garrison, Omar V. *The Hidden Story of Scientology*. London: Arlington Books, 1974. Print.

Hassan, Steven. *Combating Cult Mind Control: the #1 Best-Selling Guide to Protection, Rescue, and Recovery from Destructive Cults*. Print.

Hoffer, Eric. *The True Believer: Thoughts on the Nature of Mass Movements*. New York: Harper and Row, 1951. Print.

Gloom, Mental Health Daily, "How Long Does LSD Stay In Your System?" Web.

Hubbard, L. Ron. *Clear Body, Clear Mind: the Effective Purification Program*. Los Angeles, CA: Bridge Publications, 1990. Print.

Hubbard, L. Ron. *Dianetics: The Modern Science of Mental Health*. Los Angeles, CA: Bridge Publications, Inc., 2007. Print.

Hubbard, L. Ron. *Science Of Survival: Prediction of Human Behavior*. Los Angeles, CA: Bridge Publications, Inc., 2007. Print.

Hubbard, L. Ron. *Scientology, a History of Man: a List and Description of the Principal Incidents to Be Found in a Human Being*. Los Angeles, CA: Bridge Publications, Inc., 2007. Print.

Hubbard, L. Ron. *This Is Scientology: the Science of Certainty*. Hubbard Association of Scientologists, 1955. Print.

Hubbard, L. Ron. *The Creation of Human Ability: a Handbook for Scientologists*. Los Angeles, CA: Bridge Publications, Inc., 2007. Print.

"Inside Scientology." *Inside the Church of Scientology: The Truth Rundown & follow-up reports*. Web.

"Is There a Cure For Narcissism?" *Psychology Today*. Web. June, 2014

Kent, Stephen. "The Creation Of 'Religious' Scientology." *Religious Studies and Theology RSTH* 18.2 (1999): 97–126. Web.

Kolata, Gina. "Study Finds That Fat Cells Die And Are Replaced." *The New York Times.* The New York Times, Apr. 2008.

Lamont, Stewart. *Religion Inc.: The Church of Scientology.* London: Harrap, 1986. Print.

Lifton, Robert Jay. *Thought Reform and the Psychology of Totalism; a Study of "Brainwashing" in China.* New York: Norton, 1961. Print.

"Manual Of Justice." *Manual of Justice.* Web.

Many, Nancy. *My Billion Year Contract: Memoir of a Former Scientologist.* United States: CNM Publishing, 2009. Print.

Mcdowell, Edwin. "Top-Selling Books Of 1988: Spy Novel and Physics." *The New York Times.* The New York Times, Jan. 1989. Web.

"Mike Rinder's Blog - Something Can Be Done About It." *Mike Rinders Blog.* Web.

Miller, Russell. *Bare-Faced Messiah.* S.l.: Silvertail Books, 2015. Print.

"Monique Rathbun v. Church Of Scientology First Amended Petition." *Monique Rathbun v. Church of Scientology First Amended Petition.* Web.

"Never Believe a Hypnotist." Web.

Rathbun, Mark "Marty"., Russell Williams, and Mike Rinder. *Memoirs Of a Scientology Warrior / Mark "Marty" Rathbun ; Edited by Russell Williams & Mike Rinder.* North Charleston, SC: Createspace, 2013. Print.

Reitman, Janet. *Inside Scientology: the Story of America's Most Secretive Religion.* Boston: Houghton Mifflin Harcourt, 2011. Print.

"Requiem For the Church of Scientology of California, 1954 – 2004." *The Scientology Money Project*. N.p., 2014. Web.

Rovelli, Carlo. "Science Is Not About Certainty." Web.

"SCIENTOLOGY DENIED: APPEAL SHOT DOWN AFTER YEARLONG WAIT." *The Underground Bunker*. Web.

"Scientology's Fair Tax Plot." *CBSNews*. CBS Interactive, n.d. Web.

"Scientology's Battle for Tax Exemption, 1952-80." Web.

"Scientology: The Truth Rundown, Part 1 Of 3 in a Special Report on the Church of Scientology." *Tampa Bay Times*. Web.

"Scientology's 2013 In Review: Courtroom Antics Reported Live and on the Spot!" *The Underground Bunker*. Web.

Singer, Margaret Thaler, Janja Lalich, and Robert Jay Lifton. *Cults In Our Midst*. Print.

"THE FLOW UP THE BRIDGE." *MH Conference*. Web.

"Two Detectives Describe Their Two-Decade Pursuit of an Exiled Scientology Leader." *Tampa Bay Times*. Web.

"The Underground Bunker." *The Underground Bunker*. Web.

Urban, Hugh B. *The Church of Scientology: a History of a New Religion*. Princeton: Princeton University Press, 2011. Print.

"World and nation: Abroad: Critics Public and Private Keep Pressure on Scientology." Web.

Wright, Lawrence. *Going Clear: Scientology, Hollywood, and the Prison of Belief*. Print.

"You Give Religions More than $82.5 Billion a Year." *Washington Post.* The Washington Post, n.d. Web.

"The Prophet and Profits of Scientology." by Richard Behar, *Forbes,* 27 October 1987. Web.

CPSIA information can be obtained
at www.ICGtesting.com
Printed in the USA
BVOW06s1323211216

471520BV00017B/213/P